The Pox of Liberty

The Pox of Liberty

How the Constitution Left Americans Rich, Free, and Prone to Infection

WERNER TROESKEN

The University of Chicago Press
Chicago and London

Werner Troesken is professor of economics at the University of Pittsburgh. He is the author of *Water, Race, and Disease; Why Regulate Utilities?*; and *The Great Lead Water Pipe Disaster*.

The University of Chicago Press, Chicago 60637
The University of Chicago Press, Ltd., London
© 2015 by The University of Chicago
All rights reserved. Published 2015.
Printed in the United States of America

24 23 22 21 20 19 18 17 16 15   1 2 3 4 5

ISBN-13: 978-0-226-92217-1   (cloth)
ISBN-13: 978-0-226-92219-5   (e-book)
DOI: 10.7208/chicago/9780226922195.001.0001

Library of Congress Cataloging-in-Publication Data

Troesken, Werner, 1963– author.
   The pox of liberty : how the Constitution left Americans rich, free, and prone to infection / Werner Troesken.
        pages cm — (Markets and governments in economic history)
   ISBN 978-0-226-92217-1 (cloth : alk. paper) — ISBN 978-0-226-92219-5 (e-book) 1. Public health laws—United States—History. 2. Public health—United States—History. 3. Constitutional history—United States. I. Title. II. Series: Markets and governments in economic history.
   KF3775.T764 2015
   344.7303'21—dc23

                                                                    2014039433

♾ This paper meets the requirements of ANSI/NISO Z39.48–1992 (Permanence of Paper).

CONTENTS

I did not set out to write a book about how the American constitutional order shaped the country's disease environment and public health programs. Instead, I wanted to answer the questions: How and why have some societies come to control infectious diseases while others have let them fester? I thought there was a straightforward, almost tautological answer to this question, an answer that said strong, well-functioning governments eliminated disease, while weak, dysfunctional governments did not. I wanted, in other words, to argue that there was a simple linear relationship between disease and the quality of governance: good public health systems, like good roads or good public schools, reflected good governance and well-functioning polities, while poor public health systems, like poor roads or poor public schools, suggested inferior governance and dysfunctional polities.

I was attracted to this way of thinking by a casual empiricism. If I looked at Africa, for example, I saw a continent dominated by governments that were either too corrupt or weak to provide basic public goods such as education or public health. That these same places were also impoverished struck me not as a cause of disease, but as a symptom of the same underlying pathology: a dysfunctional state. By the same token, when I looked to richer parts of Asia or Western Europe, I saw stronger, more benevolent states where politicians seemed to have a vested interest in promoting the health and well-being of their citizenry and invested accordingly in the capital and public health systems necessary to combat disease. Given these observations, democratic institutions seemed the obvious solution to high infectious disease rates and poor public health systems. In much the same way that Amartya Sen argues that famines rarely occur in democracies because democratic leaders have stronger political incentives to combat crises than do leaders of autocratic regimes, I wanted to argue that democratic impulses drive polities to provide adequate levels of disease prevention, no matter what the climate or geography or even the level of per capita income.

While I still think there is something to this logic, history suggests that there is much more to good governance than just democracy. As explained in chapter 3, for example, public health laws are no less susceptible to the tyranny of the majority than are other areas of public policy, and protections for individual rights and liberties are no less important there than they are anywhere else in American society. The only protective mechanism that minority groups had against the encroachments of majority groups was the Constitution, enforced by an independent judiciary, and even though that was no guarantee that the majority would not still violate minority rights, it did sometimes forestall the implementation of blatantly discriminatory public health policies. By the same token, highly autocratic societies can, and often do, show greater fidelity to the principles of public health than more democratic regimes. The Soviet Union was less democratic than the United States and England, yet it eradicated smallpox much more quickly. In Brazil, smallpox lingered until a military coup in 1964 ushered in a vaccination program that was much more intrusive than had existed over the previous century or so.[1]

The Pox of Liberty is my attempt to develop a more complex and multi-faceted understanding of the relationship between the structure of the state and infectious disease rates. In developing this line of thought, I have tried to highlight the generality and unintended consequences of constitutional rules and the ideological structures that support and sustain those rules. The import of that analysis is that there is no simple correspondence between the quality of political institutions and public health outcomes. Some political institutions often thought to promote desirable political and economic outcomes can also hinder the provision of public health, and vice versa.

The Commerce and Contract Clauses, for example, were designed to address the problem of factions, powerful political lobbies that captured the state in order to use it to support their own ends at the expense of broader societal welfare. In terms of economics and politics, these and other institutional controls of factions had many desirable features. The Commerce Clause fostered competition among jurisdictions for businesses and residents, giving rise to an optimal mix of taxes and public goods. As Barry Weingast explains, the federalist structure that grew out of the Commerce Clause also allowed state governments to make credible commitments to investors about taxes and regulations in the long term, attracting fixed capital investments to the state. Similarly, the Contract Clause prevented state legislatures from altering the terms of contracts, particularly debt contracts, ex post, and this helped to revive American credit markets, which had grown moribund under the Articles of Confederation.[2]

But these clauses also directly affected the provision of public health, for good and bad. At times, the Commerce Clause obstructed the development of a coherent and rational system of quarantines to combat yellow fever, but the federalist approach it fostered also gave rise to highly effective local programs involving sanitation, which, while they did not eradicate or control yellow fever in any way, had broader public health benefits. In terms of smallpox, the Commerce Clause and the American federalist system gave rise to jurisdictional sorting that allowed anti-vaccinationists to agglomerate in small communities and thereby undermine the goal of universal vaccination in the United States (see chapter 4).

Similarly, the Contract Clause and various statutory provisions helped to promote the market for municipal debt in the United States, making it possible for cities to underwrite the construction of large and expensive public water systems. This achievement was significant on two levels. First, investments in public water systems, when taken in the aggregate, were among the largest, and might even have been *the* largest, public investments in American history. Second, investments in water systems had a larger impact on human mortality than any other public health initiative. About 60 percent of the unprecedented decline in human mortality observed during the late nineteenth and early twentieth century can be attributed to improvements in public water supplies.[3]

In *The Pox of Liberty* I have also tried to highlight the importance of ideas and how ideas about politics, economics, and science interacted to shape the American disease environment. This component of the narrative is more dynamic than the institutional component. In this ideological component, I describe how the American commitment to commerce and the rise of the germ theory of disease transformed the public health system in the United States, moving it away from one based on volunteerism and private action at the municipal level to one that was more national in scope and involved much more state intervention. Of particular importance is the way the American quest for trade both gave rise to large port cities that were vulnerable to diseases like yellow fever, and fostered a stronger and more imperialist state that helped eradicate yellow fever once and for all. Ironically, the federal government was more successful and aggressive in its efforts to control yellow fever abroad than it had been at home. For its part, the rise of the germ theory of disease had its largest impact on the structure of municipal government, inspiring a wide range of public health programs and fostering growth in the both the size and scope of municipal governments, particularly with regard to public water and sewer systems.

In writing *The Pox of Liberty*, I adopted an overtly historical and institutional approach that contrasts with the more quantitative techniques now popular in economics and political science. My decision to write and argue this way comes with costs and benefits. On the cost side, my ideas have not been formalized and subjected to statistical tests that would allow clear falsification. I have chosen to leave that course for others to follow. The reason I have chosen this explicitly historical and institutional approach is twofold. First, it enables me to analyze a broader and more complex set of institutions than a more strict quantitative treatment would have allowed. Second, and more important, this historical approach brings into sharp relief the language of history and the language of modernity and, in so doing, I hope, revives and revitalizes a historical way of thinking that has been lost.

The language of modernity says we are unhealthy despite being rich and free. But the language of history suggests that we are unhealthy, on at least some margins, because we are rich and because our legal and political institutions function well. Similarly, in the language of modernity, the geography of disease has become a sort of economic and political destiny. Tropical places, rife with disease, are doomed to poverty and poor governance; the effects of disease are so pervasive and deeply rooted in such places that they cannot be overcome. But in the language of history, a different, more hopeful rubric emerges, a rubric that says disease is a choice, a public and social choice perhaps, but a choice nevertheless.

Acknowledgments

For helpful comments and suggestions, I would like to thank Terry Anderson, Daniel Benjamin, Price Fishback, P. J. Hill, John Murray, Jonathan Pritchett, and John Wallis. Brian Beach read and commented on the entire manuscript, and I am grateful for his editorial and substantive suggestions. I presented parts of the manuscript at various colleges, think tanks, and universities and gratefully acknowledge the suggestions I received at these places, including, PERC (the Property and Environment Research Center in Bozeman, Montana), Rhodes College, Tulane University, and the University of Arizona. I am especially grateful to PERC for supporting my research with a Julian Simon Fellowship and for offering me such a wonderful and intellectually stimulating environment in which to finish this book.

ONE

An Introduction

James E. Robinson considered himself a judicial maverick. Elected to the North Dakota Supreme Court in 1918, Justice Robinson had promised voters to get "the court out of the old ruts of the law and to minister justice in a plain, common-sense, and businesslike manner." In practical terms, this meant writing brief opinions that spoke to the people; publishing those opinions in a local newspaper in a weekly column; frequently making decisions before hearing the arguments of counsel; and eschewing the practice of *stare decisis*, basing decisions on precedent. "I have little regard," Robinson explained, "for old, obsolete or erroneous decisions and prefer to decide every case in accordance with law, reason, and justice. I do never—like Pontius Pilate—wash my hands and blame the law or a precedent or party zeal for an unjust decision."[1]

Robinson's impatience with precedent and formalism earned him the ire of legal observers from coast to coast. Max Radin published a ten-page article in the *California Law Review* denouncing Robinson for his flagrant disregard of legal principle and for his refusal to apply the law in a nonpartisan and impersonal way. This characterization flowed in part from Robinson's saying openly that if a litigant before him was in the right, that person should win the case, no matter what the law or precedent said.[2] Similarly, an editorial statement in the *Harvard Law Review* admonished Robinson for relying so heavily on his own discretion and for appealing to precedent only when the precedent comported with his own ideological preconceptions.[3] But the angriest rebuke came from the country's midsection and the editors of the *Central Law Journal* in St. Louis, Missouri. In an editorial titled "Judicial Buncombe in North Dakota and Other States," the *Central Law Journal* argued that Robinson's "perfunctory opinions" would culminate in "judicial despotism," a legal system based not on the rule of law but on the vagaries of a judge's friendships, sympathies, and fears.[4]

Few decisions illustrate Robinson's approach to adjudication better than a concurring opinion he wrote in the case of *Rhea v. Board of Education*. In this case, the Board of Education of the Devils Lake School District issued an order requiring all students to show proof of a smallpox vaccination before they could enroll. The parents of Lawrence F. Rhea sued, arguing that the school district did not have the legal authority to issue and enforce such an order.[5] In ruling in favor of Rhea, Justice Robinson based his decision not on the law, but on his own views and medical opinions regarding smallpox control. Robinson acknowledged that "in writing a judicial opinion [it] is customary to fortify it by a reference to authorities, that is, to decisions in similar cases." However, he maintained such references were not possible in this case because all previous judicial decisions had been rendered "under different statutes and conditions." Given this, he felt the question was to be decided based upon something he called "the fundamental law," as well as "the statutes, common knowledge, and pure reason." Accordingly, Robinson briefly discussed a few North Dakota statutes and relevant provisions in the state constitution. He also mentioned a handful of cases from other states that he felt were loosely related. By and large, however, the decision was written as a polemic against the practice of smallpox vaccination.[6]

Like most anti-vaccinationists, Robinson believed that smallpox was caused by crowded and unsanitary living conditions. The practice of vaccination continued only because it was "promulgated and adopted as a religious creed" by physicians blinded by orthodoxy and profit, and because parents were too ignorant to understand what the procedure was doing to their children. Never one to shy away from a biblical reference, Robinson interjected: "The light shineth in darkness and the darkness comprehendeth it not."[7] Again, like most anti-vaccinationists, Robinson also believed that smallpox vaccination was an extremely dangerous procedure. He claimed that "25,000 children annually" were "slaughtered by diseases inoculated into the system by compulsory vaccination." In the same line of thought, he claimed that it had been shown, "beyond doubt," that smallpox vaccination "not infrequently" causes "death, syphilis, cancer, consumption, eczema, [and] leprosy." Robinson had little patience for those who disagreed with him on the merits of smallpox vaccination, writing at one point that anyone who held a contrary opinion "either does not know the facts, or has no regard for truth."[8]

Robinson's tenure on the North Dakota Supreme Court was a short one; he was voted out of office after serving only five years on the bench. But his views regarding the dangers of vaccination were not the reason why. On the contrary, his decision was part of a broader legal and political impulse in North Dakota and elsewhere in the United States that limited the power of public health authorities to enact and enforce compulsory vaccination programs. As late as 1975, North Dakota law prohibited state authorities from denying unvaccinated children access to public schools. In such a legal setting, it is perhaps not surprising that the death rate from smallpox in North Dakota was roughly ten times higher than in states that expressly empowered health agencies to adopt mandatory vaccination programs and compelled recalcitrant citizens to undergo the procedure. In part because of states like North Dakota, the United States had a much higher smallpox rate than most other wealthy industrialized countries. Even places like Sri Lanka, a relatively poor British colony, had a significantly lower smallpox rate than the United States.[9]

How and why did the United States—the richest, most technologically advanced democracy in the world at the time—lag behind poorer and often less benevolent societies in eradicating smallpox, as well as several other infectious diseases? In the midst of a worldwide outbreak of smallpox in 1902, an article in *Mosher's Magazine* gave the beginnings of an answer. It first noted that a century of human experience the world over had demonstrated the efficacy of vaccination in preventing smallpox. The magazine also pointed out that the leaders of the anti-vaccinationist movement in the United States and elsewhere were "the so-called intelligent ones, the professional people." It was "the lawyers, the writers, [and] the teachers" who were "most apt to deem themselves outside of the laws that make the ordinary human body sick or well." What *Mosher's* was referring to here was the mistaken anti-vaccinationist notion that smallpox originated from filth and uncleanliness, as opposed to a specific and contagious pathogen.[10]

More important than their peculiar understanding of the pathogenesis of smallpox, however, was the political ideology that undergirded the anti-vaccinationist cause. For anti-vaccinationists in the United States and elsewhere, the right to refuse and dissent from public vaccination programs was seen as fundamental as the right to free speech or private property. Efforts by state and local authorities to abridge that right were seen as despotic and tyrannical.[11] It is no coincidence, then, that anti-vaccinationists laced their polemics with the language of libertarianism. For example, in his lengthy tract against vaccination, H. B. Anderson began and ended by quoting extensively from the Declaration of Independence, the Gettysburg Address, and the Federal Constitution. According to Anderson, compulsory smallpox vaccination was equivalent to "medical slavery," and the Constitution was supposed to protect the citizenry from such bondage. Without a hint of irony, he appealed to the Thirteenth Amendment to the Constitution (forbidding slavery and involuntary servitude) as protection against mandatory smallpox vaccination.[12]

Similarly, when thousands of people gathered in Leicester, England, in March of 1885 to oppose mandatory smallpox vaccination, they, too, spoke mainly of individual liberty. One observer hailed the day as "a birthday of liberty," as a day that unified the free and principled citizens of England against an unjust policy: "From half the counties of England, from scores of towns and cities, men of all professions, of all trades, bound in close bonds of sympathy, not by tens and twenties, but by hundreds and thousands, met. Thank God for such that England has a conscience still, and a manhood and womanhood too that cannot and will not be trampled in the dust by the hoof of tyranny." Although the Leicester participants spoke much about the dangers of "horse grease," "beastly abominations," and "adulterated blood," and about how mandatory vaccination was just another phrase for "legalised compulsory medical quackery," they also made frequent appeals to libertarian ideals and principles, carrying banners that read "The price of liberty is eternal vigilance"; "Health and Liberty"; "Parental affection before despotic law"; "Men of Kent defend your liberty of conscience"; "Stand up for Liberty!"; and "We fight for our homes and freedom."[13]

Mosher's Magazine attributed the persistence of smallpox among Americans and the English to this commitment to individual rights and liberty, a commitment that in the case of smallpox endangered the broader populace. To make its case, *Mosher's* turned first to Egypt, where British colonial authorities had made smallpox vaccination compulsory. Despite the fact that the British expatriates living in Egypt had "the best" there was "in the way of comfort, cleanliness, and sanitation," their smallpox rate was "six times higher" than the rate for the Egyptians. A British government report explained that while it was "possible to enforce vaccination among the native population" it was impossible to "enforce it" among the English, who simply refused to get vaccinated.[14]

Mosher's went on to describe a "parallel case" in the Americas. Following the Spanish American War, the United States stationed troops in both Puerto Rico and Cuba. Within five years, smallpox was eradicated in both places while, at the same time, authorities in New York City and Massachusetts continued, with only limited success, to battle the disease for another fifty years. Just as with the English in Egypt, *Mosher's* reported that it was "possible to enforce" compulsory vaccination programs in Puerto Rico and Cuba but not in the United States, where the capacity to dissent and resist mandatory vaccination remained.[15] As one Pennsylvania physician explained, Americans were "accustomed to do their own thinking" and were "quick to resent every measure which seem[ed] to threaten their individual liberty."[16]

Reading this introduction, it is tempting to say the United States got it all wrong. If only the country had been less ideological and more scientific/ technocratic, the argument might go, it would not have lagged behind so many European countries in eradicating smallpox. Indeed, data presented in chapter 4 suggests that if the United States had been more like Continental Europe, it probably would have eliminated the disease fifty to one hundred years before it actually did. Nevertheless, in *The Pox of Liberty*, I suggest that we should not be so quick to dismiss entirely the American approach to disease prevention. Although the United States would have enjoyed lower smallpox rates in the absence of its commitments to individual liberty, that does not necessarily imply that the country would have been made better off by scuttling those commitments in favor of a more centralized and extensive public health network.

There are three reasons. First, the American commitment to liberty, while it hindered efforts to prevent smallpox, also promoted economic growth and political freedom, and it improved health outcomes in other contexts. Put more precisely, the same constitutional provisions and ideological beliefs that slowed the implementation of mandatory vaccination programs in the United States simultaneously fostered economic prosperity and individual liberty. Whether the benefits of increased growth and freedom outweighed the costs of smallpox I will leave for someone else to say. My goal is only to show that the trade-off existed, and that it is a trade-off with more general relevance. Understanding the American experience with smallpox in this way suggests that the United States had high smallpox rates not *despite* its being rich and free, but *because* it was rich and free. This idea inverts the way most observers think about disease—disease is typically portrayed as the result of poverty and deprivation, not riches and freedom—and it is an idea I return to, in one form or another, throughout the book.

Second, institutional and ideological commitments to liberty and economic growth were not inimical to all disease-prevention efforts; there were cases and particular diseases where the interests of public health and liberty were aligned. Chapter 5, for example, shows how constitutional rules protecting private property rights and promoting the sanctity of contracts not only fostered private investments and economic development, but also played a central role in the eradication of typhoid fever. Similarly, chapter 6 shows how the American commitment to federalism, a commitment that had decidedly negative effects on smallpox eradication programs, simultaneously encouraged regional economic prosperity and the implementation of programs that were designed to protect cities and towns from the ravages of yellow fever. Although the anti–yellow fever programs that emerged from this federalist system did not always work exactly the way their designers intended, there is evidence to suggest that they had broad public health benefits, reducing deaths not only from yellow fever but from many other diseases.

Third, history suggests that public health policies can sometimes veer away from promoting health to oppressing minority groups or promoting sectional economic interests. Perhaps the best known example of this occurred at the height of the American eugenics movement when public health officials in some states sterilized, or attempted to sterilize, individuals without their consent in order to prevent individuals with "socially undesirable" characteristics from reproducing.[17] Examples presented later in the book, while less well known, suggest that these deviations from appropriate policy occurred because politicians and public health officials were subject to the same racist and baser economic motives that animated the rest of society.[18] When one recognizes the possibility that public health officials are not above implementing the same prejudices and biases that dominate the rest of the society, the necessity of a system that protects individuals' rights and liberties becomes apparent. Of course, the cost of such protections is that, while they limit the ability of public health officials to enact objectionable policies, they also slow the adoption and implementation of policies that are effective and desirable.

The Origins of an American Approach to Disease Prevention

In the chapters that follow, I expand on these ideas and explore how the American constitutional order shaped public health in the United States from colonial times to the mid-twentieth century. Although political institutions and ideologies are the focal point of my analysis, medical and scientific discoveries play an important secondary role. Most of my analysis focuses on three diseases: smallpox, typhoid fever, and yellow fever. Smallpox is a highly infectious disease, spread mostly through the air. Typhoid is a waterborne disease spread mainly, though not exclusively, through sewage-tainted water. Yellow fever is spread by a mosquito and was a regular visitor to large port cities, especially those in the American South. All three diseases plagued the United States throughout the nineteenth century, and smallpox and typhoid remained serious public health problems well into the twentieth.

My central argument is that disease-prevention efforts in the United States were shaped by a network of ideologies and institutions. Because some of these ideologies and institutions were distinctly American, they gave rise to a system of disease prevention that was also distinctly American. The defining features of this system were fourfold. First, it was decentralized, predicated mainly on the strategies and investments of municipal governments. Second, initially the system relied almost exclusively on individual consent and private action, though over time it increasingly appealed to the coercive power of the state. Third, it relied heavily on private property rights to induce investments in health-related infrastructure. This was particularly true in the case of public water supplies, which were arguably the single most important public health initiative of the pre-1950 period. Fourth, it was heavily influenced by market processes and commercial and business interests, and those interests had a mixed effect on health outcomes, sometimes promoting healthier environments and at other times hindering them.

The ideas and ideologies that were most important in shaping the American approach to disease prevention were threefold. First, from their colonial inception, Americans showed a deep ideological attachment to forms of governance that were decentralized and rooted in private consent and voluntary action. This, in turn, fostered and helped sustain federalism in the provision of public health, despite historical and political forces that were pushing for greater centralization. Second, because Americans placed a high value on commercial success and economic prosperity, those values also influenced the practice and implementation of public health policies. While commercial and economic values are often portrayed as inimical to public health, there is evidence to suggest that such values could, at times, foster *better* public health outcomes. Third, the rise of the germ theory of disease interacted with and reshaped political beliefs and ideologies to usher in a vast expansion in the size and scope of government involvement in public health, particularly at the local level.

The institutions that mattered most in forging the American approach to disease prevention can be divided into four categories: democracy; private property rights; federalism; and protections of individual liberty. Democratic institutions allowed American politicians at all levels of government (state, federal, and local) to enjoy greater electoral success through investments in disease prevention. This aligned political and public health incentives: throughout the nineteenth century, good sanitation and disease prevention was good politics.[19] For example, when politicians invested in public health ventures that were successful, they garnered votes and political support; and when they devised ways to control and eradicate epidemics, they limited disruptions in trade, business, and tax revenues. In the case of public water and sewer, and sanitation more generally, there was an alignment of political, economic, and public health interests: as I explain in later chapters, even businesses wanted spending in these areas because it was seen as a means of promoting long-term economic growth.

As for private property rights, various provisions in state and federal constitutions constrained the future behavior of politicians and thereby enabled them to make credible promises about future behavior to potential lenders, private entrepreneurs, and taxpayers. To highlight the importance of these institutions, imagine how difficult it would have been for a city to raise the funds necessary to build a water and sewer system if potential lenders did not believe that the city would eventually pay back what was borrowed, or if there was a sizeable risk that local politicians would simply take the money they borrowed and use it for some other, less socially remunerative end. Constitutional rules governing municipal debt and prohibiting legislatures from passing laws that altered the obligation of contract ex post gave lenders and potential investors confidence that their loans would be repaid and that their capital would not be expropriated. But while these constitutional provisions made it much easier and cheaper for governments at all levels to raise the funds to finance otherwise costly public health initiatives, they could at times also hinder government efforts to regulate private enterprises engaged in activities that affected the public health.

As for federalism, during the nineteenth and early twentieth centuries, the regulatory structures of state and local governments were more vast and intrusive than those at the federal level. The decentralized nature of American public health was well suited to dealing with localized epidemics and problems, but was less adept at controlling epidemics and health problems that crossed state borders. Another benefit of this decentralized approach is that it helped to limit the mass implementation of bad ideas in relation to public health. Also, in contrast to more centralized and bureaucratic regimes, America's federalist approach to public health gave ordinary citizens multiple venues to challenge the decisions of medical experts and health authorities. If the board of health in a particular town or state announced a policy that some individuals objected to, not only could those individuals challenge the policy in court or lobby legislators to pass a law barring the implementation of the policy, but if these options failed, the aggrieved parties could move to another jurisdiction where health officials adopted friendlier policies. In turn, sorting across political jurisdictions fostered the development of communities made up almost entirely of skeptics and medical heretics opposed to the recommendations of the medical establishment. As explained in chapter 3, sorting of this variety gave rise to regional pockets of smallpox, which left the country with higher over-all smallpox rates than it would have had under a more centralized public health system that suppressed jurisdictional sorting.

As for institutional protections of individual liberty, probably the most important was the Fourteenth Amendment to the Federal Constitution. Passed in the aftermath of the Civil War, the Fourteenth Amendment guar-anteed all citizens equal protection under the law and prohibited states from taking from any individual "life, liberty, or property without due process of law." When individuals during the nineteenth and early twentieth centuries challenged any given public health measure as a violation of their individual rights and liberties, they almost always invoked the Equal Protection and Due Process Clauses of the Fourteenth Amendment. While these challenges were often unsuccessful, the litigation that grew out them could slow or delay the implementation of policy, and in some cases it might have helped popularize dissent. At a more fundamental level, the Fourteenth Amend-ment also appears to have helped galvanize ideological beliefs about the limits of state power in relation to mandatory vaccination.

In the case of mandatory smallpox vaccination, for example, when the courts upheld mandatory vaccination orders despite claims that they vio-lated Fourteenth Amendment rights, voters would simply trump the courts by securing passage of laws restricting the ability of public health officials to enforce mandatory vaccination policies. Ironically, in the political cam-paigns to legislate around the courts, those opposed to vaccination would often invoke the same constitutional provisions and protections the courts had said did not apply, suggesting that popular thinking about what the Constitution said was nearly as important, or perhaps more so, than what the courts said in shaping public health policy.

The American Constitutional Order and the Mortality Transition

As much of the discussion above suggests, it would be a mistake to believe that American political institutions had only negative effects on disease-prevention efforts. Although some aspects of the American constitutional order impaired, and continue to impair, the provision of public health and disease prevention, in many cases American political institutions fostered and promoted both public and private investments in disease prevention. The simplest way to highlight and introduce these more positive effects is by looking briefly at the history of life expectancy in the United States, giving particular attention to what demographic historians refer to as the mortality transition and the associated eradication of infectious disease.

The mortality transition took place during the late nineteenth and early twentieth centuries, when the United States (and other parts of the world) witnessed remarkable and historically unprecedented improvements in human health and longevity.[20] Between 1850 and 1950, life expectancy at birth among whites increased by 75 percent, growing from 39.5 to 69. Among nonwhites there was an even larger increase, with life expectancy more than doubling, rising from 23 to 60.8.[21] It is sometimes argued that the American mortality transition took place between 1900 and 1950, a time frame that saw American life expectancy among whites rise from 49.6 to 69. For nonwhites, life expectancy rose from 33 to 60.8.[22]

What is particularly notable about the comparatively large increase in nonwhite life expectancy is that it took place before the era of civil rights, at a time when African-Americans endured extreme economic and social deprivation relative to whites. It is possible that the catch-up among blacks stemmed from the fact that they were starting from a much lower base—after slavery, where else was there to go, but up?—but there is much evidence to suggest that investments in public health infrastructure during this period, particularly those related to water purification and distribution, benefitted blacks far more than whites. Whether one is talking about whites or blacks, life expectancy continued to rise after 1950, but the rate of improvement was one-half to one-third the rate observed in the earlier period.[23]

The improvements in health and longevity that occurred between 1850 and 1950 were associated with radical change in the country's disease and age profile. Before 1880, the leading causes of death were diarrheal diseases, such as typhoid fever and dysentery, and respiratory diseases, such as tuberculosis, influenza, bronchitis, and pneumonia. But by 1925, deaths from waterborne diseases, such as typhoid, had been largely eradicated, and respiratory diseases, while still common, were being eclipsed by heart disease and cancer as the leading causes of death in urban areas. These changes in the country's disease profile were associated with sharp improvements in child and infant mortality, because infectious diseases, such as diphtheria and diarrheal diseases, affected the young disproportionately.[24] Put another way, as the country moved from a high to low mortality environment, chronic diseases and diseases of old age replaced infectious diseases and child mortality as the leading causes of death.[25]

The eradication of infectious diseases is typically seen as a purely technological process. For some, the technological changes wrought by industrialization increased per capita incomes and made it possible for people to buy better housing and improved nutrition, which, in turn, allowed households to more effectively prevent and fight off infections such as tuberculosis. For others, improvements in the technologies associated with public health, such as water filtration and the diphtheria antitoxin, were the driving force behind the improvements in human health and longevity. Still others focus on the development of antibiotics and more modern medical treatments, though most scholars agree that these changes came along well after the greatest improvements in longevity had already been achieved.[26] But whatever technologies one wishes to emphasize, the emphasis on technology is far too simple, because new technologies, and the capital investments that fostered those technologies, were predicated on political and legal institutions.[27]

Nowhere are the connections among institutions, capital investments in public health, and the mortality transition clearer than in the history of typhoid fever. A waterborne disease, typhoid was eradicated through a series of city-level decisions to invest in water distribution networks and water filtration. Cities made these investments in response to the demands of voters who wanted effective responses to repeated typhoid epidemics and rewarded politicians with reelection for implementing such responses. White voters supported extending water distribution systems into black neighborhoods because they feared that typhoid epidemics in the black community might spread to white neighborhoods.[28] In addition, once a decision was reached to build a local water distribution and filtration system, the financing for that system relied on an institutional framework that assured potential investors that the local authorities would repay the money and invest it as promised.[29]

The social rate of return on investments to eradicate typhoid and distribute pure water were enormous, and the mortality transition in the United States would have been a much less impressive feat absent investment in public water supplies.[30] More precisely, the available demographic evidence suggests that improvements in water quality account for well over half of the reduction in mortality observed between 1850 and 1925.[31] This occurred because access to safe drinking water affected a broad range of health outcomes, not just waterborne diseases.[32] Juxtaposing the US experiences with smallpox and typhoid fever makes clear that *The Pox of Liberty* is not a wholly negative story about freedom inhibiting public health, but is a positive one as well, with American commitments to property rights and representative politics fostering an extensive effort to eliminate waterborne diseases.

Modern Relevance: Why This History Matters

Anyone who writes or teaches history inevitably has to answer the "who-cares" question: What makes this particular history relevant? For the case here, that question is no less inevitable. Why, then, should anyone today care about how the Constitution and ideological commitments to individual rights and liberties shaped the American disease environment from 1800 to 1950? First, this history can help us understand a host of modern health care debates in the United States, because many of the same Constitutional rules and structures that shaped disease-prevention efforts in the past continue to influence health outcomes today, though on a much broader scale. This is especially true of the Commerce Clause and the Fourteenth Amendment. Abortion rights; state laws regarding contraception; policies governing HIV-prevention efforts; federal spending on women's health care; medical privacy laws; the tenacity of the modern anti-vaccination movement; the extended legal and political battles over Medicare and national health insurance—all of these in one way or another harken back to an earlier time when smallpox, typhoid, and yellow fever were an integral part of the American experience.

Second, the evidence presented below suggests that disease and economic outcomes are both shaped by political institutions and that they depend on—and are products of—the structure of the state. Whether it was the American commitment to federalism as embodied in the Constitution's Commerce Clause, the Fourteenth Amendment, popular beliefs about individual liberty and the appropriate functions of government, or a variety of institutions that fostered private property rights—the American constitutional order affected both income and the provision of disease prevention. If one accepts that income and disease are both determined by the same underlying institutions and ideological preferences, the puzzle that opened this chapter—the observation that the United States was slow to eradicate smallpox—becomes much less puzzling. In particular, it is tempting to ask: Why did the United States have middling smallpox rates despite being so rich? Yet the evidence below suggests that such a question is predicated on a false sense of causality. The United States had middling disease rates for the same reason it was rich: because the institutions and ideological preferences that shaped political and economic outcomes *also* shaped health policies. To this way of thinking, the United States lagged in the eradication of these infectious diseases not *despite* being rich and free, but *because* it was rich and free.

The third and final path for making the history that follows relevant begins with the following observation. Today, when scholars look to Africa and other parts of the developing world, they often portray disease solely as the product of geography, tropical climate, poverty, and economic underdevelopment. By contrast, in the rubric of *The Pox of Liberty*, preventable diseases are as much the result of choices, both public and private, as they are of geography and climate. In the same way that societies choose the quality of their schools, their roads, their police forces, their militaries, and so forth, they also choose—or at least heavily influence—the quality of their public health systems and the associated levels of infectious diseases. Put another way, the disease environment is not just a function of geography and climate; it is also shaped by politics and individual preferences. In this setting, epidemiology is as much an exercise in political economy as it is in estimating statistical correlations. Understanding disease processes this way challenges the many scholarly claims that infectious diseases, and the biological processes that underlie the transmission of those diseases, have been inexorable forces in human history, beyond the control of either individual actors or states.

TWO

From the Ideology of the Township to the Gospel of Germs

The story of how the American system of public health was shaped by ideological beliefs begins in the early American Republic and builds heavily on the observations of Alexis de Tocqueville. According to Tocqueville, Americans forged their political identities in the context of the township, a small and cohesive community where citizens came to be inculcated with beliefs about their political rights and their duties to one another.[1] In the context of the township, a strong, state-centered response to infectious disease was not necessary; community ties and moral suasion by themselves induced cooperative behavior and allowed communities to base their public health systems not only, or even mostly, on the coercive powers of the state, but also on consent and voluntary private actions. When I refer to the ideology of the township throughout this chapter, I am referring to a system of beliefs that favored a mix of public and private activity at the local level. In this way, the ideology of the township refers to an approach to governance that emphasized local action before appeals to state and federal agencies, and an approach that involved a high degree of private cooperation, though it need not have been exclusively private. Although the ideology of the township would gradually devolve over the course of the nineteenth century, one aspect survived: municipal governments retained a strong and vital presence in the provision of public health throughout the late nineteenth century.

Tocqueville also describes Americans as a people oriented toward commerce and industry. This ideology of commerce undermined the ideology of the township through at least two processes. First, the ideology of commerce fostered centralization and concentration of political power at the federal level. While the United States would always retain a commitment to states rights, over the course of the nineteenth century the primacy of the township was slowly displaced and supplanted by the usurpations of state and federal governments and larger, more intrusive municipal governance. Second, after 1840, the American commitment to commerce gave rise to rapid urbanization and the agglomeration of populations around waterways and major port cities. It also attracted rapid immigration from Europe. As cities and towns grew larger and more heterogeneous, the volunteerism and community spirit that had animated public health in the early American Republic broke apart, and was replaced by an ideology that focused solely on the rights of individuals and not their obligations to the larger community.

Although there had always been elements in American society that pushed for a larger, more activist state in matters related to public health and disease prevention, those elements gained momentum with the rise of the germ theory of disease during the late nineteenth century. It is hard to imagine another collection of scientific discoveries that made such a strong case for a state-based system of public health as did the germ theory.[2] This is not meant to suggest that the germ theory rendered private actions irrelevant, only that they were of second-order importance when juxtaposed with the efforts of the state or state-related agencies. It was, for example, obvious to all concerned that it was much more cost-effective to have a single water purification plant (whether publicly or privately owned) in a city than to have every household spend time and resources boiling their water every few hours to assure that it was safe from cholera, typhoid, and other deadly pathogens.

Positive Externalities and Public Health

Before turning to Tocqueville and the ideology of the township, it is useful to highlight why economic theory suggests that it is difficult to sustain a system of public health predicated solely on individual consent and private action and without any state coercion. Consider an individual's decision to connect his house to the local sewer system, or his decision to get vaccinated against an infectious disease. In both cases, the decision has third-party effects: if he connects to the sewer system or gets vaccinated, positive benefits accrue not only to the purchaser and seller of the relevant service, but also to those who live with, or nearby, the purchaser. Economists call these third-party benefits *positive externalities*. The problem is that people often do not appreciate the magnitude of these third-party benefits when deciding to purchase the good or service; instead they focus solely on the private benefits—that is, on how the good or service will benefit themselves. Consequently, from a society's perspective, not enough people buy the relevant good or service, or, in the examples given here, purchase access to the local sewer system or get vaccinated.

To illustrate, imagine living in a densely populated city in 1880 or 1900. Your home is connected to the local sewer system, but your neighbor's house is not. Rather than using the public sewer, your neighbor has a privy vault (a crude septic tank, often little more than a deep hole lined with rock or wood, common during the nineteenth century). Aside from the awful smell, your neighbor's privy vault frequently overflows when it rains, potentially exposing you and your family to disease-causing pathogens. Tiring of the situation, you approach your neighbor and plead with him to hook up to the public sewer system. Your neighbor, focused solely on his own preferences, tells you that it is too expensive or not worth the trouble. Although you could respond by threatening to litigate the matter, Tocqueville suggests another, less costly solution. I call this solution the township approach.

In the context of a small, tightly knit community (like the townships described by Tocqueville), you would be able to appeal to other neighbors and friends to have them apply social pressure on your recalcitrant neighbor. If this failed, your neighbor might be ostracized or punished in some other socially acceptable way. By the same token, in a small, tightly knit community your neighbor might be more amenable to arguments about social obligations and duties and might even genuinely care about the well-being of his neighbors. In such an idealized community, conflicts like the one between you and your neighbor might never even emerge, or they would emerge with much less frequency, because all members of the community recognize and value one another as friends and neighbors. The difficulty with the township approach, however, is that it is not an especially robust institution: the available evidence suggests that it is viable only in small, cohesive groups, and even then optimal provision cannot be assured.[3]

Because of the uncertainties and fragility of private provision, conventional economic wisdom holds that some type of state intervention is desirable. Either by taxing inaction (e.g., fining individuals who fail to connect to the public sewer system or who refuse to be vaccinated) or by subsidizing the socially appropriate action (e.g., connecting to the sewer system or getting vaccinated), the state can induce the socially optimal level cooperation. As a matter of history, the sewer problem I have just described was a serious problem in cities throughout the United States because, without some form of state coercion, many urban households in nineteenth-century cities simply refused to connect to public sewers.[4] Only when local governments started to penalize households for failure to connect did cooperation emerge. Indeed, a century before the United States Supreme Court upheld the right of the federal government to tax those who did not have health insurance (which was in effect a mandate to purchase health insurance), state courts were upholding local mandates that required households to connect their homes to public water and sewer systems.[5]

Tocqueville and the Ideology of the Township

Alexis de Tocqueville began his description of American democracy by contrasting it with the structure of the typical European government. "In most European nations," he wrote, "political existence began in the higher regions of society and was communicated little by little and always in an incomplete manner to the various parts of the social body." By contrast, in the United States, political power was diffuse and decentralized, beginning first and foremost with the township and the municipality: "In America . . . one can say that the township had been organized before the county, the county before the state, [and] the state before the Union." In this way, municipal government was an organic and primordial element of the early American republic.[6] While Tocqueville obscures the legal origins of the American township—from their inception, townships in the English colonies were chartered by the king and/or Parliament, and later they would be chartered by state legislatures—his larger point remains: the township was a fundamental political institution.[7]

In Tocqueville's history, the New England township was "completely and definitively constituted" by 1650. The early colonists might have seen the British monarchy "as the law of the state," but it was in the township that one observed "real, active, altogether democratic and republican political life reigning." It was there that "interests, passions, duties, and rights" came to be defined. "One could almost say," Tocqueville wrote, that each township "at its origin was an independent nation." In the decades leading up to the American Revolution, the British monarchy grew more assertive and autocratic, but the kings "limited themselves to taking the central power. They left the township in the state they found it." And when "the American Revolution broke out," it was in the township where "the dogma of the sovereignty of the people" emerged and "took hold of the government." After the Revolution, the township retained its independence and strength, and submitted to state legislatures "only when" a question of "social interest" arose, by which Tocqueville meant a question that crossed municipal boundaries.[8]

Municipal and local governments retained their relevance because it was in the context of municipal politics that citizens discovered their civil and political identities. In Tocqueville's view, townships were the primary schools of political life,[9] in which citizens learned how to tolerate and compromise, to win and lose, to defer, submit, and lead.[10] More practically, local political conflicts helped citizens discover both their rights and their duties as members of a free society.[11] Townships were excellent schools for political life, in part, because they implemented and financed so many different sorts of projects and programs.[12] It was through the township, for example, that "the lot of the poor was made secure;" that highways were adequately maintained and managed; that deaths, births, marriages, and other vital records were recorded; that courts were operated; that officers were charged with boundaries of vacant estates and inheritances; and that primitive police forces were formed to maintain "public tranquility in the township."[13] And most importantly, from Tocqueville's perspective, townships governed primary school education: from their inception, the charters of New England townships obliged the citizenry to establish and fund primary schools.[14]

Smallpox Vaccination and the Ideology of the Township: A Case Study

Although Tocqueville mentions public health concerns only in passing, the early history of public health in the United States reflects much of what he had to say about the township and its fundamental role in American society. This can be seen most clearly in relation to the history of smallpox vaccination. When smallpox vaccination was first introduced into the United States during the early 1800s, it was mostly at the local level that policies were debated, planned, financed, and implemented, and the history that follows suggests that local responses involved a robust mix of public and private agencies.[15] One of the earliest and most heavily publicized efforts to promote vaccination began in Milton, Massachusetts, where members of the town council worked with local doctors and clergy to offer free vaccinations.[16] Similarly, in the midst of a smallpox epidemic in 1824, city authorities in Boston introduced "a general vaccination of the inhabitants," as did officials in neighboring towns.[17] Even before vaccination, townships and private local groups were enacting smallpox quarantines and promoting the practice of variolation, a crude and early form of vaccination.[18]

Newspaper accounts clearly indicate that paying for smallpox vaccination was not only an appropriate expenditure for local governments, but also a laudable one, because the decision to undergo vaccination had a substantial public benefit. As the *New York Daily Advertiser* (n.d.) recounted, "It has been the practice in many places in the country, particularly in some parts of New-England, for the towns to employ at their expense some skillful person, and have the whole population vaccinated who had not previously gone through it." "This," the paper said, is "a most valuable plan and . . . no disbursement from the treasury of such places could be more properly, or more advantageously made." As the *Advertiser* saw it, "the interest" in small-pox vaccination is "general," because "when the small pox breaks out in a neighborhood, the inhabitants are thrown into consternation, and those who have not had that disease, or [been vaccinated], have no security but in flight." The "contagious and infectious qualities" of smallpox "are such that no . . . person is safe in a place nigh the spot in which it exists."[19]

It was, moreover, not only in small New England townships that local leaders implemented smallpox vaccination programs; the same pattern was evident in larger towns and cities. For example, in 1810, officials in Newport, Rhode Island, vaccinated 3,000 of the town's 7,907 residents free of charge. One newspaper report celebrated not only the professionalism and skill of the doctors who performed the operation, but also the local clergy for "their humane exertions and personal attendance and encouragement to those unacquainted with" cowpox vaccination. The newspaper also praised "the inhabitants of the town generally for the unanimity with which they adopted the plan of [vaccination], and their general and punctual attendance at the appointed places."[20] While it is tempting to view the Newport experience as a purely state-based exercise, any public vaccination program depends on private cooperation and compliance to succeed, and the newspaper accounts above suggest that the willingness of Newport residents to undergo the procedure helped make the city's vaccination program a success. (The importance of private cooperation is made even more clear in chapter 4.)

Ten years later, after smallpox epidemics had erupted in Norfolk, Virginia, and Baltimore, Maryland, a newspaper correspondent pleaded with Newport officials to implement a universal vaccination order in the city, as had already been done in nearby Providence.[21] Similarly, in New Haven, Connecticut, a group of local physicians "instituted a thorough canvass" of the city "to discover and eradicate every vestige of the small pox, and establish general vaccination in its place." To further this end, the poor were "attended gratuitously."[22]

That it was the township's responsibility to care for and protect those vulnerable to smallpox is also evident in the isolated instances where townships failed to provide such care and protection. Consider, for example, a case from Chelmsford, Massachusetts, where a smallpox patient died not from the disease but from being quarantined in a shed that provided in-adequate protection against frigid temperatures and a raging snowstorm. A correspondent to the local newspaper described in unfortunate detail how at a town meeting, while the patient was still alive, local officials had been informed of the patient's sorry conditions but ignored the plea for help. The correspondent maintained that the patient had died from the "culpable negligence" of the town fathers, "whose duty it was to have provided a suitable hospital."[23]

A clear judicial statement on a township's responsibility in providing for smallpox vaccination comes from a case in Albany, New Hampshire. When a family there was stricken with smallpox in the spring of 1853, Albany officials requested that a local physician care for the family during their illness and vaccinate various members of the family. Once the family had recovered and the vaccination had been completed, the physician submitted a bill to the city. The city argued that because the individuals treated were not paupers, it was under no obligation to pay the physician, and that the family should pay for the services received. The New Hampshire Supreme Court, however, ruled that Albany was bound to compensate the physician for the vaccinations he performed, though the town was not obligated to pay for the other services he provided; those were to be paid by the family.[24]

Also consistent with Tocqueville's larger argument is the observation that it was at the local level that people learned about vaccination, defined their views about appropriate public policy, and, most of all, came to appreciate their duties and obligations to the larger community. Local civic leaders, ministers, doctors, and newspapers announced the efficacy of cowpox in protecting people against smallpox and encouraged everyone who was vulnerable to the disease to seek out vaccination.

One of the best examples of this comes from Baltimore, Maryland, where a group of physicians organized the Baltimore Jennerian Society during an epidemic in 1812. Aside from offering gratuitous vaccinations to the poor, the Jennerian Society divided the city into numerous districts, lobbied residents to get vaccinated if they had not already done so, and instructed the poor on how to receive vaccination free of charge from the city. When residents expressed discomfort with vaccination, the visitors "used no other than the most friendly and gentle persuasion." This sort of moral suasion proved highly effective, and within a few months' time the epidemic subsided, and there was "not one death by smallpox for nearly four years afterwards." When smallpox returned to Baltimore in 1817, the Jennerian Society resorted to the former plan, "searching [out] every person who caught [the disease], apprising all persons concerned of their dangers, and entreating them to resort to vaccination without delay."[25]

At this time, arguments about vaccination were couched not in the language of rights but in the language of duties and obligations. Sometimes vaccination was seen as a burden imposed by God the Creator. Along these lines, a correspondent to the *Salem Gazette* in 1811 argued that refusing to get vaccinated was a form of suicide, and a violation of God's will.[26] At other times, vaccination was portrayed as a duty that individuals owed to themselves or as an obligation that parents had to protect and care for their children; but perhaps most often, it was presented as a social duty, as the most effective method of protecting other members of society from a vile disease. It was in this spirit that the editors of the *Baltimore Patriot* pointedly asked, "We put it to the conscience of those who neglect this simple preservative of life, whether they are not actually destroying the lives of their children, friends, and neighbors?"[27]

Efforts by townships and private associations to vaccinate local populations during the first half of the nineteenth century engendered almost no litigation. Repeated Lexis-Nexis searches on vaccination, smallpox, and other related terms for the decades before 1850 yield only one hit for a case involving someone who was opposed to public vaccination. In that case, the town of North Hero, Vermont, levied a tax on local residents to hire a physician to vaccinate inhabitants of the town free of change. Although the tax was passed with a majority of the town voting in favor of the measure, one local property owner, Dan Hazen, objected, and refused to pay. The town's tax collector then seized one of Hazen's cows and sold it to cover the delinquent taxes Hazen owed.[28]

Hazen sued, arguing that the town did not have authority to levy taxes for the purpose of vaccinating the citizenry; he claimed that authority only existed if smallpox cases were present in the town. The state supreme court, however, held that legislation dictated that it was incumbent on Vermont townships to pay for "all prudent measures" designed to inhibit the spread of smallpox, and the court was certain that vaccination constituted a prudent measure. The tax, therefore, was appropriate, and Hazen was due no compensation from the township.[29]

Two dimensions of the Hazen case merit additional comment. First, the absence of more litigation surrounding public vaccination in the first half of the nineteenth century is remarkable when juxtaposed with the frequency of such legislation during the late nineteenth and early twentieth centuries. What changed over the course of the nineteenth century that rendered the citizenry less amenable to public vaccination? Was public health somehow more intrusive later in the century? Did personal beliefs about the efficacy and dangers of vaccination change? Second, Hazen did not couch his action in the language of individual rights. Instead, his case rested solely on the claim that the city did not have the authority to levy such a tax. This again contrasts sharply with cases in the late nineteenth and early twentieth centuries, when legal objections to public vaccination typically appealed to the principles of liberty and individual rights.[30]

What historical changes and processes rendered Americans increasingly less likely to cooperate with smallpox vaccination programs? Two changes appear to have been significant. The first important change was the ratification and adoption of the Fourteenth Amendment to the Federal Constitution in the aftermath of the Civil War. The Fourteenth Amendment states that "no state shall . . . deprive any person of life, liberty, or property, without due process of law; nor deny to any person within its jurisdiction the equal protection of the laws." The first part of this passage (the part before the semicolon) is called the Due Process Clause. The second part of the passage above (the part after the semicolon) is called the Equal Protection Clause. During the nineteenth century, the courts interpreted this clause as forbidding states from enacting laws or policies that singled out particular groups or classes for unfavorable treatment.[31]

When opponents of mandatory smallpox vaccination appealed to the Constitution for protection, they typically invoked the Equal Protection and Due Process clauses of the Fourteenth Amendment. Although these challenges were not usually successful,[32] the amendment provided a constitutional basis for the modern language of individual rights and liberties and was at the heart of legal cases opposing state-mandated vaccination. The second change was really a constellation of changes involving urbanization, industrialization, and immigration. The emergence of large, ethnically diverse cities gradually undermined the ideology of the township, the spirit of volunteerism, and the individual cooperation that it embodied. With the demise of the township and the overwhelming public health demands of the large industrial cities, state coercion in the provision of public health, particularly vaccination, grew increasingly necessary.

The Ideology of Commerce and the Irony of Federal Power

Toward the end of *Democracy in America*, Tocqueville described what he saw as the remarkable economic transformation of the United States. Once held by England in "colonial dependence," it took Americans only half a century to "become the second maritime nation" in the world, and although Tocqueville could not have known it at the time he was writing, in another half century, the United States would be richest country in the world, and in yet another fifty years, it would alone produce nearly half of the manufactured goods produced in the world. And so when Tocqueville claimed that "no people on earth" had ever made "such rapid progress as the Americans in commerce and industry," he was not far off the mark.

What forces made this transformation possible? For Tocqueville, it was because "the population as a whole" was "involved in industry." "From the poorest" to the "most opulent citizen," everyone willingly "united their efforts" in a host of commercial exploits. Railroads were built joining the "Hudson to the Mississippi," and linking "the Atlantic Ocean with the Gulf of Mexico." The longest railroads in the world, he claimed, belonged to the United States. What impressed him most, however, was not the "extraordinary greatness of a few" vast enterprises like the railroads, but the "innumerable multitude of small enterprises." Everywhere he turned, he saw people engaged in commerce; everyone seemed dedicated and committed to it. Even in agriculture, he saw farmers making a "commerce" out of planting and harvesting. Tocqueville went so far as to claim that "Americans put a sort of heroism into their manner of doing commerce."[33]

The ideology of commerce also set in motion two processes that ultimately helped undo the ideology of the township, particularly in its relation to the private provision of public health. In developing this line of thought, I do not want to say that the United States abandoned localism and private cooperation wholesale over the course of the nineteenth century, or that Americans did not continue to hold strong preferences for state and local control over a variety of policies. Neither of those propositions is true; the United States continued to use a federalist approach for many problems and a preference for decentralized forms of governance continues to this day. I only wish to suggest that because of their commitment to commerce, Americans slowly and unconsciously walked away from the civil and political life of Tocqueville's township and adopted a larger, more centralized approach to governance that relied less and less on voluntary contributions to public goods and more and more on state coercion.

In abandoning the ideology of the township, Americans were seduced by two forces: the first was the utility of federal power in promoting commerce; the second was urbanization, a process that was driven by the quest for commerce and economic gain, culminating in the disappearance of the township. I therefore begin my discussion here by describing how the ideology of commerce was reflected in the Federal Constitution, and how it gave rise to a series of Constitutional provisions that would undergird the growth of the federal government during the first century and a half of American history. Although I do not fully address the rise of American imperialism until chapter 6, it was part and parcel of the growth of the federal government, and it was driven in no small measure by the ideology of commerce. Moreover, the assertion of American military might during and after the Spanish-American War had important public health implications for both smallpox (see chapter 4) and yellow fever (see chapter 6). It is important to be clear that it was often not commerce itself that undermined the township, but the quest for commercial protections through the aid of the state. Business and mercantile interests often lobbied for expansions in the power of state and federal governments to promote their particular interests, and these expansions in governmental power often displaced the township.

As explained in the following chapter, commerce was so important to Americans that they institutionalized their commitment to it in the Federal Constitution.[34] The Fifth Amendment, for example, explicitly protected private property from uncompensated government encroachment; the Commerce Clause promoted an integrated, national market by forbidding the states from regulating interstate trade; and the Contract Clause fostered credit by forestalling legislative attempts to alter the terms of contracts ex post. These constitutional commitments to commerce stemmed from ideological preferences and financial expediency. As Hamilton explained in *Federalist Papers* 12, commerce was the life blood of government because without revenue, governments could not function, and without commerce there was no revenue. "A prosperous commerce," Hamilton wrote, "is now perceived and acknowledged, by all enlightened statesmen, to be the most useful . . . and has accordingly become a primary object of their political cares."[35]

The ideology and financial expedience of commerce also drove the Founders to push for a strong navy and federal government. In *Federalist Papers* 34, Hamilton, for example, argued that if Americans "mean to be a commercial people, it must form part of our policy to be able to defend that commerce."[36] From Hamilton's perspective, the defense of commerce appears to have been a more relevant and immediate concern than that posed by the threat of invasion or attack. Fifty years later, Tocqueville would expand on this point and argue as follows: "Reason indicates and experience has shown that there is no lasting commercial greatness if it cannot unite in case of need with military power."[37] More generally, when the Founders spoke of the benefits of supplanting the confederated states with a single unified nation, they pointed repeatedly to how the new Union would promote commerce by forestalling trade wars among the states and by regularizing the regulations and tariffs that governed trade with foreign nations.[38]

Hamilton's views about the necessity of a strong federal government were inconsistent with the ideology of the township. As Tocqueville explained, the flip side to the ideology of the township was a deep skepticism and fear about the power of the federal government and a belief that the centralization of political power at the federal level posed a threat to liberty. "Americans are . . . preoccupied with one great fear," he wrote. "They perceive that among most peoples of the world, the exercise of sovereignty tends to be concentrated in few hands, and they are frightened at the idea that in the end it will be so with them." Tocqueville himself considered the fear of an excessively powerful central government entirely unfounded, and believed that in the United States the federal government was growing weaker with time, not stronger. "I avow," he wrote, "these fears of many Americans to be entirely imaginary. Far from dreading . . . the consolidation of sovereignty in the hands of the Union, I believe that the federal government is becoming visibly weaker."[39]

History would offer Tocqueville mixed support on this last point, however: while data on government spending are supportive of Tocqueville's point, many events suggested that the federal government was, at least in a political sense, growing stronger over time. These events include the Louisiana Purchase, the Nullification Crisis, the Civil War, Reconstruction, and the Spanish-American War. Events like these helped erode, or at least redirect, the ideology of the township. This process of federal power eroding and redirecting local governance can be seen clearly in the history of yellow fever control. As explained in chapter 6, yellow fever afflicted New Orleans more than any other American city, and that city benefited more than any other from efforts by the American military to combat the disease during and after the Civil War, yet few cities in the United States seem to have resented the assertion of American military might and federal control more than New Orleans, at least not initially. Only with time did New Orleans and the State of Louisiana relent and come to cooperate with the federal government in its efforts to control yellow fever. Federal intervention, for example, appears to have been at least partly responsible for driving New Orleans officials to invest more heavily in sanitation, an improved sewer system, and mosquito eradication during the early 1900s.[40]

Ironically, while Americans feared that expansions in federal power would threaten individual rights and liberties, some of the most important safeguards of individual rights and liberties embodied in the Federal Constitution—among them the Fourteenth Amendment—grew out of Reconstruction, one of the largest and most significant assertions in federal power in American history. In the aftermath of the Civil War, the federal government launched an effort to reshape Southern institutions and political structures so as to include and fully integrate the recently emancipated slaves into Southern life.[41] Deeply opposed and resented by nearly all white Southerners, Reconstruction was supported and maintained only by the presence of Union troops in the South. During the time when Union troops occupied the South, from 1868 to 1877, blacks could vote and were getting elected to political office for the first time in American history, but once Northern troops pulled out of the South, all of that gradually disappeared.[42]

An integral part of Reconstruction was passage of the Thirteenth, Fourteenth, and Fifteenth Amendments to the Federal Constitution, the so-called Reconstruction Amendments. The Thirteenth and Fifteenth Amendments were narrow and focused in their words and affect: the former prohibited slavery, and the latter prohibited states from passing laws that denied individuals the right to vote on account of "color, race, or previous condition of servitude." By contrast, the Fourteenth Amendment was a broad measure designed to prevent Southern states from passing laws that singled out blacks for discriminatory and unequal treatment. In the century and a half following its adoption, the Fourteenth Amendment has been at the heart of almost every significant legal battle where assertions of state power conflicted with individual rights and liberties. The Fourteenth Amendment, for example, has played a decisive role in the jurisprudence of privacy rights, abortion rights, educational funding, protections against self incrimination, sexual orientation, the apportionment of voting districts, religious freedom, and zoning laws.[43]

Urbanization and the Demise of the Township Approach to Public Health

Over the course of the nineteenth century, as American municipalities gradually abandoned the township approach to public health (i.e., an approach that mixed public and private agencies, with a heavy emphasis on the latter), they replaced it with one based more on government intervention and coercion. In the discussion that follows, I explore the central and multifaceted role that urbanization played in the demise of the township approach. As figure 2.1 shows, between 1790 and 1940, the proportion of America's urban population living in Tocqueville-sized townships (towns with populations between 2,500 and 5,000) was more than halved, falling from around 22 percent to less than 10 percent. Over the same period, the proportion of the urban population living in cities with populations greater than 100,000 rose from 18 percent in 1820 to nearly 50 percent in 1940. (There were no cities with populations greater than 100,000 before 1820.) Urbanization was driven, in large part, by industrialization and the quest for commerce. In particular, the rise of manufacturing, mostly in larger cities, increased wages in urban areas relative to outlying areas, attracting migrants from small towns and the countryside.[44]

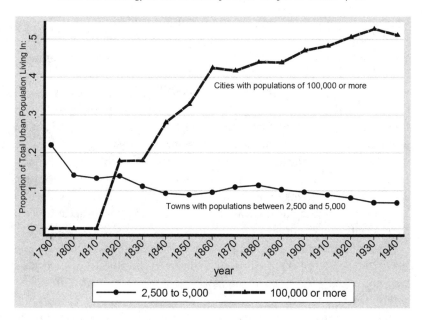

Figure 2.1. Urbanization and the demise of the New England township: 1790–1940. (Data from *Historical Statistics of the United States*; see chap. 1, n. 21.)

The rapid migration into larger cities undermined the township approach to public health in at least three ways. First, to the extent that people were abandoning Tocqueville-sized townships for larger cities, one might say that urbanization was literally destroying the wellspring of the ideology of the township, the place where it was born and nurtured. Second, rapid migration into very large cities meant that people were increasingly moving to environments where it was harder to secure voluntary contributions to public health. As explained at the outset of this chapter, it is much harder to get individual cooperation in larger groups (i.e., big cities) than in small ones (i.e., small, Tocqueville-sized townships). Third, as city size grew and population densities increased, the urban disease environment, which was already bad, became even worse. Illustrative of broader trends, New York saw its crude death rate rise from around 25 deaths per 1,000 persons in 1800 to just under 35 by 1860, an increase of nearly 40 percent.[45] That death rates were growing worse with time suggests that the existing township approach to public health was overwhelmed.[46]

Urbanization was heavily focused on port cities, cities dedicated to commerce and trade, particularly foreign trade. From 1790 onward, the fastest growing counties in the United States were those located alongside major waterways, such as the Mississippi River, or those with major ocean seaports. In addition, urban growth in the United States has always been especially pronounced for towns and cities located at the confluence of one or more major waterways. Even today, more than 50 percent of the American population lives in coastal counties alongside oceans, navigable rivers, or the Great Lakes, despite the fact that those counties make up less than 15 percent of the country's total landmass.[47] Why did the American population agglomerate around waterways? Although many factors might account for this pattern, two of the most important must have been the American quest for commerce and the advantages that accrued to industry from locating alongside rivers and major ports. And arguably the single greatest industrial advantage of locating near a waterway was access to the cheapest form of transportation at the time.[48]

The concentration of the American population around waterways and port cities rendered the country particularly vulnerable to diseases that were correlated with trade and migration, notably cholera and yellow fever. Yellow fever, in particular, was not amenable to a township approach to disease prevention. Even during the late seventeenth and early eighteenth centuries, the heyday of the township approach, American cities and towns tried to control the disease by initiating large-scale and intrusive, state-based interventions. These interventions included massive investments in sanitation, putting quarantines on commercial trade, and, in some extreme cases, shutting down trade entirely. While private groups often undertook steps to complement and assist the state, these private actions were aimed not at preventing or forestalling the disease, but at providing relief for the ill and for those who survived. Throughout the nineteenth century, for example, the Howard Association functioned much as the Red Cross does today. It solicited relief funds for cities stricken by yellow fever; set up camps for those fleeing epidemics; recruited doctors, nurses, and pharmacists to care for the sick and dying; and established orphanages for the many children left parentless by yellow fever epidemics.[49]

The urbanization of the United States was also associated with a rate of immigration that has few parallels in human history. As figure 2.2 shows, between 1800 and 1850 the annual immigration rate to the United States (the number of immigrants per thousand residents) increased by a factor of seven, and immigration rates continued at high levels throughout the nineteenth century, so that between 1850 and 1900 the proportion of the American population that was foreign-born bounced around between 10 and 15 percent. Just as the concentration of the population in port cities

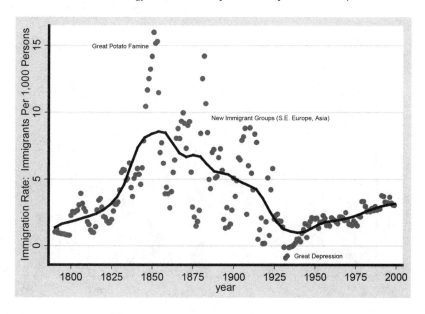

Figure 2.2. Immigrants per thousand persons: 1800–2000.
(Data from *Historical Statistics of the United States*; see chap. 1, n. 21.)

made the United States increasingly vulnerable to yellow fever, so too did immigration, especially immigration from Northern Europe. In places such as New Orleans, which had frequent exposure to the disease, yellow fever was known as "Stranger's Disease" because immigrant and migrant populations with no prior history of exposure were much more vulnerable to the disease than were native-born populations with a prior history of exposure.[50]

Immigration altered the ethnic profile of the United States. In 1790, more than half of the American population could trace their ancestry back to the British Isles (England, Wales, Scotland, or Ireland). And, as figure 2.3 shows, as late as 1850, 60 percent of the foreign-born population in the United States was of British heritage. It was not by accident that when the American revolutionaries tried to rally public support, they frequently appealed to the "Rights of Englishmen" and argued that the king was routinely violating those rights. But as effective as this rallying cry might have been in 1776, it would have fallen flat by 1920, when only 15 percent of the foreign-born in the United States were from the British Isles, and if one ignores the Irish, that percentage falls to 8 percent. Compounding the effects of rapid in-migration, increased ethnic fractionalization eroded Tocquevillian com-

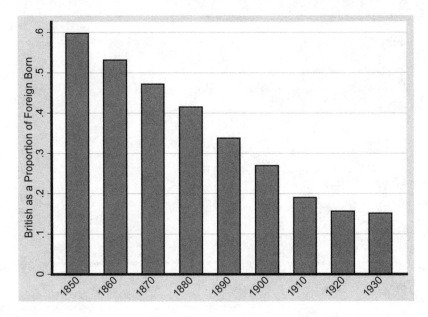

Figure 2.3. British residents as a percentage of the foreign-born: 1850–1930. (Data from *Historical Statistics of the United States;* see chap. 1, n. 21.)

munity ties and made it harder to assure cooperation on public health issues like the "sewer problem" that opened this chapter.

The Ideological Imperatives of the Germ Theory of Disease

The breakdown in the township approach to disease prevention and the worsening of the infectious disease environment put increased pressure on local politicians to address the problem. The rise of the germ theory of disease put still more pressure on local politicians to act, making it much harder to argue that disease could be prevented solely through voluntary private action. If, as the early science seemed to suggest, germs and pathogens were everywhere, hard to destroy, and so easily spread, private action was a necessary first step but was, by itself, insufficient. External effects this difficult to prevent and control called out for state intervention, or, at the very least, a centralized private response.

Put crudely, with the germ theory, public health officials "got religion," and that is why medical historians now often refer to the social and political imperatives suggested by the germ theory as the Gospel of Germs. In part because so many aspects of this new gospel did, in fact, have a firm scientific foundation and were so effective in practice, people were sometimes too quick to believe in and recommend as public policy even the most absurd ideas if they were couched in the nomenclature of the germ theory. More importantly, for those who wished to use the coercive power of the state to oppress minority groups, the germ theory gave great cover—the claim could always be made that any minority group was somehow less clean and carried more germs than other "more desirable" groups. This is well illustrated by the efforts of whites in San Francisco, who used fear of the plague to oppress and abuse the Chinese community in the city.[51]

The Gospel of Germs also interacted with the ideology of commerce. Whether one considers expansions in local water and sewer systems in the battle to conquer typhoid fever (chapter 4) or improved sanitation to combat yellow fever (chapter 6), business and commercial groups were in the vanguard of the municipal public health movement, because they believed the eradication of infectious and preventable diseases would promote the long-term economic development of the city and region. By the same token, adherents to the Gospel of Germs routinely adopted the language of commerce and business to justify large investments in public sanitation. One can see this in the case of yellow fever, where observers routinely claimed that no other "disease interferes so seriously with commerce."[52] This was also true in the case of typhoid fever, where public health officials routinely tallied up the costs of all the workdays lost due to sickness and death to justify large investments in public water systems.[53] More modern economic analyses support their conclusion that such investments yielded impressive social rates of return.[54]

The new religion of germs helped to fuel and guide a vast expansion in the size and scope of state and municipal governments. This expansion can be seen in the creation of hundreds of municipal boards of health across the country. During the first two decades of the new American republic, only a handful of large cities had any sort of formal board of public health, and the powers of these early boards were circumscribed. But, as figure 2.4 shows, the number of municipal boards of health in the United States grew ninefold during the late nineteenth century, from around 25 in 1850 to just under 225 in 1890. What the graph cannot show is that not only did the number of boards of health grow sharply, but their powers grew as well, increasing from some limited police powers to impose quarantines and isolation in a narrow set of circumstances to include the power to regulate water quality and sewer connections to homes, to impose fines and penalties on individuals and firms that helped spread disease, and to forcibly vaccinate school children.[55]

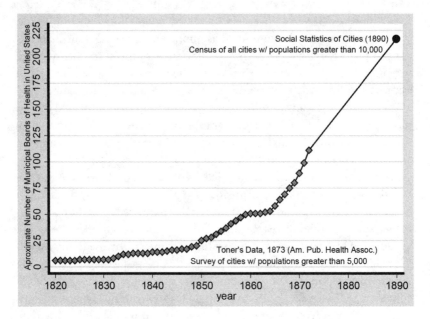

Figure 2.4. Number of municipal boards of health: 1820–1890.
(Data from John M. Toner, "Boards of Health in the United States," *Public Health Reports and Papers Presented at the Meetings of the American Public Health Association in the Year 1873* (New York: Hurd and Houghton, 1875); and Bureau of the Census, *Social Statistics of Cities* (1880 and 1890 volumes).

A Brief History of Some of the Policies and Programs Fostered by the Germ Theory of Disease

The germ theory of disease inspired a wide range of public health policies and programs, most of which were associated with expansions in the size of the state. These programs included anti-tuberculosis campaigns, pasteurization, development of the diphtheria antitoxin, and water purification. The history of anti-tuberculosis programs begins in 1865, when the French scientist Jean Antoine Villemin injected material from humans infected with tuberculosis into rabbits, who then contracted the disease. This established that the disease was caused by a specific (yet unknown) agent. Villemin's experiments remained much contested until 1882, when Robert Koch showed that one could give animals tuberculosis by inoculating them with the tubercle bacillus from human patients.[56]

Seizing on the discoveries of Villemin, Koch, and other researchers, municipal health boards across the United States launched a series of anti-tuberculosis campaigns. These campaigns involved advertising to inform people about the dangers of crowded living conditions and the benefits of fresh air, municipal ordinances that forbade spitting on streets and other public places, laws requiring physicians to report cases and deaths from tuberculosis, and ordinances requiring the quarantine and isolation of particularly infectious cases of the disease.[57] In Massachusetts and other states, it was not uncommon for cities to forcibly remove people infected with tuberculosis from their homes and place them in state-run sanitariums. When those removed were the primary breadwinners, the family could become destitute and dependent on state and local relief.[58]

One of the most successful public health initiatives that was shaped by the discovery and identification of harmful bacteria such as the tubercle bacillus was pasteurization. Pasteur began studying the beneficial effects of boiling wine and beer during the 1860s and 70s, but it was not until the late 1880s and 1890s that other scientists noticed that heating raw milk could destroy harmful bacteria, and that feeding the heated milk to infants could greatly reduce infant mortality from diarrheal diseases. A large study of infants in Paris found that those who consumed unpasteurized milk had mortality rates two to three times greater than those who did not. What made this study especially compelling was that the children who were ingesting unpasteurized milk were drawn from the wealthiest sections of town, while those drinking pasteurized milk were from the poor sections of town.[59]

Another famous study found that unpasteurized milk sold in markets contained as much bacteria as raw sewage. Researchers also identified *salmonella typhi*, the bacillus that causes typhoid fever, in raw milk. And during the early 1900s, investigators repeatedly found evidence that raw milk sold in urban markets contained tubercle bacilli: 7 to 16 percent of the milk sampled in Chicago, New York, and Washington, D.C., for example, was tainted with bacteria from diseased cows. In addition to typhoid, tuberculosis, and diarrheal diseases, tainted milk was also implicated in the spread of diphtheria, scarlet fever, and other streptococcal infections.[60]

The discovery that unpasteurized milk could carry so many disease-causing pathogens prompted local governments to initiate milk inspection programs and to mandate that milk sold within their jurisdictions undergo pasteurization. In part because of these programs, infant mortality rates in large American cities dropped sharply over the course of the late nineteenth and early twentieth centuries. In Chicago, for example, the infant mortality rate fell by 75 percent between 1870 and 1920. Similarly, in New York, the infant mortality rate fell by 66 percent, from 273 deaths per 1,000 live births in 1885, to 94 in 1915.[61]

As evidence that pasteurization played a significant role in the decline in infant mortality, historical observers frequently pointed to how pasteuri-

zation altered the seasonal distribution of infant deaths. Before the introduction of pasteurization, infant diarrhea deaths in American cities exhibited a sharp summer peak. This peak was highly correlated with bacterial
counts in raw milk: during the summer months, raw milk sold in urban
markets contained far more bacteria than did milk sold during the winter,
early spring, and later fall.[62] After the introduction of pasteurization, bacteria counts in milk were low throughout the year, and the summer peak in
infant deaths from diarrheal disease vanished.[63] There is also evidence from
large American cities that passed ordinances mandating pasteurization hastened the decline in typhoid fever.[64]

In 1883, a year after Koch established the role of the tubercle bacillus in
transmitting tuberculosis, Edwin Klebs identified C. diphtheria, the bacteria
that causes diphtheria, and in the following year Friedrich Löffler developed
a medium on which to grow the bacillus, which was important because it
was a fragile organism. The findings of Klebs and Löffler laid a foundation
for Emil Behring's highly effective antitoxin a few years later. Early studies showed that, introduced promptly in the treatment of the disease, the
antitoxin reduced the case fatality rate among hospitalized children from
around 40 or 50 percent to between 15 and 25 percent, and these numbers
improved with time as physicians gained more skill in using the antitoxin.[65]

To maximize the efficacy of the antitoxin, it had to be introduced early
in the course of disease, at the first sign of symptoms. Mortality rates rose
sharply if the administration of the antitoxin was delayed more than twelve
hours after the onset of a sustained increase in temperature.[66] Figure 2.5 illustrates the efficacy of the antitoxin for a paradigmatic case reported in the
literature. For this diphtheria patient, before the onset of fever and other
symptoms (the first five days) the patient's temperature hovered between
96.8 and 98.6 degrees Fahrenheit (36 and 37 degrees centigrade), but on
the sixth day, the fever set in and the patient's temperature spiked, reach-
ing 107.6 degrees (42 degrees centigrade). But at the end of day six, 10 cc
of the antitoxin were administered and within twenty-four hours the fever
was gone.[67]

Once city health departments in the United States noticed how effective and useful the antitoxin could be, they began offering it free of charge
to the poor, regulating and promoting its use among ordinary physicians,
and overseeing its production and distribution in cities to assure safe and
adequate supplies.[68] These campaigns, which began during the mid to late
1890s, were incredibly successful, as diphtheria went from being a leading cause of death among children to a minor one.[69] As an illustration of
more general trends, consider figure 2.6, which plots the mortality from

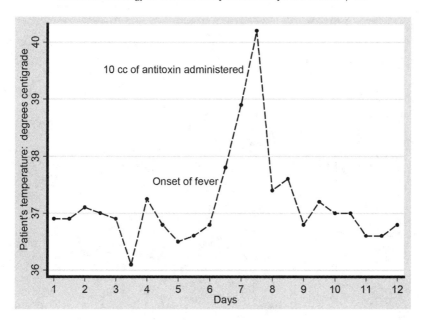

Figure 2.5. The diphtheria antitoxin and the course of the disease.
(From J. W. Schereschewsky, "Diphtheria: Its Prevention and Control," supplement no. 14 to the United States Public Health Service, *Public Health Reports*, April 17, 1914 [Washington, DC: Government Printing Office].)

diphtheria for Chicago. Notice that in the years before the antitoxin was introduced in the mid-1890s, diphtheria rates rose from around 0.5 deaths per thousand to 1.5, a threefold increase. This trend, however, was reversed at roughly the same time the antitoxin was introduced, and the rate fell to around 0.3 deaths per thousand by 1905, a reduction of nearly 80 percent.[70]

For the purposes of this book, probably the most important germ-related discoveries were related to waterborne diseases such as cholera and typhoid fever. During the 1840s, William Budd demonstrated that typhoid was spread by food and water. Later, during the 1870s, Budd published a famous article documenting the importance of purifying and protecting public water supplies. Discoveries by Carl Eberth and Edwin Klebs in 1880 (identifying the typhoid bacillus in the intestinal tract), and by Georg Gaffky in 1884 (culturing the typhoid bacillus from a patient's lymph nodes) laid the foundation for more accurate diagnostic techniques, such as the Widal test, and for the development of an anti-typhoid vaccine. As for cholera, William Budd published work in 1849 describing microscopic bodies in the excreta of cholera patients. Then, in 1854, John Snow famously traced an outbreak of cholera in England to local water supplies. It was another

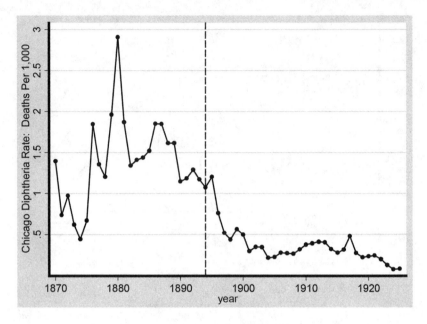

Figure 2.6. Diphtheria in Chicago: 1867–1924.
(Data from Chicago Department of Health, *Annual Reports*.)

twenty-nine years, however, before Robert Koch would identify the microbe that caused cholera (*V. cholerae*). The discoveries of Budd and Snow, along with the proselytizing of scientists like William Sedgwick, drove municipalities across the United States and Europe to invest in public water and sewer systems. For municipal governments, these investments were of a massive and unprecedented scale. As explained in chapter 4, they were also incredibly effective, not only reducing deaths from waterborne diseases, but also eliminating deaths from the sequelae of typhoid fever.[71]

The Germ Theory of Disease as an Encroachment on Individual Rights

The expansions in the size and scope of municipal government that came with the rise of the germ theory did not pass unnoticed or uncontested. One of the most ardent critics of these expansions was H. B. Anderson, the secretary and treasurer of the Citizens Medical Reference Bureau. In *State Medicine: A Menace to Democracy*, Anderson pointed to the germ theory as the inspiration for a host of laws and regulations inimical to the Constitution and the principles of a free society: "The germ theory," he wrote, "has been the basis for numerous laws, rules and regulations antagonistic to personal liberty." As evidence for this position, Anderson cited a host of actual and proposed laws involving mandatory smallpox vaccination, government-led initiatives promoting the use of the diphtheria antitoxin, the identification and isolation of tuberculosis patients, and local laws that would have mandated medical examinations for anyone wishing to work as a domestic, lest they spread tuberculosis and typhoid.[72]

Anderson wrapped his indictment of legislation based on the germ theory in a short constitutional exegesis that at its best had a common sense appeal, but was often nothing short of bizarre. The aspects of his analysis that appealed to common sense, though not formal legal precedent, invoked the Fourth Amendment (barring unreasonable search and seizure), the Fifth Amendment (eminent domain), and the Ninth Amendment (the protection of unenumerated rights). Certainly one could acknowledge at least the plausibility of an argument that laws requiring physicians to report certain diseases or dictating medical examinations for certain professions might violate the Fourth Amendment; or that laws requiring individuals to undergo vaccination might violate the Ninth Amendment, even if the courts routinely rejected such arguments. But as noted in the introduction, Anderson grew more bizarre when he likened vaccination to slavery and then claimed that mandatory vaccination therefore violated the Thirteenth Amendment (which prohibited slavery). Anderson also seemed to imply that government policies predicated on the germ theory violated the First Amendment prohibition against government establishment of religion.[73] Other anti-vaccinationists were no less enthusiastic in wrapping their arguments in appeals to legal precedent and the Constitution.[74]

Whether or not Anderson was correct in his assessments and interpretations, dissent like his was often successful in blocking new public health regulations or in getting newly passed regulations repealed. In several cities, for example, ordinances designed to check the spread of tuberculosis had to be repealed because of loud protests from the citizenry, who argued that municipalities were turning tuberculosis patients into lepers by quarantining them in sanatoriums, so-called pest houses, and isolation hospitals.[75] Public health officials typically characterized such popular dissension as misguided and based on a poor understanding of the relevant science. Yet, as Anderson correctly pointed out, there really was very little in the way of solid scientific evidence *at the time* to justify the claim that isolating and quarantining tuberculosis patients stemmed the spread of the disease,[76] and at least some of the leading experts in the country were arguing that state-sponsored anti-tuberculosis campaigns were doing little to hasten the decline in the disease.[77] At a more general level, the germ theory, though usually rooted in a firm scientific foundation, was malleable and easily bent to serve dubious ends.[78]

Concluding Remarks

This chapter has described the evolution and interaction of three ideological impulses in American society, each with important implications for both economic development and public health. The first of these was the ideology of the township, which fostered a system of public health that was highly localized and predicated on individual consent and private action. The history of smallpox vaccination suggests that this township approach worked well so long as communities were small, ethnically homogeneous, and tightly knit. But as America industrialized and urbanized, a process shaped and driven by what Tocqueville described as the American commitment to commerce, the ideology of the township began to break down. As city size expanded, communities became fragmented; and individuals lost sight of their obligations to the larger community and focused solely on their rights as individuals. This process was hastened by the adoption of the Fourteenth Amendment, which created a new language and rhetoric of individual liberty that affected not only civil rights but economic rights as well. Indeed, as the next chapter shows, during the nineteenth and early twentieth century, the litigation surrounding the Fourteenth Amendment had more to do with economic liberties than with civil ones.

The rise of the germ theory directly undermined the ideology of the township because the public health initiatives it suggested, such as sanitation and improved water quality, rendered state action, or action by large private enterprises, far more effective than measures based solely on individual behavior. This occurred partly because the new germ theory inspired technologies that exhibited scale economies, thus making large firms or the state more efficient providers of disease prevention than individual consumers or small groups. Consider the case of providing clean water. As noted in the next chapter, an individual family could be assured that its drinking water was safe by boiling it, or a single company could simply filter and treat the water before distributing it. The latter option was much cheaper than the former. The germ theory of disease was also promoted by the ideology of commerce, as businesses and merchants saw improved sanitation and disease-prevention technologies as means of fostering long-term economic development.

THREE

The Constitutional Foundations of Health and Prosperity

Philadelphia, the first capital of the United States and the site of Constitutional Convention in 1787, was struck by a series of yellow fever epidemics during the 1790s and early 1800s. The epidemic of 1793, which came only seven years after the Constitutional Convention, killed 8 percent the city's population. A second epidemic in 1797 killed 2 percent; a third in 1802 killed almost 0.5 percent; and a fourth in 1805 killed just under 5 percent. Earlier epidemics in 1741 and 1699 were no less deadly, killing 2.5 and 10 percent the city's population, respectively. What happened in Philadelphia was not unusual. Diseases such as yellow fever, malaria, and smallpox ravaged American cities and settlements throughout the seventeenth, eighteenth, and nineteenth centuries. For example, in 1721, a smallpox epidemic in Boston killed one of every ten city residents. Similarly, a smallpox epidemic in Charleston, South Carolina, in 1698–99 might have killed up to a quarter of the city's population.[1]

So common were smallpox, yellow fever, malaria, and other diseases in early America, that one could *almost* say that it was a republic forged in the crucible of disease. However, I emphasize the word "almost" because, while American institutions might have been created in the midst of a harsh disease environment, that harshness had no perceptible effect on constitutional structure or the political thinking of the Founders. There is no explicit reference to disease or disease prevention anywhere in the Constitution. Nor do Hamilton, Madison, or Jay discuss the Constitutional significance of biological diseases anywhere in the *Federalist Papers*; the only substantive use of the word *disease* involves Madison's metaphorical reference to the political pathology he famously called "faction." Although the disease of faction turns out to have important implications for the provision of public

health in the United States, the larger point remains: disease in a strictly biological sense was not a salient factor in the American founding.

Building on these observations, this chapter explores how the Constitution shaped the American response to epidemic diseases. I develop two
interrelated arguments. First, the Constitution was not designed to control
disease in the most effective ways possible, but rather to promote economic
and political freedoms. Because the Constitution was designed around economic and political principles, not public health imperatives, its effects on
disease-prevention policies were indirect, unintentional, and probably suboptimal from a disease-prevention standpoint. Second, the same constitutional provisions that fostered economic prosperity in the United States also
influenced, for good and for bad, public health policies and the prevalence
of infectious diseases.

To demonstrate how the Constitution came to shape economic and
public health outcomes simultaneously, I organize the chapter around four
economic and political problems that were fundamental concerns to the
Founders: the tyranny of the majority, interstate commerce, factions, and
debtor-creditor relations. Describing how specific constitutional provisions
and structures were designed to mitigate these problems, I also discuss how
those same provisions and structures affected public health policies. In the
case of the tyranny of the majority, the discussion that follows shows how judicial independence not only limited the ability of majorities in the United
States to enact public health policies that oppressed minority groups, but
also helped check the power of legislatures to enact popular and politically
expedient policies that otherwise would have stifled economic development. In the case of interstate commerce, the discussion shows how, in an
effort to promote interstate commerce and forestall interstate trade wars, the
Constitution also gave rise to a highly federalist and decentralized system
of public health. As for factions and debtor-creditor relations, the discussion shows how institutions designed to minimize the influence of special
interest groups and promote the sanctity of private contracts helped foster
private investments in public health systems.

The Tyranny of the Majority and an Independent Judiciary

The Founders recognized that while democracy in some form might have
been a necessary precondition of a free and just society, they also recognized
that by itself democracy was not sufficient. For James Madison and others,
the fact that a policy was chosen through democratic means did not make
it just or legitimate; nor did it necessarily imply that it was the product

of a truly consensual process. Although Madison made frequent reference to ancient Greece to make his point, today we need look no further than the past two-hundred odd years of American history to show that democracy alone is not enough to guarantee consensual governance. Throughout American history, whites have been in the majority and have been able to use that majority status to oppress and exploit minority groups through their dominance over the legislative process. That their choices to segregate schools and deny blacks equal access to a host of public services were made democratically did not make those choices legitimate or imply that blacks consented to them. Put another way, democratic outcomes reflect the preferences and pathologies of voters. If the majority of voters are corrupt in some way, it is difficult to see how the choices they make at the ballot box would not reflect and embody that corruption.

Tocqueville referred to this general phenomenon as the tyranny of the majority; the Founders used language that was less evocative but expressed the same idea and fundamental concern about populism run amuck. In one often-quoted letter to James Madison (March 15, 1789), for example, Thomas Jefferson wrote, "The executive power in our Government is not the only, perhaps not even the principal, object of my solicitude. The tyranny of the Legislature is really the danger most to be feared, and will continue to be so for many years to come." Similarly, Madison believed that, because of the tyranny of the majority, pure "democracies have ever been spectacles of turbulence and contention; have ever been found incompatible with personal security, or with rights of property; and have, in general, been as short in their lives, as they have been violent in their deaths."[2] For Tocqueville, an enfranchised majority could pose a greater threat to individual liberty than the most rapacious king. A king, he explained, ruled by force alone, while the majority possessed both force and a claim to moral legitimacy. The king could never control the hearts and minds of his people, while a truly democratic state was the political embodiment of those very same hearts and minds.[3]

Because of their concerns regarding the tyranny of the majority, the Founders created a constitutional republic, not a direct democracy. Under a constitutional republic, voters influence policy indirectly by choosing their government representatives who then enact policy. In addition, a constitution puts limits on the policies that the majority could enact and enforce through their representatives. These constitutional limits do not assure universal consent, nor have they always provided adequate protection to the dispossessed, but they have offered some modicum of protection to minority groups who might otherwise find themselves without any recourse to legislative tyrannies, such as the Jim Crow South.[4] Among the many constitutional provisions designed to check the power of the majority, arguably the single most important is an independent judiciary. As the only branch of government immune to the short-term electoral and political pressures that animate the legislative and executive branches, it alone has the power to maintain constitutional protections of individual rights in the face of powerful and potentially misguided democratic majorities and corrupt special interest groups.[5]

That the Founders saw an independent judiciary as a guardian of individual rights in the face of legislative encroachment is evident in *Federalist Papers* 78. As Alexander Hamilton explained there, to fulfill their obligations faithfully and effectively, judges should hold permanent tenure: "If then the courts of justice are to be considered as the bulwarks of a limited constitution against legislative encroachments, this consideration will afford a strong argument for the permanent tenure of judicial offices, since nothing will contribute so much as this to that independent spirit in judges."[6]

Only if judges held permanent tenure and were immune to electoral pressures could they effectively block and forestall "the injury of the private rights of particular classes of citizens by unjust and partial laws." The "firmness of the judicial magisteracy" was, Hamilton wrote, of "vast importance in mitigating the severity and confining the operation of such laws." In Hamilton's view, not only would independent judges strike down laws that were constitutionally unsound in their effects on individual and minority rights, but they might also actually discourage legislatures from passing such laws in the first place.[7]

The available evidence suggests that the American commitment to judicial independence had, and continues to have, important implications for both economic prosperity and public health policy. Historically, judicial checks have been an important source of economic growth because they forestall both legislative and executive attempts to expropriate private property when such expropriation is politically popular. The history of American railroads and public utilities suggests that in the absence of judicial protection from such actions, private companies would have been unwilling to invest in fixed plant and distribution systems because of fear of expropriation.[8] More broadly, formal statistical studies document a strong correlation between judicial independence and economic performance: controlling for other factors, countries with independent judiciaries are richer and have faster economic growth than those without.[9]

An example many economic historians point to in highlighting the importance of an independent judiciary involves England's Glorious Revolution in 1688. Before 1688, the English judiciary was subservient to the Crown and could do little to check the king when the king unilaterally decided to renege on loans or otherwise abridge private property rights. Because of this, private capitalists were reluctant to lend the king money or even invest in England, hindering the country's growth and development prospects. But with the Glorious Revolution, the relative power of the English judiciary rose and, as a result, it could now impose meaningful checks on the power of the sovereign. Of particular importance in this regard were legal structures that prevented the Crown from reneging on its promises to lenders and private investors. As a consequence, the Crown was able to gain credit at much lower interest rates, and private investment in England expanded rapidly, laying the foundation for the English Industrial Revolution and the onset of modern economic growth.[10]

An Example of the Tyranny of the Majority in the Provision of Public Health: Plague Prevention and the Chinese in San Francisco

The experience of the Chinese in San Francisco illustrates how an independent judiciary can prevent majorities from tyrannizing minorities under the guise of protecting the public health. In 1900, there were 13,954 Chinese residents in San Francisco out of a total population of 342,782, or 4.6 percent of the city's population.[11] The Chinese were, therefore, in a distinct minority, and, given the racial attitudes of the day, they were subjected to a legislative campaign very similar to the ones Southern cities launched against African Americans. As a consequence, the Chinese frequently found themselves in court challenging one discriminatory ordinance or another, because, whatever else one might say about San Francisco politicians at that time, they were persistent and dedicated servants of the city's white majority.[12]

On May 18, 1900, the San Francisco Board of Health adopted a policy requiring all Chinese residents in the city to get vaccinated against the plague with the Haffkine Prophylactic. They were also barred from leaving the city without first getting the Haffkine vaccine. Failure to comply was met with imprisonment. Immediately after adopting this measure, the board of health began rounding up the city's Chinese residents and forcibly vaccinating them. One Chinese resident, Wong Wai, sued in federal court, asking that the court enjoin the city health department from further coercive efforts to vaccinate the Chinese community.[13]

In granting Wai the injunction, the court explained that the board of health's order was a clear violation of the Fourteenth Amendment's Equal

Protection Clause.[14] There was no compelling rationale for singling out the Chinese community for vaccination; the city presented no evidence that the plague was more pronounced or limited in any way to the Chinese community. If there was a risk of plague, the city should have vaccinated everyone, not simply the Chinese. As the court wrote, "[The regulations] are directed against the Asiatic race exclusively, and by name. There is no pretense that previous residence, habits, exposure to disease, method of living, or physical condition has anything to do with their classification."[15] Moreover, the court found that the city's plan, even taken on its own terms, was counterproductive and exposed the Chinese to grave and unnecessary risks. The Haffkine vaccine was only indicated for use among individuals who were not already infected with plague; vaccinating someone who was already ill greatly increased the risk of serious complication and death. By the court's reasoning, if there already was much plague among the Chinese, vaccinating the entire community, many of whom by the city's logic were already infected, would have only increased the number of deaths.[16]

The court's written opinion had a scolding and impatient air about it, and with good reason. This was not the first time the city had singled out the Chinese community for unequal treatment. From the moment the Chinese arrived in San Francisco, they were targeted. During the 1870s, all ships arriving from Hong Kong were automatically detained in a lengthy quarantine until the passengers were all forcibly vaccinated for smallpox and the ship was fumigated. Passengers on boats arriving from other ports were only quarantined and detained if there was strong evidence of a contagious disease aboard. According to the San Francisco Board of Health, this policy was motivated by the belief that "Chinese coolies" had "no regard for sanitary laws," and brought with them "diseases of a most contagious character." The "immense hordes of Chinese" immigrants were, in the board's view, "filthy beyond description," having made their passage in boats that "resembled the slave ships of former times."[17]

The efforts of the white majority in San Francisco to tyrannize the Chinese minority did not stop there. In June of 1876, San Francisco passed an ordinance requiring the city jailer to clip the hair of all prisoners to uniform length, one inch from the scalp. Although the city claimed the ordinance was passed for purposes of sanitation and public health, a federal court ruled that its "real purpose" was to disgrace Chinese prisoners who were forced to shave off the long ponytails they wore down their backs. Accordingly, the court struck down the ordinance as a violation of the Equal Protection Clause.[18] Similarly, in 1880, the San Francisco City Council passed an ordinance mandating that laundries in the city be operated in buildings made of brick or stone; any laundry operated in a wooden structure had to secure permission from the board of supervisors. Again this was passed under the guise of protecting the public's health and safety. Because almost all Chinese laundries in the city operated out of wooden buildings, the law and its enforcement fell almost entirely on the Chinese: hundreds of Chinese businesses were fined and many owners were jailed. The United States Supreme Court held that the ordinance was clearly designed to single out Chinese-owned laundries and that it therefore violated the Equal Protection Clause of the Fourteenth Amendment.[19]

It is important to note, however, that the American court system did not always rise above the politics and prejudices of the majority. This was particularly true in state courts, where judges were often elected and subject to the same political forces that animated legislative behavior; by contrast, judges in federal courts were appointed with lifetime tenures. In South Carolina, for example, the state supreme court refused to quarantine a wealthy white woman ill with leprosy in a pest house solely because the house was beneath her social station, while at the same time, the court allowed public health officials to quarantine African Americans sick with smallpox in the very same pest house. In a dissenting opinion, one justice explained that if the house was appropriate for African Americans, it was also appropriate for whites.[20]

There is also the unfortunate story of Mary Mallon, better known as Typhoid Mary. A poor woman of Irish descent, Mallon had the unfortunate characteristic of being a typhoid carrier. Officials quarantined Mallon on two occasions because she refused to stop working as a cook and was the source of several infections. Historians often point to Mallon's isolation as evidence of disparate treatment, because typhoid carriers from more advantaged backgrounds were not quarantined.[21] Finally, probably the strongest evidence of disparate treatment in the provision of public health comes from the history of smallpox, where public health officials in the United States were much quicker to impose draconian vaccination policies and isolation procedures on African American communities than they were on white communities.[22]

Federalism, Economic Prosperity, and Public Health

Through the Constitution, the Founders created a peculiar form of federalism that circumscribed the powers of both state governments and the federal government. Although the Founders appear to have been most interested in preventing the trade wars that hindered the movement of commerce among the states under the Articles of Confederation, the American system of federalism had economic benefits beyond simply promoting cross-border trade flows; it also gave rise to a state regulatory climate conducive to economic growth.[23] As for its influence on public health, federalism in the United State had two effects. First, it promoted localized and state-based responses to diseases. In some contexts, the localized response worked well, while in others it gave rise to a sort of regional parochialism that hindered effective responses to epidemic diseases that crossed city and state borders. Second, state and local governments sometimes used public health concerns as a thinly veiled cover for enacting protectionist trade policies that had few, if any, benefits in terms of disease prevention.[24]

The American system of federalism begins and ends with the Commerce Clause, which reads:[25] "The Congress shall have Power . . . to regulate Commerce with foreign Nations and among the several States." Through these words, the Constitution expressly grants the federal government the authority to regulate *inter*state trade and commerce, and, by implication, bars it from regulating *intra*state trade and commerce. More precisely, the Commerce Clause has been interpreted by the courts to give the federal government the sole authority to regulate matters that cross state boundaries, but the clause prohibits the federal government from interfering with local, instate issues and activities.[26] In addition, judicial interpretation of the Commerce Clause has generally prevented the states from regulating interstate matters, except those that were related directly to the states' police powers and public health. In the words of one circuit court judge during the nineteenth century, "The power of congress is supreme over the whole subject" of interstate commerce, which should be "unimpeded and unembarrassed by state lines or state laws." "In this matter," the court continued, "the country is one, and the work to be accomplished is national." State interests, jealousies, and prejudices could demand no consultation. Simply put, "in matters of foreign and interstate commerce, there are no states."[27]

The Founding Fathers inserted the Commerce Clause in the Constitution because of the abject failure of interstate trade policies under the Articles of Confederation. Prior to the Constitution, state governments regularly engaged in trade wars, erecting tariffs against one another in an effort to promote industries within their own borders; in the end, however, they accomplished nothing more than stifling economic activity and technological innovation.[28] Also problematic were states that served as passageways for more productive states, and burdened the goods that passed through their jurisdiction with heavy taxes. By preventing the states from imposing tariffs on one another, the Constitution created a free-trade zone or common market that fostered the flow of goods and services across state borders.[29]

As James Madison explained in *Federalist Papers* 42, the Commerce Clause, by giving the federal government ultimate authority over interstate trade, was designed to forestall such beggar-thy-neighbor trade policies: "A very material object of [the Commerce Clause] is the relief of the states which import and export through other states, from the improper contributions levied on them by the latter. Were these at liberty to regulate the trade between state and state, as must be foreseen, that ways would be found out to load the articles of import and export, during the passage through their jurisdiction, with duties which would fall on the makers of the latter, and the consumers of the former."[30]

Given the experience of the American states under the Articles of Confederation, Madison was confident that the problem of passageway states imposing tariffs on more productive states would continue and that it would "nourish unceasing animosities" and probably culminate in "serious interruptions of the public tranquility."[31] Madison went on to argue that such a situation would inflame the passions of the productive states that were harmed by such taxes and would redirect trade to less economical routes: "The desire of the commercial states to collect in any form, an indirect revenue from their uncommercial neighbors . . . would stimulate the injured party . . . to resort to less convenient channels for their foreign trade."[32]

Building on many of the justifications for federalism offered by Madison and Hamilton, modern economists and political scientists suggest a number of avenues through which federalism might promote economic growth. The first is through sorting across jurisdictions. Individuals who prefer a state that taxes heavily to provide many government services, move to that state; individuals who prefer low taxes move to states that provide low levels of government service.[33] There is, for example, some theoretical evidence to suggest that, at least in reference to spending on public education, such jurisdictional sorting might have positive implications for growth by promoting savings and capital accumulation.[34]

Another avenue through which federalism might foster economic growth involves interjurisdiction competition, which discourages any one state from enacting policies that are unduly onerous. Along these lines, Barry Weingast has introduced the concept of market-preserving federalism to characterize political systems in England, the United States, and China. He argues that federalism in these places functions as a commitment device, allowing governments to credibly promise to potential investors and businesses that they will not expropriate their investments ex post because expropriation would only discourage other businesses from locating in the state. In the absence of such a credible promise, businesses, especially those wanting to invest large amounts in fixed and immovable capital, would be reluctant to invest and locate in the state.[35]

Historians have long suggested a more general version of Weingast's argument. In particular, in characterizing the origins and effects of the municipal reform movements during the Progressive Era, urban historians have described how local citizen groups tried to promote and attract economic activity to particular cities and municipalities by improving municipal governance and eradicating the political corruption that had dominated the urban landscape throughout the nineteenth century. This line of thought suggests that the corruption of local governments disrupted the provision of local public goods and services, which in turn, discouraged in-migration from businesses and workers. As a result, by eliminating corruption and making local governments more responsive to the electorate, reform was thought to have a positive influence on subsequent urban growth.[36]

While jurisdictional competition and sorting likely promoted better political and economic outcomes in states and localities, its effects on public health were mixed. On the positive side, it seems likely that through demonstration effects (defined below), federalism and decentralization probably encouraged otherwise recalcitrant cities to invest in public water supplies. To appreciate the importance of demonstration effects, imagine two cities, A and B. City A begins filtering its water; city B is reluctant to invest in the process because it is unsure of the benefits. Once A begins filtering its water, typhoid rates in the city plummet and convince voters and authorities in B that they too should invest. In the absence of such demonstration effects and localized experimentation, investments in public health would have been slower to diffuse, as it would have been much harder to convince authorities in B of the benefits of the process. In a more centralized system, it is possible that B's recalcitrance might have prevented any sort of investment and thereby undermined demonstration effects. Indeed, Louis Cain and Elyce Rotella document the significance of demonstration effects in the construction of urban water and sewer systems in the United States and Europe.[37]

On the negative side of federalism and public health, consider how jurisdictional competition and sorting would have undermined efforts to achieve universal vaccination. Imagine a country with one hundred individuals. Ninety of them favor and willingly obey laws mandating that all citizens undergo vaccination, but there exists a small, vocal community of ten dissenters who strongly oppose vaccination and favor policies that allow individuals the freedom to refuse public vaccination orders. In one setting, call it the non-federalist setting, vaccination policy is set by a central government that enacts the policy favored by the majority. Because ninety of the country's one hundred residents favor mandatory and universal vaccination, the non-federalist setting generates a national mandatory vaccination law that does not permit individuals to opt out, and all members of society are vaccinated.

By contrast, consider a federalist setting that allows individuals to sort into smaller communities and where the decision to implement mandatory vaccination policies is decentralized. In this world, it is easy to imagine scenarios where the ninety individuals who favor mandatory vaccination sort into a single community (or a group of communities) where 100 percent of the populace favors vaccination, and universal vaccination is quickly and easily achieved, while at the same time, the ten dissenting individuals sort into their own community. Assuming that democratic institutions apply, this community of dissenters would adopt policies that reflect their values and preferences, including rules that allow individuals to make their own decisions regarding vaccination. By allowing sorting, federalism would allow communities of dissenters to develop and flourish, and, in turn, undermine attempts to achieve universal vaccination, which would have been achievable under a more centralized, national system. The discussion in chapter 4 suggests that federalism might have played a role in the relatively high smallpox rates observed in the United States and Switzerland during the late nineteenth and early twentieth centuries.

Federalism, the Courts, and Public Health

Madison's rationale for the Commerce Clause has been reiterated and reconsidered countless times by the courts, but one of its most important nineteenth-century treatments came from Chief Justice John Marshall in *Gibbons v. Ogden* in 1824. At issue was a conflict between a New York law and federal legislation governing the interstate waterways. The New York law granted Robert Livingston and Robert Fulton a monopoly over the right to operate steamboats on New York waterways, even those that bordered other states. Livingston and Fulton, in turn, licensed Aaron Ogden to operate their monopoly. Federal legislation, however, had at the same time empowered Thomas Gibbons to operate his own steamboat service between New York, New York, and Elizabethtown, New Jersey. Ogden sued, requesting a New York court to enjoin Gibbons from operating a competing steamboat line. Gibbons, however, argued that under the Commerce Clause, the federal government had the exclusive right to regulate interstate commerce, which included the navigation of interstate waterways.[38]

Although the New York courts ruled in favor of Ogden,[39] the United States Supreme Court deemed the New York legislation "repugnant to the Constitution" and held that the federal government had supreme authority over interstate waterways.[40] In striking down the New York monopoly, Justice Marshall argued that it was "the inconveniences" of state regulation (explained above) that led the United States to abandon the Articles of Confederation and adopt the new Constitution that limited state powers and granted the federal government supremacy in matters related to interstate commerce.[41]

Over the course of the nineteenth and early twentieth centuries, Marshall's logic was applied to a wide range of regulatory activities, including railroad regulation (states could not regulate the rates on routes that crossed state borders);[42] retail licensing (states and municipalities could not discriminate against retailers and peddlers handling goods manufactured in other states);[43] meat inspection (states could not impose heightened regulatory standards on meat slaughtered in other states);[44] liquor sales (states could not bar citizens from purchasing liquor from other states);[45] and taxes (states could not tax transcontinental railroad routes, immigration, or other forms of interstate commerce).[46] The economic significance of these rulings is that they prevented states from using regulations and taxes to discriminate against out-of-state businesses and operations. While such discrimination would have promoted the interests and well-being of a narrow class of individuals, it would have done so at the expense of broader societal and consumer interests.[47]

State and municipal governments could only intervene in interstate matters when they could make a legitimate argument that the intervention fell within their police powers, such as protecting the populace from contagious and epidemic disease. For example, in St. Louis, Missouri, the city council passed an ordinance that any steamboat with more than twenty passengers originating south of Memphis, Tennessee, and arriving at the Port of St. Louis would be quarantined for no less than forty-eight hours. The stated purpose of this measure was to prevent the spread of infectious diseases such as smallpox, yellow fever, and cholera from the deep South, particularly New Orleans. In the early 1850s, the owner of a steamboat who was fined for violating the ordinance appealed his conviction, arguing that the city did not have the authority to interfere with interstate commerce.[48]

In upholding the conviction, the Missouri Supreme Court affirmed "the authority and power of the city make quarantine regulations, for the preservation of the health of its citizens" and maintained that the defendant could only prevail if the ordinance imposed burdens that were not justified by the demands of public health and safety. This, however, was not the case. In the court's view, city authorities did well in "supposing contagious and pestilential diseases were found more prevalent on crowded boats" and from boats originating south of Memphis.[49] To the extent that interstate commerce was affected by the ordinance, that effect was incidental, and not by design or intent.[50]

Three decades later, in the *Morgan's Steamship* decision, the United States Supreme Court upheld a Louisiana quarantine measure aimed at the Port of New Orleans. In that case, the court began by observing that "if there is a city in the United States which has need of quarantine laws it is New Orleans."[51] Because it was so involved with trade from warm and tropical climates, the city was especially vulnerable to epidemics and disease.[52] Furthermore, while the court was unwilling to speak directly to the specific mechanisms through which cholera and yellow fever spread, it saw New Orleans as their North American entrepôt.[53] In the court's view, effective quarantine measures in New Orleans were necessary and could serve as a laboratory for what strategies might work best in preventing the spread of epidemic diseases.[54]

According to the court, the steamship company litigating the quarantine law denied none of this. What was at issue was a fee schedule Louisiana imposed on all boats entering and leaving the Port of New Orleans. The steamship company argued that the fees were a tax on interstate commerce. The court disagreed, arguing that the fee merely compensated state authorities for the costs associated with inspecting, fumigating, and isolating the ship, its cargo, and its occupants.[55] The steamship company's refusal to pay the fee left the court flummoxed, as the steamship was itself a primary beneficiary of the quarantine policy and the associated system of inspection and certification of the boat as disease-free. The court reasoned that in the absence of New Orleans's inspection policy, the steamship would have been under frequent suspicion in more Northern ports, where officials would be concerned that the boat might introduce diseases into their jurisdictions.[56]

In addition, if New Orleans failed to adequately inspect all ships, the court felt this would only force the city to adopt more draconian and invasive policies over the long run.[57] As to the question of whether "the law under consideration" was "void as regulation of commerce,"[58] the court recognized that quarantines had a substantial and material effect on interstate commerce,[59] but the justices "did not think it necessary" to review the body of law that classified quarantines as a necessary component of the state's police powers—any law governing the "health, comfort, and security" of the populace would have fallen under the rubric of the state's police powers.[60]

Significantly, should the federal government have wished to forestall, supersede, or otherwise limit state quarantine laws like those in Louisiana, it could have done so easily under the Constitution by creating or empowering a relevant federal agency. As the court explained, should Congress ever pass legislation for a "general system of quarantine" or create a National Board of Health, "all State laws will be abrogated" in so far as they are inconsistent with federal law.[61] But the history of federal legislation left little doubt that Congress had chosen to defer to the states in matters related to public health and the quarantine of interstate commerce.[62] Given these observations, the Court was forced to conclude that quarantine laws belonged "to that class of State legislation which . . . [is] valid until displaced or contravened by some legislation of Congress."[63] Yet Congress had clearly chosen not override the states in matters of public health; the legislative history cited by the court made it abundantly clear that Congress wanted the federal government to play second-fiddle to the states in terms of preventing and controlling epidemic diseases.

The congressional choice to leave it to the states is striking when one considers the frequency and severity of various epidemics in America's port cities during the nineteenth century. As the court explained, Congress, for nearly one hundred years, never passed a quarantine or any other measure to prevent the invasion of contagious diseases, despite the ever-present threat of disease in port cities, especially those in the American South. The court cited, in particular, the American experience with yellow fever and cholera.[64] What explains this inaction? The court believed it stemmed from an ideological commitment to states' rights and to the corresponding belief that the states were better at protecting the public health and quarantining ports.[65] From the court's perspective, it was a wise and practical decision for the federal government to show deference to the states, because every state and every port was different, and state officials better understood what was happening in their jurisdiction than more distant observers from Washington, DC.[66]

The court, however, probably overstated the wisdom and practicality of this decentralized approach. While purely local responses made sense for localized epidemics, such approaches were problematic for epidemics that crossed borders, for the reason that state and local governments did not fully appreciate how their actions might adversely affect neighboring jurisdictions. Moreover, it is not at all clear that every port in every state was so different as to require a unique plan. It is equally plausible that all ports were fundamentally similar, and that it was redundant in the extreme to have each port or each state reinvent quarantine plans that were working well. Perhaps a single, centralized authority would have learned more quickly from those lessons than individual states. Along the same lines, it is also possible that larger enterprises were more efficient and cost-effective providers of disease prevention than small enterprises, so that a single, centralized provider would have been the superior organizational structure.

A good example of the difficulties associated with localized responses to epidemic diseases involves a lengthy court battle between the Sanitary District of Chicago and St. Louis, Missouri. During the 1890s, the Sanitary District of Chicago enlarged the flow of wastes into the Chicago River, which in turn entered a tributary of the Mississippi River and eventually reached the water supply of St. Louis, Missouri. This decision had positive benefits for Chicago: typhoid rates in the city fell once the sewage flow was diverted away from Lake Michigan (the city's water source) and into the Chicago River. St. Louis residents, however, believed that Chicago's decision caused typhoid rates in St. Louis to increase. As a result, St. Louis officials filed suit in federal court to enjoin the Sanitary District from emptying more sewage into the Chicago River. Although St. Louis eventually lost the suit, the case illustrates the conflicts that can arise when authorities combat disease from a local, as opposed to a regional or national, perspective.[67]

Constitutional Solutions to the Problem of Faction and Their Effects on Public Health and Economic Performance

In *Federalist Papers* 10, James Madison offered his famous discussion of the problem of faction: factions were political pressure groups, whether organized around populist impulses, narrower economic or ideological interests, or sectional animosities. When factions of any variety capture the state, they twist and distort policy outcomes to their own ends and in the process impose costs on other groups in society. For Madison, faction was a disease endemic to all free and democratic societies, both modern and ancient. "Liberty is to faction, what air is to fire, an aliment without which, it instantly expires," he wrote. Yet failure to control factions was fatal to all democratic governments.[68] Democracy, therefore, was no cure for the problem of faction and was subject to the worst form of faction: a faction of the majority, or what Tocqueville called a tyranny of the majority.[69] Only well-designed institutions could limit the adverse effects of faction: "Among the numerous advantages promised by a well constructed union, none deserves to be more accurately developed, than its tendency to break and control the violence of faction."[70]

Recent research in economic development suggests that the formation of at least certain types of factions, or what economists and political scientists call rent-seeking behavior, is an important barrier to economic growth. Through rent-seeking, business groups lobby and bribe lawmakers to enact policies that inhibit market entry and protect incumbent firms from competition. The result is legislation that stifles innovation, inhibits market entry, and raises consumer prices, all of which conspire to undermine economic growth. Rent-seeking not only undermines economic progress through its direct effects on innovation and competition, but also by encouraging firms and individuals to redirect their investments and spending away from productive pursuits (e.g., manufacturing or providing needed consumer services) to purely redistributive activities (e.g., lobbying or bribing lawmakers for friendly legislation). Rent-seeking is also pervasive and is not limited to lesser-developed countries or countries with poor governance, though one would expect it to be a more severe problem in places with poorly developed political institutions.[71]

At least three provisions in the federal Constitution help to curb the pernicious influence of factions and rent-seeking: the Commerce Clause; the Equal Protection and Due Process Clauses of the Fourteenth Amendment; and the Contract Clause. As suggested by the discussion in the preceding sections, the Commerce Clause undermined the formation of factions in relation to state-level trade policies. In particular, in the absence of the Commerce Clause, business groups and labor would have conspired to lobby state and local governments for protectionist legislation that would have insulated them from out-of-state competition. While that legislation would have raised the profits of the firm and the wages of the associated laborers, it also would have imposed significant costs on the rest of society in the form of higher consumer prices, disruptions in trade, and reduced productivity growth. By forbidding states from regulating interstate trade and commerce, the Commerce Clause, in theory, would have eliminated any incentive for factions to form around the lines of state-level trade policy.[72]

The effectiveness of the Commerce Clause in reining in trade-related factions at the state level is well illustrated by two cases: *Barber v. Minnesota* and *Louisiana v. Texas*. In both cases, state legislatures used public health concerns as a ruse for protecting a narrow class of domestic business interests at the expense of broader societal and consumer interests. At issue in *Barber v. Minnesota* was a state law passed in April 1889 requiring that Minnesota health officials inspect all animals no more than twenty-four hours before slaughter if meat from those animals was to be lawfully sold in the state. The ostensible goal of the law was to prevent the consumption of diseased meats; at the time, diseases such as bovine tuberculosis and trichinosis were widespread.[73]

Within a few months of passage of the law, Henry E. Barber was convicted and jailed for selling one hundred pounds of uncured meat that had been butchered in the State of Illinois and had not been inspected and certified as safe by Minnesota authorities. Barber filed for a writ of habeas corpus, arguing that the Minnesota statute violated the Commerce Clause. Minnesota claimed that the law was designed solely to promote public health and was therefore, a reasonable exercise of its police powers. In striking down the Minnesota statute and upholding Barber's release from a county jail, the Supreme Court explained that the law was, in effect, an outright prohibition of meat slaughtered out of state.[74]

"It is one thing," the Court wrote, "for a State to exclude from its limits cattle, sheep or swine actually diseased, or meats that, by reason of their condition, or the condition of the animals from which they are taken, are unfit for human food, and punish all sales of such animals or of such meats within its limits." But, the Court reasoned, it was quite another thing "for a State to declare, as does Minnesota by the necessary operation of its statute, that fresh beef, veal, mutton, lamb or pork . . . shall not be sold at all for human food . . . unless the animal from which such meats are taken is inspected in that State, or as is practically said, unless the animal is slaughtered in that State."[75] What the Court could not quite bring itself to say in this case was that the measure disrupted interstate trade to protect the interests of Minnesota butchers at the expense of large, out-of-state meat-packing plants, without any compelling reason to believe that the out-of-state meat was any more prone to disease or taint than the meat slaughtered in-state.[76] However, that statement was made by the Court only a year later when it struck down a nearly identical meat-inspection law in Virginia.[77]

The efficacy of the Commerce Clause in reigning in factions, however, was limited by both an ideological preference that favored state and local regulation over federal, as well as other Constitutional provisions that shaped regulatory policies in the United States. To appreciate the origins and significance of these limits, consider the case of *Louisiana v. Texas*. In the summer of 1899, there was an outbreak of yellow fever in New Orleans. Although this was the third straight summer in which yellow fever had appeared in the city, by historical standards this was a trivial outbreak. Nevertheless on September 1, 1899, Joseph D. Sayers, the governor of the State of Texas, and William Blunt, the state's chief health officer, imposed an embargo against all persons and things originating from New Orleans and other Gulf Coast places where yellow fever was present. Moreover, Sayers and Blunt initiated the quarantine despite pleas from federal authorities associated with the United States Marine Hospital Service and public health officials from Mississippi and Alabama, who, after visiting New Orleans for several days, issued a statement that it would be "unnecessary and unwise for any State or city to quarantine against New Orleans under present conditions."[78]

The quarantine had a significant effect on the amount of interstate trade shipped through New Orleans. Before the quarantine, New Orleans was the "greatest cotton exporting port of the United States," and handled 25 to 30 percent of the Texas cotton crop. After the embargo, however, less than 15 percent of the Texas cotton crop was exported through New Orleans, and almost the entire trade was diverted to the Port of Galveston in Texas. In light of this, Louisiana officials believed that the quarantine against the state was a sham and "nothing less than a commercial war" against New Orleans and other ports and cities in Louisiana. The quarantine, in their view, was not enacted for the "bona fide purpose of protecting the health of the State of Texas," but was instead, enacted "for the purpose of increasing the trade and commerce of the State of Texas and of her ports, cities, and citizens, to the great damage" of the citizens of Louisiana.[79] Louisiana sued, asking the United States Supreme Court to enjoin the Texas embargo.

Texas did not dispute any of the allegations made by Louisiana; it only argued that the United States Supreme Court did not have original jurisdiction. In his decision, Chief Justice Fuller agreed with Texas and dismissed the case for want of jurisdiction, ruling that the Supreme Court only had jurisdiction over disputes between two States; in the case at hand, however, the dispute was between the citizens of Louisiana, particularly those in New Orleans, and the State of Texas. The State of Louisiana, Fuller explained, filed suit "from the point of view" that Texas was "intentionally absolutely interdicting interstate commerce as respects the State of Louisiana by means of unnecessary and unreasonable quarantine regulations." Yet the harm suggested by this action was inflicted on the citizens, businesses, merchants, and property owners who resided in Louisiana, and not the state itself.[80] Fuller's sharp distinction between the State and the people who resided within the State's borders might strike some readers as little more than a semantic game, but it was a distinction that was based on Article III of the Federal Constitution, as well as subsequent federal legislation.[81]

Aside from a brief of discussion of a state's right to enact quarantines, Fuller did not discuss the merits of the case against Texas. In two concurring opinions, however, Justices Brown and Harlan signaled greater sympathy for Louisiana's cause. Brown, for example, likened Texas's quarantine against Louisiana to a "preliminary declaration of war."[82] Brown conceded that there was little the court could do to aid Louisiana in the current case, but suggested that some sort of judicial inquiry, perhaps in state courts, into the motives of Texas authorities was appropriate. "While I fully agree," Brown wrote, "that resort cannot be had to this court to vindicate the rights of individual citizens, or any particular number of individuals, where a State has assumed to prohibit all kinds of commerce with the chief city of another State, I think her motive for doing so is the proper subject of judicial inquiry."[83] Justice Harlan was more explicit in his rebuke of Texas authorities, stating clearly that if the allegations against Texas were true, they had overreacted to the outbreak of yellow fever and unnecessarily interfered with interstate trade in violation of the Commerce Clause, though he conceded that the Supreme Court was powerless to intervene in this instance for want of jurisdiction.[84]

Factions, Public Health, and the Equal Protection and Due Process Clauses

In an earlier section, I described how the Equal Protection and Due Process Clauses prevented the white majority in San Francisco from imposing a discriminatory vaccination order that required Chinese citizens to undergo vaccination for plague but imposed no such obligation on the residents of the city who were not of Chinese descent. One might easily describe what happened in San Francisco as an example of the dangers of what Madison called a "faction of the majority." In this section, I broaden and expand on these ideas to describe how the Equal Protection and Due Process Clauses not only affected public health policies but simultaneously suppressed factions and promoted a specific kind of economic prosperity. The discussion here pays particular attention to what legal historians call substantive due process. Predicated on the Equal Protection and Due Process Clauses, substantive due process dominated judicial thinking from the late 1870s to its demise in the late 1930s, and it shaped economic policies and regulations in a number of industries and market settings.[85] I give particular attention to two types of regulation: the legislative grants of monopoly rights and other special privileges to businesses; and the regulation of railroad and utility rates by state and local commissions.

To see how the doctrine of substantive due process limited rent-seeking and the formation of factions in these three areas, consider first the problem of legislatures granting firms monopoly rights and special privileges. Suppose that by granting an individual firm a monopoly right over a particular market, that firm over its lifetime would earn a million dollars more than it would have earned in the absence of that monopoly status. In that case, the firm would be willing to spend up to one million dollars lobbying and bribing legislatures to secure that monopoly status. Such rent-seeking would undermine economic growth in at least two ways. First, by granting the firm monopoly status, the legislature would discourage competition and prevent entry by new and more innovative enterprises. The result for consumers would be higher prices, reduced quality, and technological stagnation. Second, the million dollars the firm used to lobby and bribe legislators could have been put to productive (as opposed redistributive) ends, such as improving the firm's plant and capital.

When special interest groups lobbied for and secured this sort of favorable treatment from legislatures, the resulting legislation accomplished nothing except to grant a few privileged firms monopoly status, with no countervailing social benefit. In particular, by creating a monopoly in production, the legislature would benefit the producer at the expense of consumers, in effect redistributing income away from the latter to the former. By the logic of substantive due process and equal protection, this was constitutional anathema, and undermined the political creation of monopolistic and growth-inhibiting enterprises through two avenues. First, when legislatures created a monopoly, or special privileges that somehow benefited one group over another, the courts usually struck down such legislation as a violation of the Equal Protection Clause.[86] Second, the threat that the Court would strike down class-based legislation would, in theory at least, have deterred legislatures from passing laws that treated groups unequally and denied individuals their due process rights.

The courts carved out an important and sensible exception to this approach, however: they allowed legislatures to create monopolies and grant special privileges when such grants were consistent with broader societal interests. In particular, the courts allowed legislatures to grant monopolies and special privileges to businesses in situations where public health was a concern, or where the relevant market was characterized by natural monopoly—that is, when a single provider of a good or service was more efficient than multiple providers. In the case of public health, the courts usually sustained municipal legislation that restricted entry into slaughtering and other offensive trades in order to control diseases and limit damages to neighboring properties, even if those restrictions had redistributive effects.[87] Similarly, the courts also upheld local laws granting monopoly rights to gas companies and other public utilities such as electricity and water because competition among multiple companies in those settings worked so poorly: cities only required a single set of mains or wires to distribute gas, electric, and water, and competition resulted in the costly duplication of capital and higher consumer prices.[88]

But the creation of these rational monopolies came with a cost: in the absence of market forces, these new industries had to be regulated. As a result, by the late-nineteenth century, city and state governments had developed vast regulatory apparatuses to control the prices charged by railroads, public utilities, and other industries "affected with a public interest" and therefore subject to rate regulation.[89] The difficulty with these regulatory structures is that they were vulnerable to something akin to the Madisonian faction—what economists and historians refer to as industry capture. Capture occurs when some well-organized and politically savvy group gains control of the regulatory process and uses it to distort the results toward their own ends.[90]

Historically, regulatory bodies have been captured at different points in time by both industry and consumer groups. When industry captures the regulatory process, the results are higher consumer prices and lower quality for consumers. When consumer groups capture the regulatory process, the results are very low prices and a gradual erosion of the industry's capital base. Substantive due process worked to prevent and limit the effects of capture by consumer groups. During the 1890s and early 1900s, politically active farmers and farm groups in the Midwest worked to capture state railroad commissions and have those commissions impose dramatic rate reductions on the railroads. In cases where those reductions were so large that they left railroads teetering on the edge of bankruptcy, the courts intervened and barred enforcement of the rate reductions on the grounds that they violated the railroads' due process and equal protection rights.[91]

The logic underlying these decisions was that rate structures that did not allow railroads and public utilities to earn a reasonable rate of return in effect confiscated the capital and property of the railroad or utility company and redistributed it to the consumer, in much the same way that the creation of an unregulated monopoly redistributed property and income away from consumers toward producers. This way of thinking about railroad and utility regulation—that it is vulnerable to capture by consumers as well as producers—is alien to the standard logic of political economy, which suggests that consumers are too large and diverse a group to form effective lobbies.[92] Yet the available historical evidence suggests that the capture of state and local regulatory commissions by consumer groups was not uncommon during the late nineteenth and early twentieth centuries, and on a purely intuitive level this should not be too surprising.[93]

More generally, the evidence suggests that institutional structures like substantive due process that insulated railroads and public utilities from politically motivated and confiscatory rate regulations fostered the following: long-term investment in the associated industry; well-functioning private markets; and higher-quality services and delivery systems.[94] As explained further in chapter 5, these institutional safeguards for capital investments had implications for public health. In particular, they encouraged water companies to invest more in distribution mains and water purification systems, investments they would not have made if there were a sizeable risk that sometime down the road local regulators might use the promise of lower water rates as a mere pretext for winning reelection. In turn, increased investments in distribution and water purification played a central role in reducing waterborne disease rates in cities, and because cleaner drinking water had diffuse health effects, the benefits for overall human health were significant.[95]

Factions, Public Health, and the Obligation of Contract

On April 26, 1787, the *Columbian Herald,* a newspaper in Charleston, South Carolina, published a lengthy plea for the ratification of the new Federal Constitution and the unification of the states under a stronger central government. The newspaper's plea ended with the following five sentences:[96] "It is time to render the federal head supreme in the United States. Conventions have too long, and indeed, too unequally divided power. Until this is effected, we cannot depend upon the success of any plans of reformation. When this is done we ought to attempt the revival of public and private credit. With what decency can we pretend, that republics are supported by virtue, if we presume upon the foulest of all motives—our own advantage—to release the obligation of contracts?"

To modern readers, the first two sentences strike the right tone: they sound weighty and broad-minded. The same cannot be said of the final two sentences, which sound petty and narrowly economic: the newspaper is suggesting that the success of the newly formed nation and newly adopted Constitution depended on the "revival of public and private credit." It would be a mistake, however, to dismiss the final two sentences as either superfluous or anachronistic merely because they do not immediately resonate with a modern ear.

By equating the ratification of the Constitution with the revival of American credit markets, the *Columbian Herald* identified a key source of economic stagnation and decline under the Articles of Confederation and helped explain how the Constitution was supposed to address that decline. As the following narrative highlights, the demise of American credit markets was driven by the formation of factions and rent-seeking behavior on the part of debtors, who were continually lobbying state legislatures to abrogate their debt commitments. Because debtors far outnumbered creditors, their cause was politically popular, and state politicians responded with laws relieving them of their debt obligations. Recognizing how quick American legislatures were to respond to the demands of debtors, creditors, both foreign and domestic, grew reluctant to lend, fearing that future legislatures would behave no differently than those of the past. Only because the new Constitution included provisions that discouraged rent-seeking and the formation of factions around debtor/creditor issues did American credit markets rebound during the 1790s and early 1800s.[97]

To illustrate how factions undermined American credit markets, and, in turn, gave rise to Constitutional provisions protecting creditors, consider the experience of South Carolina, where planters and townspeople alike found themselves increasingly indebted to British merchants. Unable to meet their obligations, debtors portrayed the British merchants as rapacious and opportunistic, and, more importantly, lobbied the South Carolina legislature for laws that would forestall collection efforts. Perhaps the most outspoken critic of the British mercantile class was Aedanus Burke, a South Carolina lawyer and farmer. Burke, while opposed to many of the more vindictive policies passed against British loyalists, also resented the ease with which British loyalists and newly arrived English immigrants were able to achieve citizenship in South Carolina. As time passed, his anger grew as he watched a "standing army" of British merchants and clerks "out-maneuver, undersell, and frighten away [French and Dutch merchants]."[98]

To hear Burke describe it, the British merchants "monopolized our trade, speculated on our necessities, and holding out every object of temptation, plunged us into a debt." They "seduced us to contract." The British merchants, in Burke's view, were conspiring to retake America through debt peonage. "There is a much surer way," Burke wrote, "for the British [to regain their] influence in America than by fleets and armies." This "surer way" employed "linens, woolens, silks, and haberdashery" to "feast on men in power," and "to tamper with men without." It was a strategy that held "out every object to tempt and corrupt," and involved "all orders of men, from the wealthy rice planter to the wagoner."[99] In response to Burke and other prominent citizens, South Carolina passed a series of stay laws restricting the ability of British merchants to collect on their debts.[100] The first stay law was passed on March 26, 1784, and established a moratorium of sorts, imposing a strict time schedule for collecting on debts incurred. A second law, passed on October 12, 1785, provided that if a debtor offered land valued at three-fourths of the total amount of debt outstanding, the creditor was obliged to accept the land as payment in full. According to one British journal, "these acts and others, and the general conduct of [the South Carolina legislature]" were "greatly complained of" by British merchants and subjects.[101]

South Carolina's experience was representative of a broader national trend. On November 3, 1784, Massachusetts passed a law "suspending the payment of interest" to creditors. On July 12, 1782, the legislature of the State of New York enacted a measure that "precluded" British merchants from collecting interest on their debts and forbade them from repossessing principal for three years. Stay laws were also passed in Pennsylvania, New Hampshire, Maryland, Virginia, North Carolina, and Georgia. In some states, the courts simply refused to hear cases where British creditors sued to collect, while in other states, where the courts were willing to entertain such actions, lawyers were often too afraid to prosecute for British debts.[102]

Not everyone agreed with Burke's depiction of British merchants as lecherous and conniving, or with the laws relieving debtors of their obligations. One of Burke's most eloquent critics, who signed his correspondence "A Friend to Civil Government," argued that Burke missed entirely the benefits that British creditors had conferred upon the newly independent American states. Describing how America rose from the ruination of nine years of war, "A Friend" wrote,[103]

> After the ravages of a nine year war, we beheld nothing but desolation and ruin in almost all parts of the Continent. Our inhabitants destitute of all kinds of necessaries, and with but little money, and our cities laid in ashes—And now in the space of four years, behold the contrast—Our cities are rebuilt in a style of magnificence far surpassing their pristine state; our citizens, though perhaps bare of gold and silver, abounding not only in all the conveniences of life, but even luxuries, never thought of in former times, and perhaps not to be surpassed in the voluptuous and opulent cities in Europe.

From "A Friend's" vantage point, it was trade with Britain and the liberal extension of British credit that allowed Americans to prosper and surpass the "voluptuous and opulent cities" of Europe. Yet after enjoying the fruits of British trade, Americans repaid their benefactors by refusing to honor their debts and by claiming that they were all duped by tempters and unscrupulous lenders.[104]

"A Friend's" scorn highlighted the disconnect between Revolutionary language—which often lamented the yoke of British paternalism—and Burke's contention that the patriots, like the perpetual children of rich parents, were now unable to conduct their financial affairs without endless indulgence. In this way, Burke's rhetoric and the policies it ultimately spawned were a rebuke of the very principles on which the country was founded. Burke's policies and arguments were "a mean and pitiful evasion, unworthy of Americans."[105]

As to Burke's contention that the British extended mercantile credit with abandon in an effort to retake the American colonies, "A Friend" mocked the logic of a scheme that left so many British creditors destitute themselves. If anyone was duped and misled, it was the British creditor. As "A Friend" saw it, British creditors had been "lulled" into "a fatal security" by the Americans who had promised to repay, only to find themselves "wretchedly disappointed" and their mercantile houses "broke or tottering." It was the "perfidious and ungenerous" conduct of the Americans that was the source of the problem, not Burke's duplicitous merchant.[106]

In addition to his moral indictment of Burke, "A Friend" emphasized the dire economic consequences of legislation allowing debtors to escape or defer their obligations to creditors. Access to credit depended on trust. The lender had to believe there was some probability that he would be repaid in a timely fashion; absent such trust, trade and commerce stagnated. "It is impossible to carry on trade," "A Friend" wrote, "without placing a very great confidence in mankind, which can never be preserved but by strict honesty and punctuality in all their dealings." But in transforming themselves from "laborious farmers" into a "petty peddling people," Americans had betrayed that trust—"as a mercantile people our character must be blasted and we [are] undone"—and, according to "A Friend," had justly earned the "censure of the world." The French and the Dutch, not to mention the British, were now too afraid to extend much of anything to the Americans in the way of credit for fear that the courts and state legislatures would repudiate the debt. "A Friend" contrasted the policies of Europe, where a clear and stable body of bankruptcy law facilitated the orderly and just discharge of debt, to those of South Carolina, where the legislature and the courts were beholden to the interests of farmers and largely ignored the interests of creditors, especially those from Britain and other American states.[107]

As creditors, both foreign and domestic, grew increasingly reluctant to lend, the new American confederacy found itself being crushed under the weight of a moribund economy. In an argument before the Supreme Court some twenty years later, the great orator and lawyer Daniel Webster described the situation this way: "Commerce, credit, and confidence were the principal things which did not exist under the old Confederation." "A vicious system of legislation had completely paralyzed industry, threatened to beggar every man of property, and ultimately ruin the country." While Webster believed that the "relation between debtor and creditor" was always delicate and fraught with conflict, under the Articles of Confederation, debtor-creditor conflicts were especially divisive and "threaten[ed] the overthrow of all government." In Webster's view, a second "revolution was menaced, much more critical and alarming than that through which the country had recently passed."[108] Given all this, it is useful to recall the puzzling juxtaposition the *Columbian Herald* made at the start of this section: first, the United States should ratify the Constitution; and then it should revive its credit markets. For Webster, the two went hand-in-hand: credit markets could not have been revived without the Constitution, and the decline of American credit markets served as an impetus for ratifying the Constitution.[109]

Webster was not alone in his concern that the hostility between debtors and creditors might threaten the viability of the American state. In *Federalist Papers* 7, Alexander Hamilton explored the conditions under which the American states might make war upon one another. Aside from territorial disputes and tariffs, he was particularly concerned about stay laws, moratoria on debt collection, and other laws "in violation of private contract." Of special note is Hamilton's reference to a dispute between Connecticut and Rhode Island: "We have observed the disposition to retaliation excited in Connecticut, in consequence of the enormities perpetrated by the legislature of Rhode Island; and we may reasonably infer, that in similar cases, under other circumstances, a war not of parchment, but of the sword, would chastise such atrocious breaches of moral obligations and social justice."[110]

Although Hamilton did not offer much in the way of historical context, Rhode Island had passed a series of stay laws that angered creditors from other states who were trying to collect. Creditors in Connecticut were especially upset, and lobbied their state legislature for a retaliatory law relieving Connecticut debtors of their obligations to Rhode Island creditors. When this measure faltered, Connecticut petitioned Congress for assistance in 1787.[111]

Given this historical backdrop, it is not surprising that the Federal Constitution contains several provisions specifically aimed at reviving American credit markets and making more credible the promises of debtors to repay their loans. Of these provisions, the one that proves most important for its effects on public health is the Contract Clause (Article 1, Section 10, Clause 1), which reads, in part: "No state shall . . . pass any . . . ex post facto Law, or Law impairing the Obligation of Contracts." Just as the Commerce Clause grew out of widespread dissatisfaction with state-level trade wars and policies under the Articles of Confederation, the Contract Clause was a response to the failure of the states to foster and protect credit markets under the Articles. It is important to be clear about exactly what the phrases "ex post facto law" and "impairing the obligation of contracts" came to mean in the early American Republic. As interpreted by courts, the Founders wanted to prevent state legislatures from passing laws that retroactively altered the terms of debt contracts. Bankruptcy laws, for example, were constitutionally sound so long as they operated prospectively on future contracts, but those laws could not then go back in time and grant borrowers more generous terms than they had originally bargained for.[112]

Today, the Contract Clause is largely dead-letter law. Like the Ninth Amendment, which protects rights not otherwise specified and enumerated in the Constitution, the clause is almost never appealed to by either plaintiffs or defendants, and when it is appealed to, it is almost never successful. But it was not always like this. Before 1840, the Contract Clause was frequently invoked to challenge a variety of state and local laws that were alleged to have interfered somehow with private contracts. While the Contract Clause continued to influence policymaking and policy outcomes throughout the nineteenth and early twentieth centuries, the courts slowly chipped away at the clause, allowing states ever more latitude in altering the terms of preexisting contracts. Nevertheless, as long as the Contract Clause was in force, it would have minimized the political risks associated with lending—that is, the possibility that debtors might form factions and secure a law relieving them of their promises to repay their debts. This, in turn, kept borrowing costs lower than they would have been and helped finance all sorts of economic activities from agriculture to industry.[113]

The death knell for the Contract Clause came in the wake of a New Deal decision by the Supreme Court, *Blaisdell*, upholding a mortgage moratorium in Minnesota. In *Blaisdell*, the Court returned the United States to a legal regime similar to the one that had prevailed under the Articles of Confederation, where debtors and their legislative representatives could change the rules of the game midstream by appealing to economic exigency. Following *Blaisdell*, interest rates in states enacting mortgage moratoria rose relative to those without, as lenders grew increasingly reluctant to lend in those states that were quick to relieve debtors of their obligations.[114]

The Contract Clause mattered for public health mostly through its effects on the development of urban water supplies. As explained in chapter 5, urban water systems were very expensive—indeed, on a per capita basis, they represented some of the largest public investments in American history— and as a consequence their construction relied heavily on debt financing. When public and private companies went to the debt market to secure the funds necessary to install mains and construct water filters, the Contract Clause as well as a series of institutional mechanisms (described below) helped assure creditors that their loans would be repaid and thereby kept borrowing costs reasonable. In addition to shaping debt contracts and keeping borrowing costs low, the Contract Clause made it possible for cities and private companies to enter into binding contracts that encouraged private companies to invest adequately in the city and provide disease-free water at low cost.[115]

To appreciate this second point, note that private water companies and cities made binding contracts through what were called franchises. Through franchises, local governments granted private water companies various privileges—such as the right to lay water mains along streets in a particular city. In return for these rights, the private enterprise would agree to certain conditions—a water company might promise to set its rates below a certain threshold and/or to distribute its water at specified levels of pressure and purity. For much of the nineteenth century, the courts interpreted charters and franchises as contracts between the states or municipalities and the private enterprises. As such, those contracts were inviolable, but over the course of the nineteenth century the courts gradually moved away from this strict contractual interpretation to one that interpreted franchises as a collection of suggestions rather than legally binding contracts.[116] As interpreted by the Marshall Court during the early 1800s, even contracts made before the American Revolution could not be abrogated by state governments, as occurred when New Hampshire famously tried to alter the charter of Dartmouth College.[117]

So long as franchises were interpreted as contracts, they helped protect both cities and private water companies from each other's opportunistic actions and helped assure a well-functioning market for clean water. By binding the company to particular rates and service quality, the franchise, at least in theory, protected cities from the most egregious forms monopolistic behavior on the part of the private water companies. In part because of the commitments they made through franchises, private water companies regularly invested in water purification systems and did so more often than public companies. There was, however, a downside to insulating private companies from public competition: such protections made it difficult for municipalities to punish those companies for charging monopolistic rates or providing poor service.[118]

Concluding Remarks

This chapter has described how—in an effort to solve the problems of factions, interstate trade rivalries, the tyranny of the majority, and debtor-creditor relations—the Constitution simultaneously affected economic outcomes and public health policies. For example, one of the strongest constitutional protections against the encroachment of tyrannical majorities bent on abrogating individual rights and liberties was the Fourteenth Amendment. The Fourteenth Amendment, however, not only prevented a racist white majority in San Francisco from imposing a discriminatory vaccination program against the Chinese in that city, it was also instrumental in preventing legislatures from imposing confiscatory rate ordinances on railroads and public utilities. This, in turn, fostered investments in price-regulated industries, such as water.

By the same token, this chapter described how the jurisdictional competition associated with federalism promoted good governance and growth-promoting policies on the part of state governments, but also gave rise to pockets of anti-vaccination resisters, undermining efforts to achieve universal vaccination for smallpox in the United States. I return to this observation in the next chapter and show how other countries with federalist systems had relatively high smallpox rates, given their level of income (e.g., Switzerland). The chapter also emphasized debtor-creditor relations and the importance of the Contract Clause. Provisions like the Contract Clause helped promote credit markets, which not only had broad and important implications for American economic growth, but, as explained in chapter 5, were instrumental in the construction of public water and sewer systems that had large and beneficial effects on human health.

FOUR

The Pox of Liberty

It is sometimes argued that no single disease, not even the plague, killed or maimed more human beings than smallpox. Sir Gilbert Blane (1749–1834) claimed that "smallpox has destroyed a hundred" lives "for every one that has perished by plague." So prevalent was the disease that it became a rite of passage; among adults in the eighteenth century, probably more than 90 percent had been afflicted with smallpox at one point in their life. During the mid-1700s, the French scientist and explorer Charles Marie de La Condamine estimated that at any given moment smallpox was killing, blinding, or otherwise disfiguring one-quarter of the world's population. In regions where the disease struck isolated populations with no prior history of exposure, smallpox decimated whole societies and races, killing anywhere from 50 to 95 percent of the population.[1]

Even though a safe and highly effective vaccine for smallpox was discovered in 1796, the disease remained endemic in many parts of the world for more than a century, and for nearly two centuries in some parts of the world. Given the prevalence of smallpox and the horrors most societies and cultures associated with it, it is not clear why any government would have chosen not to initiate widespread public vaccination and eradicate the disease; yet, that is just what many countries decided to do. More puzzling still is the performance of the United States in terms of smallpox eradication. By 1900, the United States was the richest country in the world, yet its death rate from smallpox was thirty-one times greater than Germany's, nearly seventy times greater than Denmark's and Canada's, and six times greater than Switzerland's. Even the British colony of Ceylon (Sri Lanka) had a smallpox rate one-third that of the United States.[2] By the 1930s, the Soviet Union had lower smallpox rates than the United States, despite the fact that before the Communist Revolution, Russia's public vaccination programs were much weaker and less effective than US programs.[3] Perhaps the most surprising aspect of the American experience with smallpox is that, while most state and local governments in the United States allowed the disease to linger for decades, the US military eradicated smallpox within a few years time in colonial settings.[4]

Why, then, were smallpox rates so much worse in the United States than in other industrialized countries, and even in some nonindustrialized countries? Why too did the United States allow smallpox to fester on its mainland while quickly eliminating the disease in its colonial possessions? Surely it was not because American politicians cared more about their colonial subjects than the citizenry of the United States. In this chapter, I build on the ideas introduced in previous chapters to argue that smallpox prevention in the continental United States was hindered by its commitment to federalism, the Due Process and Equal Protection Clauses, and popular access to a strong and independent judiciary. In particular, federalism gave rise to a patchwork of laws and regulations that varied sharply across states and municipalities: some places adopted stringent anti-smallpox measures; others were more lax. Also, while the courts typically gave public health officials broad authority to implement mandatory vaccination programs in the midst of epidemics, that authority was more limited in non-exigent circumstances. Compounding the impact of litigation, politicians frequently passed legislation expressly forbidding public health officials from adopting mandatory vaccination policies.[5]

While this chapter focuses on the disease of smallpox, the large themes of the chapter are really about the institutions and ideologies that shaped efforts to combat disease in general. Looking at vaccination debates today, the history of smallpox could just as easily be replaced with the history of some other infectious disease, and one would see how the American commitment to liberty hindered public vaccination programs with those diseases as well. In other words, the history of smallpox vaccination, and how that history was shaped by institutions and ideologies, is meant to illustrate a much broader story about the political economy of disease prevention and vaccination.[6]

A Brief History of Smallpox

An ancient disease of uncertain origin, smallpox probably first appeared in Asia or Northern Africa. Recent work mapping the genetic origins of smallpox suggests it emerged from a rodent-borne, variola-like virus in Africa 16,000 to 68,000 years ago. Whatever its origins, by 1600 CE, smallpox was pervasive, and affected human populations the world over.[7] Smallpox was highly contagious and was typically transmitted when a vulnerable individual inhaled the virus, absorbing it into his or her upper respiratory tract. Historically, the disease might have infected up to 90 percent of the population at risk. There were two kinds of smallpox, *Variola major* and *Variola minor*. The former was more serious and had a case fatality rate of around 25 percent, while the latter produced relatively minor symptoms and had a case fatality rate of 1 percent or less. Once a vulnerable individual was exposed to smallpox, there was an incubation period of about twelve days. After this, the disease erupted in a high fever, head and muscle aches, vomiting, and convulsions. About three-quarters of all cases, however, developed a rash, with pustules eventually appearing on the face, hands, feet, and other parts of the body.[8]

The breadth and severity of smallpox epidemics depended, in part, on environmental conditions. Smallpox, like measles and other infectious diseases, thrived in environments with high population densities and quickly fizzled out in rural areas without the requisite level of agglomeration. Smallpox was also positively correlated with cold and dry weather. Many historical observers, particularly those opposed to vaccination, also argued that the incidence of smallpox was correlated with other diseases and that it struck those in already unhealthy environments the most.[9] Claiming that there were simultaneous declines in cholera, diarrheal diseases, and smallpox, these observers argued that smallpox epidemics were caused mainly by poor sanitation, including poverty, crowded housing tenements, inadequate sewerage, and poor water supplies. Formal econometric tests, however, indicate that such claims are untrue.[10]

The single most important determinant of a given population's vulnerability to smallpox was immunity status, and smallpox devastated isolated populations with little or no prior exposure to the disease. Perhaps the best known cases of such devastation involve the first European contact with the indigenous peoples of the Americas, but other examples can be found from Greenland, Iceland, and Japan.[11] Evidence of the importance of immunity status is also apparent from the age distribution of deaths. In endemic areas before the introduction of vaccination, smallpox was primarily a disease of the young, as those who survived enjoyed a much-heightened immunity status, and the most vulnerable in terms of their immunity were quickly weeded out of the population.[12] Between 1700 and 1859, in Britain, around 90 percent of all smallpox cases occurred in children five years old or younger.[13] This age profile shifted with the introduction of vaccination, as an increasing proportion of older and unvaccinated individuals perished.[14]

Early Treatment and Prevention

Early treatments for smallpox were either ineffective or counterproductive. During the Middle Ages and Early Modern period, it was not uncommon for European doctors to encourage patients to drink red or purple liquids and wrap themselves in red or purple blankets. Later physicians recommended exposing patients to red light. Other treatments included ointments, such as palm oil in West Africa, consuming dried horse manure in Brazil, piercing smallpox pustules with a gold or silver needle, and eating donkey fat in medieval Arabia. Subjecting the patient to extreme temperatures, either hot or cold, was also a common treatment. In seventeenth-century Europe, bleeding and leeches were common treatments, as was a drink made from sheeps' dung. Physicians used the latter in the belief that such a repulsive concoction might exorcize the demon that caused smallpox.[15]

Before the advent of modern vaccination, variolation helped to protect individuals from smallpox infections. Variolation was a primitive form of vaccination that involved deliberately infecting vulnerable individuals with mild cases of smallpox. It is not clear when or where exactly the practice of variolation began. In China, variolation is well documented for populations after the eleventh century, and the practice likely began in the southwest of the country, along its border with India. The Chinese aged the scabs from mild smallpox cases in an effort to attenuate the virus, and then blew the scabs up the nostrils of the inoculated individual. In the Americas and Europe during the eighteenth century, various practitioners of folk medicine took pus from smallpox victims and scratched it into the skin of vulnerable individuals.[16]

There were at least two problems with variolation, however. First, the variolated individual became contagious before the onset of any symptoms and could help spread the disease as long as he or she had an active case. Second, between 1 and 4 percent of all those variolated developed fatal cases of smallpox. In light of these risks, most people did not resort to variolation unless in the midst of an epidemic, in which case the dangers of inoculation were outweighed by the dangers of contracting a more virulent strain of the disease. Because so many people refused to undergo variolation, it appears to have been a less effective prophylactic than vaccination would prove to be. One can see this by looking at what happens to smallpox rates after the introduction of vaccination. If variolation was widely used and highly effective, one would expect that the introduction of vaccination would have had a small-to-modest effect. However, if variolation was not commonly practiced, the introduction of Edward Jenner's vaccine would have had a large effect, reducing smallpox rates by a significant amount from previous levels. The evidence presented below indicates sharp and very large reductions in smallpox rates after Jenner's vaccine was introduced.[17]

Modern forms of vaccination were developed when Edward Jenner (among others) noticed that individuals who had previously suffered from cowpox (a relatively mild pox disease spread by cattle) did not exhibit the symptoms of smallpox, even after inoculation. Building on this observation, Jenner injected several people, including his own son, with cowpox. He then exposed these individuals to smallpox through inoculation. When the test subjects failed to develop smallpox, Jenner knew he had made a major discovery. His original procedure, which was followed by physicians for decades and mimicked earlier inoculation procedures, involved transferring pustule material from the inflamed arm of a vaccinated individual into the arm of an unvaccinated individual.[18]

Arm-to-arm vaccinations proved dangerous—sometimes spreading other infectious diseases from one individual to another—and by the middle of the nineteenth century, physicians had adopted a safer and more effective procedure. With this new procedure, physicians used a scalpel or sharp pin to make at least four shallow incisions on the upper arm. The lymph of a diseased cow was then rubbed into the incisions. The procedure left scars, collectively referred to as a cicatrix. Observable decades later, the cicatrix was used to assess whether or not the vaccination "took." Pronounced, long-term scarring signaled a successful vaccination; limited scarring suggested partial success; and no scarring suggested that the vaccination was probably a failure.[19]

Opposition to Vaccination

When Edward Jenner first submitted his findings to the Royal Society, the editors rejected his paper and suggested that he halt his experiments. But Jenner continued his research anyway, and eventually published a pamphlet in the summer of 1798. After publication, his findings spread rapidly across Europe, parts of Asia, and North America. By 1801, England had vaccinated more than a hundred thousand persons, and in the years that followed, France, Germany, Russia, and Spain vaccinated thousands more. Between 1808 and 1811 alone, France vaccinated nearly two million people. Vaccination, however, was not adopted evenly and without dissent. In China, practitioners of traditional forms of inoculation opposed and worked to suppress Jennerian vaccination. Elsewhere in Asia, it was thought that smallpox was divinely inspired and that man should not interfere with the disease for fear of angering the gods. In Ceylon (now Sri Lanka), the indigenous population believed that the "permanent cicatrix" that was associated with most vaccinations would "enable the Government at a future time to recognise individuals and to call them out for personal service."[20] Ceylon's experience was not unusual. In colonial settings, mandatory vaccination was often widely opposed and required a sizeable military force to enforce it.[21]

Much like modern debates about the safety of modern childhood vaccines, the historical debate over smallpox vaccination was highly contentious and often degenerated into an exchange of unsystematic anecdotes or poorly constructed statistics. For example, after a few early vaccinators transmitted infections across multiple children through arm-to-arm vaccinations, anti-vaccinationists began claiming that such transmissions were widespread and frequent, and that vaccination routinely resulted in childhood syphilis.[22] Whatever their predilection toward vaccination, few people cited the relevant statistic of how often vaccinated individuals perished as a direct result of the procedure, which appears to have been somewhere between one per hundred thousand and one per million.[23] By the 1920s, however, some anti-vaccinationists were making the reasonable argument that smallpox had become so rare and mild (with the introduction of *Variola minor*) that there were more deaths from vaccination than from the disease itself.[24]

For many anti-vaccinationists, their opposition was part theology, part anecdotal reasoning, and part medical intuition. In their writings and testimony before government inquiries, these anti-vaccinationists would first characterize the procedure as an abomination against both God and Nature and then go on to relate a story about how someone they knew, or knew of, had died or fallen ill following vaccination. Still other anti-vaccinationists appealed to the ideologies of free trade or radical labor movements. In England, the free trade arguments held special appeal for practitioners of irregular or nontraditional medicines, who saw laws mandating vaccination as yet another attempt on the part of the state to suppress their practice and promote mainstream medicine.[25]

As an illustration of how ideas about religion, unorthodox medical practices, and personal experience might converge to produce an anti-vaccinationist argument, consider the words of Rev. W. Stoddart, a Unitarian minister from Whitby, England. In 1885, Stoddart was summoned before an English court for his refusal to have his son vaccinated. Although he was threatened with both fines and imprisonment, Stoddart was steadfast in his opposition. "I am determined," he testified, "to submit to any fine, and if necessary to imprisonment, rather than allow the blood of my child to be poisoned." He explained what he saw as his obligation to protect the health and innocence of his child this way: "I consider it my bounden duty to endeavor to keep my child in perfect health, and not to allow him to be infected with disease by the operation called vaccination."[26] It should be noted, however, that clergy among other denominations and in other places, notably France and Sweden, actively supported efforts by the state to secure universal vaccination.[27]

Stoddart maintained that it was "unnatural and immoral to cut through the protecting skin of a child, and to inject into his blood the virus of cow-pox, and perchance the germs of other worse diseases, as syphilis." For Stod-dart, the safest and most effective means of warding off disease was to eat right, get plenty of exercise, and lead a moral and active life: "I maintain that the proper and natural way to ward off disease is by keeping the body in a healthy and vigorous condition, not by defiling the very springs of life."[28] The ideas Stoddart expressed were an integral part of the broader anti-vaccination movement, which saw vaccination as a process that adulterated the blood of innocent children and disrupted the natural social order. One prominent anti-vaccinationist argued that vaccination "corrupted" the physical body and "debased the moral life-blood of all who submitted to it."[29]

More revealing still are the following passages from William White's *The Story of a Great Delusion in a Series of Matter-of-Fact Chapters*. White argued that vaccination was immoral because it tempted people into ignoring the natural laws of clean living and proper sanitary practices. Vaccination was, according to White, nothing more than an attempt to swindle God and Nature:

> The vaccinator says: "Come, my little dear, come and let me give you a disease wherewith I will so hoax Nature, that henceforth you may live in what[ever] stench you please, and small-pox shall not catch you." But can Nature be hoaxed? Mr Lowell, in praising the genius of Cervantes says, "There is a moral in *Don Quixote*, and a very profound one it is—That whoever quarrels with Nature, whether wittingly or unwittingly, is certain to get the worst of it." There is sometimes an apparent triumph over Nature. We do wrong, and fancy we may evade the penalty by some cunning contrivance, but ere long we perceive with dismay that the consequences were only concealed or staved off, and that we have to answer to the uttermost farthing.

Vaccination was, therefore, an unnatural and unholy hoax:

> Vaccination is a dodge, kindred with incantations and similar performances whereby it is hoped to circumvent the order of the Highest, and compel his

favour apart from obedience to his will. By artifice it is attempted to obviate a consequence of ill-living, while persisting in ill-living; but if it were possible to escape small-pox by such means, we should have equal punishment in some other mode. No: small-pox will have its alternatives, and equivalents can only be avoided through compliance with the old-fashioned prescription, "Wash you, make you clean; cease to do evil, learn to do well."[30]

If smallpox were God's retribution for unclean living, vaccination was to be abhorred because it obviated the punitive will of the Divine and undermined private incentives to live a clean and moral life. The result was "nullity and disaster."[31]

In the United States, prominent anti-vaccinationists also presented a mix of motivations and rationales in defense of their positions. Consider the case of Lora Little. While living in Yonkers, New York, in 1895, Little's only child, a seven year-old-boy named Kenneth, died soon after undergoing smallpox vaccination, a procedure required for entrance into the public schools in Yonkers. Some time later, she moved to Minneapolis, only to be abandoned by her husband for unknown reasons. While in Minnesota, she edited and published a journal called *The Liberator*, which focused on health and lifestyle issues, particularly those related to anti-vaccination. In her capacity as editor, Little spoke out against the ill-gotten gains of Rockefeller and Carnegie; roundly criticized the morality of Comstock, while celebrating women who were "strongly sexed"; and criticized the "tyranny of state medicine," which, in her view, manifested itself in compulsory vaccination programs that bore disproportionately on the poor and African Americans. Little's concern that compulsory vaccination infringed on the rights and liberties of the dispossessed was not unique to American critics of state medicine. In England, too, anti-vaccinationists in the late nineteenth and early twentieth centuries were concerned that British missionaries and state officials were abusing indigenous populations in colonial settings through mandatory vaccination programs.[32]

Between 1906 and 1909, Little traveled widely to lecture on the dangers of smallpox vaccination, and, in 1909, she finally left Minneapolis permanently to make Portland, Oregon, her home. While there, she spearheaded two important efforts. The first was to block the state from passing a mandatory sterilization law. Whether one agrees or disagrees with Little's position on vaccination, it should be emphasized that the same ideological and scientific beliefs that led her to oppose compulsory vaccination also led her to work against mandatory sterilization laws for criminals and the mentally "unfit." In the early 1900s, mandatory sterilization laws and other eugenics-inspired legislation were not uncommon, and it is noteworthy that those committed to the anti-vaccinationist cause were among a handful of individuals who worked against such odious legislation. Little's second important political effort was her work for the passage of a city-wide referendum that would have banned compulsory vaccination in Portland. The measure, though receiving 55 percent of the vote, failed to become law.[33]

Little's arguments against vaccination seem to be almost a century before their time, mixing the language of a new kind of libertarianism with an evangelical commitment to pure air, good food, and clean living. According to Little, opposing vaccination was about much more than just "personal liberty," because it was not only the person undergoing an involuntary vaccination who was harmed. On the contrary, the social and political structures that brought about mandatory vaccination had broad effects that suppressed a whole range of health-promoting practices and institutions. Little was, for example, troubled by the fact that the state suppressed natural approaches to medicine, such as homeopathy, but at the same time promoted such unnatural practices as "drugging" urban water supplies with chlorine. Little also believed that the industrialization of the nation's food supply undermined the consumption of whole grains, which she saw as far healthier than refined flours that "quickly became rancid and wormy." In the same regard, Little repudiated market processes and the division of labor, hoping to return American society to a less specialized and smaller-scale economic structure. Anti-vaccination, therefore, was but one part of Little's larger critique of state medicine and American political economy in general.[34]

On the Efficacy of Vaccination

In contrast to Little, nineteenth-century proponents of vaccination cited three types of evidence to make their case that vaccination worked: time-series data (i.e., variation in smallpox rates before and after the publication of Jenner's findings); comparisons of the incidence rates and case-fatality rates across vaccinated and unvaccinated populations; and the experiences of various armies and navies with compulsory vaccination. While each of these evidentiary sources has its problems, they all point to the same general conclusion: vaccination was highly effective. In particular, the available data suggest that smallpox vaccination reduced an individual's risk of contracting the disease by 90 percent, and the risk of dying from the disease by 96 percent.[35]

Before turning to a review of the historical evidence, however, two caveats are in order. First, vaccination with cowpox was not risk-free; a small fraction

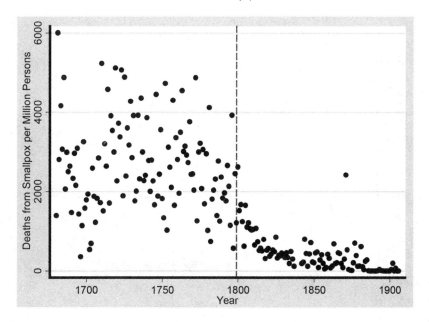

Figure 4.1. Smallpox in London, 1675–1905.
(Data from *Second Report of the Royal Commission*, 289–90; see chap. 4, n. 19.)

of individuals died as a result of Jenner's procedure.[36] In Germany during the late nineteenth century, out of 2.275 million vaccinations, there were thirty-five deaths.[37] Second, whatever the merits of vaccination, the decision to get vaccinated rested on an individual and subjective assessment of relative risks: did the risk associated with getting vaccinated outweigh the risk of contracting smallpox? If so, a rational person would have chosen to forego vaccination. This is exactly what Justice Robinson argued in the North Dakota case discussed in the introduction: because population densities were so low in the Great Plains, the risk of smallpox breaking out was very close to zero, while the risks associated with getting vaccinated were immediate, and, to Robinson's way of thinking, nontrivial.

In terms of time-series evidence on the efficacy of vaccination, the experiences of London and Sweden are representative. Figure 4.1 plots the death rate from smallpox in London from 1675 to 1905.[38] Between 1670 and 1800, there were, on average, 2,700 deaths from smallpox per million persons every year, about 10 percent of all deaths. After the introduction of vaccination around 1800, there is a clear and unmistakable break in the trend, with the annual death rate falling by roughly 75 percent to 684 deaths per million. Note, too, that it is not just the mean level that plummets, but

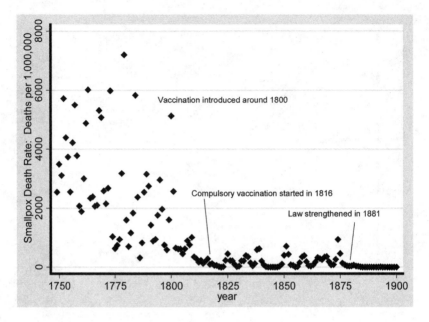

Figure 4.2. Smallpox in Sweden, 1750–1900.
(From General Board of Health, *Papers Relating to the History and Practice of Vaccination*
[London: Her Majesty's Stationary Office, 1857]; and Edward J. Edwardes, *A Concise History of
Smallpox* [London: H. K. Lewis, 1902].)

also the variance in annual deaths. Before 1800, the smallpox death rate frequently spiked at levels as high as 5,000 or 6,000 per million, while between 1800 and 1905, the death rate was much more stable, and, with the exception of the 1872 pandemic, never rose above 2,000.[39]

Along the same lines, figure 4.2 plots the smallpox death rate in Sweden before and after vaccination. As with London, there is a clear break in the trend around 1800. The magnitude and patterns of decline are similar to those observed in London. Between 1750 and 1800, the death rate averaged about three thousand deaths per million persons, and fell to less than five hundred after 1800. Sweden, though, adopted a policy of mandatory and universal vaccination, while England, except for a thirty-year interval at the end of the nineteenth century, adopted a policy of voluntary vaccinations. That Sweden adopted mandatory vaccination might explain why its death rates were lower than England's for much of the nineteenth century. At a more general level, though, the same patterns as those observed in London and Sweden have been documented for cities and countries throughout Europe; the introduction of vaccination around 1800 was associated with sharp declines in the death rate from smallpox.[40]

As noted above, a standard trope of the anti-vaccinationists was that smallpox was the product of unsanitary living conditions and that it could be best prevented through improved sanitation. As a result, when anti-vaccinationists looked at data like those just presented for London and Sweden, they would argue that smallpox rates fell after the adoption of Jenner's discovery, not because of the spread of vaccination, but because cities began to improve their sanitary conditions.[41] There are at least three problems with this line of thought. First, cities did not begin improving their sanitary conditions for another 50–100 years, long after Jenner's vaccine was introduced. Second, it is decidedly untrue that smallpox rates were associated with a broader mortality decline. Indeed, as explained in chapter 2, the early 1800s were often associated with rising mortality rates and worsening health in urban areas. Third, when laws mandating vaccination were introduced, smallpox rates fell, and when they were loosened, smallpox rates rose.[42]

Aside from time-series evidence, proponents of vaccination also pointed to a series of cross-sectional studies that looked at smallpox rates among vaccinated and unvaccinated populations. One of the most thorough of these studies was conducted during an epidemic in Sheffield, England, in the 1880s. Soon after the epidemic subsided, health officials undertook a vaccination census of the city. Surveying every household in Sheffield, census takers asked questions about the vaccination status of every member of the household; about who in the household had contracted smallpox; and about who had died from it. As another way to highlight the efficacy of vaccination, the discussion below provides a brief review of the data and evidence found in the Sheffield survey.

The results of the Sheffield vaccination census are reported in table 4.1, and are broken down by districts. Out of the 316,288 individuals included in the census, 308,830 (97.6 percent) were vaccinated, while 7,458 (2.4 percent) were not, indicating that only a small fraction of Sheffield residents had not undergone vaccination during or at some point prior to the epidemic. For every 1,000 vaccinated individuals, 16 contracted smallpox, and less than 1 perished. Among the vaccinated who contracted smallpox, the case fatality rate was 4.7 percent. By contrast, for every 1,000 unvaccinated individuals, 138 contracted smallpox (9 times the rate among the vaccinated), and 43 perished (54 times the rate among the vaccinated). Similarly, the case fatality rate for the unvaccinated was 31.1 percent, 6.6 times the vaccinated rate.

Further evidence that vaccination was highly effective comes from military settings. The Franco-Prussian War (1870–71), for example, was frequently cited by the proponents of vaccination as evidence of the efficacy of

Table 4.1. The vaccination census of Sheffield

| District | Vaccinated population | | | | Unvaccinated population | | | |
| | N | Rate per 1,000 | | Case fatality rate | N | Rate per 1,000 | | Case fatality rate |
		Attacks	Deaths			Attacks	Deaths	
Attercliffe	35,370	14	0.8	5.7	722	96	37	39.1
Brightside	60,184	16	0.8	4.6	1,548	94	30	31.3
North Sheffield	38,260	28	1.4	5.0	981	290	80	27.4
Sheffield Park	19,981	10	0.9	4.6	470	147	49	33.3
South Sheffield	17,661	13	0.6	4.4	416	175	65	37.0
West Sheffield	12,811	25	1.5	5.9	562	250	75	30.0
Ecclesall	75,775	10	0.5	4.5	1,310	100	37	36.6
Nether Hallam	45,948	15	0.7	4.5	1,421	83	21	27.3
Upper Hallam	2,840	4	0.4	8.3	28	30	0	0.0
Entire borough	308,830	16	0.8	4.7	7,458	138	43	31.1

Source: Second Report of the Royal Commission Appointed to Inquire in the Subject of Vaccination; with Minutes and Evidence and Appendices (London: Her Majesty's Stationary Office, 1890), appendix 4, 248–49, Diagrams A–E.

vaccination. This proves to be a compelling example, because Prussia adopted a policy of universal vaccination of its troops but adopted loose sanitary measures, while the French, on the other hand, did not vaccinate their troops, but were fastidious when it came to food, water, and waste disposal. The result? The death rate from smallpox was 38 times greater among the French than among the Prussians,[43] while at the same time the combined death rate from typhoid fever and dysentery (both diseases are typically spread through the fecal-oral route and are highly correlated with sanitation) was 1.5 times greater among the Prussians.[44] Had the anti-vaccinationists been correct, the smallpox rate would have been lower among the French.[45]

A lesser known military example is more complicated, but is also more compelling. Reported in table 4.2, the data for this example come from the Italian army and cover the period from 1877 to 1897.[46] The table is divided into two panels according to immunity status at time of enlistment. The top panel is for soldiers with a compromised immunity status. These are men who, at time of enlistment, satisfied both of the following criteria: (1) they had never been vaccinated for smallpox; *and* (2) they had never contracted smallpox. The bottom panel is for soldiers with elevated immunity status. These are men who, at time of enlistment, had been vaccinated for smallpox.[47] Within each panel, there are three subcategories: (*a*) recruits who had not yet been vaccinated by the army; (*b*) recruits who had been vaccinated while in the army but whose scarring indicated that the vaccination was not a success (as noted above, limited scar tissue was a sign the vaccine did not induce an immune response in the subject); and (*c*) recruits who had received a successful vaccination while in the army. While it is difficult to argue that there was random assignment across the two panels,[48] assignment across subcategories was random, particularly assignment into category (*a*). Because all new recruits were in the army for weeks before they were vaccinated, every soldier would have fallen into this category at some point during his enlistment.

The column labeled "Average strength" indicates the average number of soldiers (at any one point in time over the 1877–1897 study window) that fell into the various subcategories. The next two columns indicate annualized morbidity and mortality rates per ten thousand soldiers. Several patterns in these data are consistent with the notion that vaccination was effective, and it is useful to consider both the efficacy of childhood immunization and immunization in the military. Notice first the stark differences in rates across the two panels that separate soldiers by their immunity status at time of enlistment. Regardless of their treatment once in the military, it is clear that those who had been exposed to smallpox as children or had previously

Table 4.2. Vaccination in the Italian Army, 1877–97

Prior history	Army experience	Average strength	Rate per 10,000	
			Morbidity	Mortality
Never vaccinated nor had smallpox before enlisting	Not yet vaccinated in the corps	67	319.8	71.1
	Vaccinated in corps w/o success	1,533	28.6	2.2
	Vaccinated in corps w/ success	3,228	10.0	0.4
Vaccinated or had smallpox before enlisting	Not yet vaccinated in the corps	2,727	55.9	4.5
	Vaccinated in corps w/o success	88,108	7.4	0.3
	Vaccinated in corps w/ success	108,314	4.6	0.1

Source: Ridolfo Livi, "On Vaccination and Small-Pox in the Italian Army," British Medical Journal, 29 April 1899, 1017–21.

undergone vaccination with cowpox had much lower morbidity and mortality rates than those who entered the military with a compromised immunity status. Among those not yet vaccinated by the military, early life exposure to smallpox or cowpox reduced the risk of contracting the disease by 82.5 percent, and the risk of dying by 94 percent. Moreover, even among those successfully vaccinated in the military, there was a sizeable reduction (roughly 50 percent) in the risk of contracting smallpox if there had been a childhood vaccination.

Another way to approach the problem is to compare those who entered the military with compromised immunity status, and explore how military vaccination affected their ability to fight off smallpox. In terms of early life selection, these groups are the same: they consist entirely of individuals whose parents chose not to have them vaccinated. Among those entering the military with compromised immunity status, the incidence of smallpox for those not yet been vaccinated was 3.2 times higher than among those who had been vaccinated successfully (with full scarring). The contrast is even starker if one looks at mortality rates: the smallpox death rate for the not-yet-vaccinated exceeds the rate for the successfully vaccinated by a factor of 177. Among those entering the military with a prior history of exposure (either through vaccination or by surviving smallpox itself), the same patterns emerge, though they are not as pronounced. The not-yet-vaccinated incidence rate exceeds the successfully vaccinated incidence rate by a factor of 12, while the not-yet-vaccinated mortality rate exceeds the successfully vaccinated mortality rate by a factor 45.

Smallpox and the American Constitutional Order

During the early twentieth century, legal commentators frequently argued that the Constitution posed no bar to mandatory or compulsory vaccination; they claimed that public health authorities in the United States could compel individuals and communities to undergo vaccinations whenever they deemed it appropriate.[49] While such a claim seems to conflict with the larger argument I am developing here, it is not without historical support and it proves a useful starting point for thinking about the problem of mandatory smallpox vaccination in history. And so I begin this section by exploring a court case that seems, at first glance, to run exactly counter to my larger argument and make an airtight case that the American constitutional order was no barrier to mandatory smallpox vaccination programs.

In 1897, in Cambridge, Massachusetts, the local public health department ordered all Cambridge residents who had not recently undergone vaccination to get vaccinated, free of charge, by local public health officials.
The order was made because of an outbreak of smallpox in the town. It
was not uncommon for local health departments in the United States to
deny unvaccinated students access to public schools, particularly in the
midst of smallpox epidemics, but the Cambridge order applied not only to
school children, but also to adults. While such orders were commonplace in
Europe, they did not often happen in the United States, unless in the midst
of an epidemic. The Cambridge board of health derived its power to compel
vaccination from a state statute (Mass. Rev. Laws ch. 75, 137). Nevertheless,
when Cambridge officials ordered Albert M. Pear and Henning Jacobson
to undergo the procedure, both men refused to comply and were fined five
dollars (about one hundred dollars in current dollars).[50]

Pear and Jacobson not only refused to get vaccinated; they also refused
to pay the negligible financial penalty and instead filed suit in state court
for injunctive relief. They argued, among other things, that the statute from
which Cambridge derived its authority was unconstitutional, a violation of
their rights under the state and federal constitutions, particularly the Equal
Protection Clause of the Fourteenth Amendment. Jacobson's counsel argued
that the statute treated adults and children differently, offering children a
way to opt out of vaccination without penalty if they or their parents objected, while adults had no such option: they had to submit or pay the fine.
Whatever the legal merits of his case, if we take Jacobson's personal concerns
at face value his objections do not sound at all unreasonable. He claimed
that as a child he had been vaccinated and soon after suffered a long and
debilitating sickness that caused him "great suffering." When he had his
own son vaccinated, he too became sick.[51]

It is difficult to see anyone with Jacobson's personal history complying
with the town's mandatory vaccination order. That said, in court he was
unable to offer any direct evidence documenting post-vaccination illness,
either on his part or his son's. The best Jacobson could do was solicit testimony from other anti-vaccinationists saying that they heard similar stories.
The court, however, refused to entertain that testimony, arguing that the
state legislature had already decided to embrace the scientific consensus,
which was overwhelmingly in favor of vaccination.

In an impatient decision, the Massachusetts Supreme Court rejected
every aspect of the Pear and Jacobson cases. The court explained that it was
well established that legislatures could interfere with personal rights and
liberties to compel vaccination or any other restriction on freedom when-

ever the interest of the public was threatened: "The liberty of the individual may be interfered with whenever the general welfare requires a course of proceedings to which certain persons object because of their peculiar opinions or special individual interests." Similar statutes had been upheld, for example, by state courts in both Georgia and North Carolina, and, more generally, courts had long upheld the government's authority to quarantine sick people and ships, to limit how property might be used if it adversely affected the broader community, and even allowed for conscription at moments of national peril.[52]

As to how the Massachusetts statute treated children and adults differently, the courts had always recognized that children and adults had different rights and obligations under the law. As to Jacobson's concern that a vaccination might injure him again, the court explained it was a simple matter to avoid that risk: pay the fine.[53] Although the court did not spell out the logic behind that statement, it comports well with how an economist would think about the problem: the fine would compensate society for the risk Jacobson was imposing on his friends, family, and neighbors for refusing to undergo vaccination. A fine, in many ways, was the ideal way to balance out Jacobson's interests and those of the broader Cambridge community.[54]

The magnitude of the costs Jacobson imposed on the rest of society depended on several factors. The first was the size of the unvaccinated population with whom Jacobson interacted and the population who would have faced the greatest risk of infection should he forego vaccination. While most of the unvaccinated were very young children, there was a small proportion of the adult population that remained unvaccinated. The second factor was the rate at which the efficacy of the smallpox vaccination decayed, because, as explained above, the vaccine did not remain effective over time. Nor, as explained above, was the cowpox vaccine always 100 percent effective; the vaccinated could become sick with the disease. As a result, some proportion of the vaccinated population remained vulnerable and faced a heightened risk of disease from Jacobson's refusal to undergo vaccination. If the vulnerable populations were tiny or far removed from Jacobson's social orbit, his decision to refuse vaccination would not have imposed significant costs on the rest of society. Like a decision to ride a motorcycle without a helmet, the decision to forego vaccination in such a context might be foolhardy, but would not have significant effects on the rest of society.

Rejected by the Massachusetts Supreme Court, Jacobson appealed to the United States Supreme Court. The court's decision was written by Justice Harlan, whose legal decisions typically exhibited a strong libertarian impulse and a deep sympathy for concerns over individual rights and liberties.

Harlan was also not afraid to go his own way. When, for example, the Supreme Court struck down one of the country's first civil rights laws, passed in the wake of Reconstruction, Harlan dissented. Similarly, when the rest of the court infamously upheld a law mandating segregated railway cars in 1897, Harlan was the lone dissenter. Anticipating *Brown v. Board of Education* by half a century, Harlan refused to be defined and governed by the orthodoxies of his day. Jacobson, in other words, probably could not have asked for a better Supreme Court justice: if any great legal mind was going to find merit in his case and rebuke legal and medical consensus it would have been Harlan.[55]

Yet, like the Massachusetts Supreme Court, Harlan rejected Jacobson's arguments wholly and completely. When Jacobson complained that the Massachusetts court did not allow him to present testimony from his anti-vaccinationist experts, Harlan dismissed his concerns, questioning the competency of any scientist who would claim that vaccination was not effective. Later in his decision, he quoted earlier state court rulings that explained that legislatures did not require 100 percent scientific consensus to move ahead with legislation; that would have imposed an unreasonable barrier, because science was always contentious, and there was no area of science where there was complete agreement.[56] When Jacobson complained about the infringement to his individual liberty, Harlan explained that the "liberty secured by the Constitution . . . does not import an absolute right in each person to be, at all times and in all circumstances, wholly freed from restraint. There are manifold restraints to which every person is necessarily subject for the common good."

More than that, Harlan believed that the Massachusetts legislature had an affirmative responsibility to enact laws controlling smallpox and other social afflictions, even if such laws left Jacobson and others like him uncomfortable; the legislature's job was to protect the many and not let the interests of the many become hostage to the interests of a few.[57] Nor would the court countenance judicial reasoning that enabled one person, or a minority of persons, to use the Constitution to dominate the majority, unless there was a clear violation of a constitutionally protected right to life, liberty, or property.[58]

In *Jacobson*, the highest court in the land rebuked most of the elements of the anti-vaccinationist cause and upheld the right of a state to enact compulsory vaccination programs. The only question the courts left open was how much force the state could use in enforcing a mandatory vaccination. In the litigation preceding the Supreme Court decision, the Massachusetts Supreme Court ruled that, in cases like *Jacobson*, the state could not use physical force to compel vaccination, and in his decision Harlan suggested that even in the midst of an epidemic, the state could go too far in enforcing mandatory vaccination orders, though in the case at hand it had not.[59] Some anti-vaccinationists also embraced the aspects of the *Jacobson* decision that suggested vaccination could not be imposed on someone if it posed a serious risk to their health and safety.[60] Nevertheless, it is not surprising that so many observers have cited *Jacobson* as evidence that the Constitution was no barrier to mandatory vaccination in the United States.[61] Such reasoning, however, reflects an unduly literal reading of the decision and broader failure to appreciate the myriad of ways that Constitutional structure has shaped public health in American history, especially principles related to federalism.

To see this, it is useful to reconsider a passage from the *Jacobson* decision itself. Harlan quoted the following passage from a New York ruling to justify excluding Jacobson's so-called experts from testifying and allowing the Massachusetts legislature to proceed even without 100 percent scientific consensus:[62]

> The fact that the belief is not universal is not controlling, for there is scarcely any belief that is accepted by everyone. The possibility that belief may be wrong, and that science may yet show it to be wrong, is not conclusive; for the legislature has the right to pass laws which, according to the common belief of the people, are adapted to prevent the spread of contagious diseases. In a free country, where the government is by the people, through their chosen representatives, practical legislation admits . . . no other standard of action; for what the people believe is for the common welfare must be accepted as tending to promote the common welfare, whether it does in fact or not. Any other basis would conflict with the spirit of the Constitution, and would sanction measures opposed to a republican form of government.

The central idea here should not be missed: in a republic such as the United States, the people acting through their legislative agents, not scientific experts, choose policy. In this setting, there is no guarantee that democratic outcomes will be in accord with scientific consensus. Divisions between scientific expertise and policy can emerge whenever the majority is confused or when small, highly mobilized dissenting groups exercise disproportionate influence on the legislative process or in the courts.

Indeed, in most American states, Jacobson probably never would have gone to court, because no one would ever even have tried to vaccinate him. Of the forty-five states then in the Union, only eleven had compulsory vaccination laws that approached the Massachusetts law in their stringency;

three-quarters of states had no laws compelling vaccination, and at least two states had laws expressly forbidding public health authorities from adopting compulsory vaccination programs.[63] Moreover, even in states with strong, statewide laws for vaccination, local doctors and public health officials resented the interference of state and federal authorities and refused to cooperate. Nor did federal officials do much to foster more aggressive state and local responses to smallpox. During the early 1900s, the United States Marine Hospital Service (the forerunner to the United States Public Health Service) expressly stated that it would operate in accordance with the principles of federalism and defer to state and local officials.[64]

Although there is evidence to suggest that failure to submit to compulsory vaccination laws in some states could, at times, result in heavy penalties,[65] the norm in the United States appears to have been fairly loose vaccination policies, and even in states with compulsory vaccination laws, enforcement of those laws was often lax, geographically circumscribed, and limited to children.[66] And even in this context, the Massachusetts law was itself a fairly tame measure, with a low fine and no threat of jail or imprisonment for those who refused to comply. Massachusetts stood in stark contrast to Continental Europe, where those who refused vaccination were subject to stiff fines and imprisonment.[67] In short, in the United States, the republican institutions defined by the Constitution *generally* were not fostering the same sorts of aggressive vaccination policies one observed in more centralized and less representative forms of government. This is despite the fact that public health officials in the United States almost universally saw the strong compulsory policies of Germany as a model for what should be done here.[68]

In another passage in the *Jacobson* decision, Harlan explains that vaccination policies are state and local decisions, not under the purview of the federal government.[69] As in so many other areas, federalism was a controlling principle. This meant that each state was free to choose whatever policies it wished. However, the difficulty with a federalist approach to preventing infectious disease is that neighboring jurisdictions do not adequately consider or take into account how their policies might adversely affect their neighbors. If, say, Indiana chooses to abandon a public vaccination program, it will not give enough weight to the concerns of people in neighboring states such as Illinois, Kentucky, Michigan, and Ohio.

The logic here is no different than the free-rider problem described in chapter 2. When dealing with externalities, both individuals and groups do not adequately consider the repercussions of their actions on their neighbors, some third-party intervention in the form of taxation or punishment is necessary to induce compliance and optimal provision of the public good.

Hence, *solely from a disease-prevention standpoint*, it would have been preferable to have vaccination policies established by the federal government, assuming that the federal government would have adopted and mandated national vaccination policies that were more aggressive than those adopted by the most lax states.[70] Because lax states also tended to have smaller populations, and more populous states had more aggressive policies, it seems likely that the majority of American voters would have pushed for a relatively aggressive federal vaccination program. In addition to this, as explained in chapter 3, under federalism there is sorting across jurisdictions. This allows groups (such as anti-vaccinationists) who might be a minority at a national level to sort into states or regions where they are majorities and secure the passage of otherwise nationally unpopular laws at a state level.

Two court cases from Illinois and Wisconsin highlight another aspect of the American constitutional order that hindered and slowed the implementation of mandatory smallpox vaccination programs. These cases make it clear that state constitutions established procedures and rules for the implementation of mandatory vaccination. Public health officials could not simply issue an order that everyone undergo vaccination and have it enforced without question. The state had to first vest those authorities, clearly and unambiguously, with those powers. Only then, could the appointed officials act.

In the Illinois case, the state supreme court maintained that school boards and public health departments could not exclude unvaccinated students unless expressly authorized to do so by the state legislature.[71] "It is a matter of common knowledge," the court wrote, "that the number of those who seriously object to vaccination is by no means small, and they cannot, except when necessary for the public health and in conformity to law, be *deprived of their right* to protect themselves and those under their control from an *invasion of their liberties* by a practically compulsory inoculation of their bodies with a virus of any description, however meritorious it might be [emphasis added]." Using identical logic, the Wisconsin high court held that while the state's police power "enables it to prohibit all things hurtful to the comfort and welfare of society," such power could only be derived from an express legislative fiat and could not simply be assumed or asserted by state agencies.[72]

These cases become all the more significant when one notes that, in the United States, public health officials were not working to achieve universal smallpox vaccination: there were no nationwide programs mandating the vaccination of children who attended private school (only public schools); nor were there any attempts to regularly revaccinate adults whose immunity status had declined over time. Authorities worked mainly to vaccinate children attending public schools. By contrast, polities such as Denmark and Germany sought to vaccinate every child and maintained a policy of regularly revaccinating older children and adults.[73] Moreover, during an epidemic in the early 1900s when American authorities in some states adopted more aggressive European-style policies, enforcing vaccination orders at gunpoint with soldiers or police, those efforts were frequently met with violent protests and elaborate evasion schemes.[74] Significantly, the American courts might have helped fuel such protests by leaving open questions about just how far public health officials could go in enforcing mandatory vaccination orders.[75]

Although Jacobson's legal counsel claimed in his argument before the United States Supreme Court that smallpox rates were no lower in states with compulsory vaccination laws than in those without, a closer look at the data suggests otherwise. In 1921, James P. Leake and John N. Force analyzed the incidence of smallpox rates across nineteen American states. Based on the information they provided, those states can be categorized into one of two groups: those with strong legal environments and those with weak ones. In states with strong legal environments, there was some sort of mandatory vaccination statute that was enforced and generally respected. By contrast, in states with weak legal environments, there was no mandatory vaccination law, or the law simply was not enforced because of widespread public opposition. There were thirteen states with weak legal environments: Alabama; Indiana; Kansas; Louisiana; Michigan; Minnesota; Mississippi; Ohio; Oregon; Vermont; Virginia; Washington; and Wisconsin. There were only six states with what Leake and Force described as strong legal environments: Connecticut; the District of Columbia; Maryland; New Jersey; New York; and South Carolina.[76]

For the years 1915 to 1920, the incidence of smallpox was ten times higher in states with weak legal environments than in those with strong ones. More precisely, the incidence of smallpox in weak-law states was 1.03 cases per thousand persons, while the incidence in strong-law states was only 0.1 cases per thousand persons.[77] While simple cross-sectional comparisons such as these are always subject to concerns about selection bias, the same conclusions emerge when we look at time-series data. After the State of California repealed its mandatory vaccination law in 1911, smallpox rates in the state reversed a long-term downward trend, and more than doubled within a few years time. Similarly, when the State of Washington repealed its mandatory vaccination law in 1919, the incidence of smallpox in the state shot up by a factor of 3.5, from 1.27 cases per thousand in 1918 to 4.44 cases in 1920.[78] As in California, this represented a significant deviation from long-term trends in the state.[79]

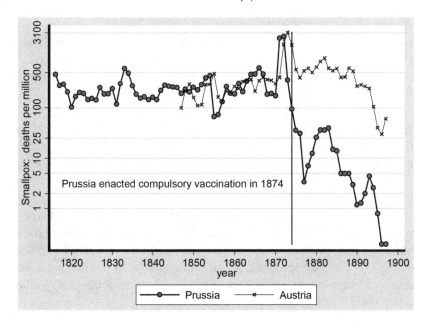

Figure 4.3. Smallpox rates in Prussia and Austria, 1820–1900.
(From General Board of Health, *Papers Relating to the History and Practice of Vaccination*; and
Edward J. Edwardes, *A Concise History of Smallpox*.)

Perhaps the single best historical example of abandoning a decentralized approach to smallpox prevention and moving to a centralized one comes from German history. Before unification in 1871, the German territory was made up of twenty-seven constituent states, the largest of these being the Prussian state, which accounted for about 60 percent of German territory. This loose confederation was not unlike the situation in the United States, where individual states and municipalities had primary authority over public health matters, particularly as they related to smallpox. With unification, however, the German state abandoned this federalist structure and become far more centralized. Driven in part by the Prussian military, centralization affected many dimensions of German society, including smallpox vaccination.[80]

Accordingly, three years after unification, Germany enacted a strong mandatory vaccination law that not only required vaccination of young children but also revaccination of adults. The impact on smallpox rates was astounding. Prussia, for example, went from having among the highest smallpox rates on the European continent to among the lowest. This dramatic shift can be seen in figure 4.3, which juxtaposes the smallpox death rates in Prussia and Austria. Before 1874, smallpox rates in Prussia and Austria hovered between 100 to 500 deaths per million persons, as neither country had compulsory vaccination. But soon after Prussia enacted its mandatory vaccination law, smallpox rates plummeted, falling by more than 95 percent in a few years' time, a reduction that appears to have also benefited the Austrians, who were in close geographic proximity. As figure 4.3 shows, by 1900, Prussia and other German states had, for all practical purposes, eradicated the disease; America, however, would have to wait another fifty years before they were in a similar situation.

Post-unification Germany had two advantages over the United States. As already suggested, the first was its more centralized approach to disease prevention. The second was its more authoritarian governance structure. In contrast to those in the United States, public health officials there did not have to build consensus among the citizenry or worry so much about popular support for their policies. Expert beliefs about appropriate policies, in public health or in any other area, could be implemented without extended public debates and litigation. Expert opinion, for good and for bad, was more likely to be implemented in the German system.

Ironically, the way the United States and other democratic societies built consensus around smallpox vaccination was to wait for smallpox epidemics. To understand the logic behind this approach, it is useful to appeal to a small literature in economics one might call the "rational epidemics" literature.[81] In this literature, epidemics are characterized as the pathological social outcome of an otherwise rational individual thought process. Models of rational epidemics begin with the observation that, during epidemics, people are much more compliant and willing to undergo vaccination. The individual calculus that generates this result is simple: any rational agent balances the costs of getting vaccinated against the benefits. When the costs of vaccination are higher than the benefits, the agent foregoes vaccination. In the midst of an epidemic, the benefits of vaccination rise sharply because the risk of contracting the disease in the absence of vaccination is so much higher. Obviously, while this cost-benefit calculation is rational on a purely individual level, it is not probably optimal from the standpoint of disease prevention. On the contrary, it seems likely that social behavior such as this leaves societies more vulnerable to epidemics than they otherwise would be.[82]

More precisely, for an epidemic to break out, there must be a sufficiently large population of individuals vulnerable to the disease (i.e., individuals who are not vaccinated or otherwise immune to the disease). In any region without mandatory vaccination programs, the population of vul-

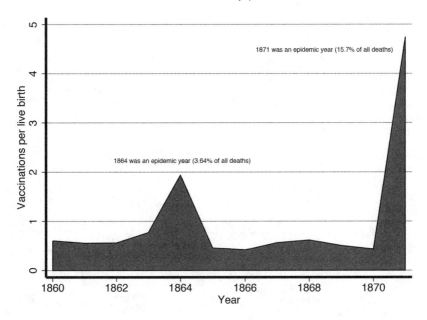

Figure 4.4. Vaccinations and smallpox epidemics in Berlin, 1860–1872. (Data from *Second Report of the Royal Commission*; see chap. 4, n. 19.)

nerable individuals would rise over time as people, each beholden to their own individual cost-benefit calculations, grow increasingly indifferent and apathetic to vaccination, which in turn causes the population of vulnerable individuals to expand and the likelihood of an epidemic to rise. Compounding all of this is the logic of herd immunity. Herd immunity suggests that recalcitrant individuals who refuse to get vaccinated nevertheless enjoy disease-protection benefits from the other members of society who get vaccinated. As more and more people get vaccinated, the vaccinated reduce the probability of an epidemic breaking out, and this reduction in risk confers a benefit upon those who do not undergo vaccination. In this way, the unvaccinated ride free off of the investments of those who undergo vaccination. In an extreme case, imagine a community of one hundred individuals where ninety-nine of them get vaccinated. The one who refuses to get vaccinated gets 100 percent protection from disease without ever incurring the cost of getting vaccinated, because everyone else gets vaccinated. (This, of course, assumes there is no in-migration.)[83]

As an empirical matter, there is clear evidence that vaccination rates spiked upward in the midst of smallpox epidemics. This can be seen in figures 4.4 and 4.5, which plot vaccination rates in Berlin and Dublin (before

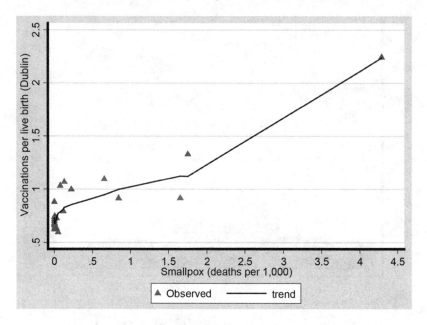

Figure 4.5. Vaccinations and smallpox in Dublin, 1863–1887.
(Data from *Second Report of the Royal Commission*, 258, table D; see chap. 4, n. 19.)

unification and mandatory vaccination). Note that the vaccination rate is defined as vaccinations per live birth, and any number above one implies that it was not only infants receiving vaccinations but older children and adults as well. In both Berlin and Dublin, the vaccination rate spiked upward during epidemics. The inefficiency and waste implied in these two figures should not be missed. There is also anecdotal evidence to support the claim that people are much more willing to undergo vaccination during epidemics than they would be otherwise.[84] If all those older children and adults who waited until the epidemic to get vaccinated had done so earlier, there might never have been an epidemic to begin with.

To the extent that smallpox epidemics imposed significant disruptions on trade and economic activity, as well as loss of life, there would have been broader economic benefits had the recalcitrant members of society simply gotten vaccinated in an earlier (non-epidemic) year. By refusing vaccination at an early stage, those who chose to delay vaccination imposed costs on others in society, especially those who were responsible and sought out vaccination early and still had to experience the economic disruptions associated with an epidemic. What mandatory vaccination programs accomplished was to spread out and flatten the vaccination profile, so that vaccinations were not all clumped in epidemic years. This, in turn, significantly reduced the number of epidemics.

It is tempting to look at the German experience and argue that if only the United States had been more like Germany—more centralized, more authoritarian—it too could have eradicated smallpox quickly and efficiently. The difficulty with this line of thought is that it was more than just political institutions like federalism and democracy that hindered the American effort to eradicate smallpox—it was also American attitudes. Even in the American states and cities that adopted aggressive, European-style vaccination programs, those programs were often met with riots and opposition so strong that authorities had no choice but to yield and abandon compulsion.[85] Attitudes and ideological beliefs, in other words, drove policy. This can be seen most clearly when one looks at how legislatures responded to court decisions that upheld efforts by local health boards to mandate vaccination. For example, immediately after state courts in Minnesota, South Dakota, and Utah upheld decisions by local school boards to exclude unvaccinated children from school, legislatures in those states passed laws that prohibited local school boards from denying unvaccinated children access to school. In short, given the representative and democratic nature of American political institutions, if local policies did not comport with local preferences and attitudes, those policies were quickly changed.[86]

It is important to be clear, however, about whose preferences were carrying the day, because it is not at all obvious that laws restricting the ability of school boards to enforce mandatory vaccination programs appealed to most voters; they might only have appealed to a minority of voters with unusually intense preferences. In this way, one might liken the politics of vaccination to the politics of tariffs. There is a large literature that cuts across both economics and political science that explains the persistence of (nonoptimal) tariffs on international trade as the result of a democratic pathology. With any tariff, there will be winners and losers. The winners will be all those protected by the tariff, who otherwise would have been displaced or injured by the presence of foreign competition. Typically, this includes the laborers who work in the protected industry and the owners of capital in that industry. The losers will be all those who would have benefited from the presence of foreign competition. Typically, this includes all consumers of the products of the protected industry. So, for example, a tariff on steel would help steel workers and the owners of steel mills, but hurt the consumers of steel, such as auto companies or anyone who buys an automobile from a domestic auto manufacturer who had no choice but to purchase steel in a market where prices are propped up artificially by tariffs.

The difficulty for anyone concerned with the formation of efficient tariff policies is that, even when the costs of a potential tariff to consumers far exceed the benefits to labor and capital, labor and capital often win the political battle and secure passage of nonoptimal tariffs. This occurs because laborers and capitalists are a small, tightly knit group with very high private incentives to engage in the political process. As a result, they can easily organize and lobby for the tariff. By contrast, consumers are a dispersed and loosely connected group with only limited private incentives to lobby— while a steel worker's livelihood might depend on the tariff, the individual consumer only stands to pay slightly higher prices for automobiles and other products made of steel. That said, because consumers far outnumber steel workers, it is typically the case that, *in the aggregate*, the losses to the former far exceed the benefits to the latter. Given that consumers face higher costs of organizing and lower individual payoffs even if they succeed in organizing, capital and labor have, until recently in the United States, dominated the political process with regard to tariffs.[87]

A critic of laws like those passed in Minnesota, South Dakota, and Utah— which, as noted above, forbade school boards from excluding unvaccinated children from school—might reasonably argue that a parallel process was at work in those states. The winners from such laws were small, tightly knit groups of anti-vaccinationists who believed that vaccination put each of them in mortal peril: anti-vaccinationists like Henning Jacobson believed that there was a very high probability that smallpox vaccination would lead to an extended and serious illness and might even culminate in death. Like a laborer in an unprotected industry, where the cost of no tariff might have been his or her livelihood, individuals opposed to vaccination believed that they had a lot to lose if the state had the capacity to compel vaccination.

One does not have to read the testimony of anti-vaccinationists at trial or before government investigators for long to see how deeply and intensely they feared the procedure. Whether those subjective fears were based an objective reading of the evidence is dubious, but the larger point remains. By contrast, those who were willing to undergo vaccinations probably represented a much larger and diverse group. Not unlike consumers in the tariff example, their individual preferences were much less intense than those opposed to vaccination, even if there were many of them. Yet, because anti-vaccinationists were better organized and more highly motivated than the larger, more diverse majority group, the anti-vaccinationists might well have been able to secure legislation that was at odds with the preferences of the majority. Having developed this line of thought, I do not wish to suggest that opposition to mandatory vaccination was always and everywhere a minority

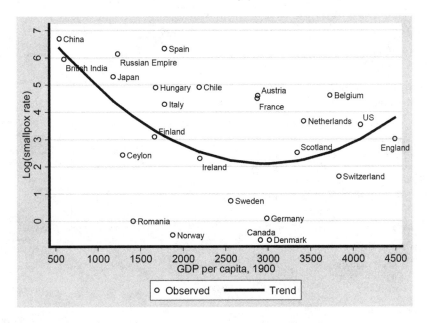

Figure 4.6a. Smallpox versus GDP per capita, 1900.
(Data for both 4.6a and 4.6b are from United States, Bureau of the Census, *Mortality Statistics* [1906 volume]; Samuel W. Abbott, "Progress in Public Hygiene," *Boston Medical and Surgical Journal* 146.18 [1902]: 465–67; Angus Maddison, *The World Economy: A Millennial Perspective* [Paris: OECD, 2001], 264–65.)

position. On the contrary, there are well-documented cases where majorities favored less coercive vaccination programs. For example, in 1916, voters in Portland, Oregon, considered a local referendum banning compulsory vaccination in the city. Partly because of Lora Little's organizational efforts, the measure enjoyed the support of 55 percent of the voters going to the polls.[88]

The American Experience in the International Context

Using international data from the turn of the twentieth century, Figure 4.6a plots the smallpox mortality rate against GDP per capita. The sample of countries is small ($N = 28$), but includes all countries for which data on GDP and smallpox rates are available. What is interesting about this graph is that the data reveal a clear, U-shaped pattern. Middle-income countries have the lowest smallpox rates, while rich and poor countries have higher rates. The uptick in smallpox rates for rich countries is statistically significant. In particular, regressing the log of smallpox rate against (GDP per capita) and (GDP per capita)-squared yields the results shown in table 4.3.

Table 4.3. Smallpox and income

Variable	β	t-statistic	p-value
GDP per capita	−.004	−2.47	.021
(GDP per capita)-squared	.646	1.94	.064
Constant	8.49	4.73	.001
Adjusted R^2 .256			
No. of obs. 28			

Table 4.4. Smallpox, Catholicism, and income

Variable	β	t-statistic	p-value
GDP per capita	−.006	−4.93	.001
(GDP per capita)-squared	.112	4.25	.001
= 1 if predominantly Catholic	3.42	4.77	.001
Constant	9.68	7.39	.001
Adjusted R^2 .602			
No. of obs. 28			

Notice, however, that in Figure 4.6a there are at least three countries in which smallpox rates look unusually high, notably Spain, Austria, and France. What these countries have in common is that they are predominantly Catholic. If we add a dummy variable for countries that were predominantly Catholic to the regression discussed above, we obtain the results shown in table 4.4.

Note that the Catholic control is highly significant and improves the fit. The following countries are defined as predominantly Catholic: Belgium, Italy, Spain, Austria, Hungary, Chile, and France. The results are robust to alternative categorizations of Catholic countries. The theoretical motivation for including a dummy for Catholic countries is that opposition to vaccination on the part of the lay population appears to have been unusually high.[89] To facilitate visualization of these results, figure 4.6b plots the residual from a regression where the log of the smallpox rate has been regressed against a dummy variable for predominantly Catholic. This figure highlights how controlling for Catholicism sharpens the results shown in Figure 4.6a and makes the U-shaped relationship between income and smallpox even more pronounced.

The patterns highlighted in Figures 4.6a and 4.6b are surprising. If one looks at either historical or modern data for diseases other than smallpox,

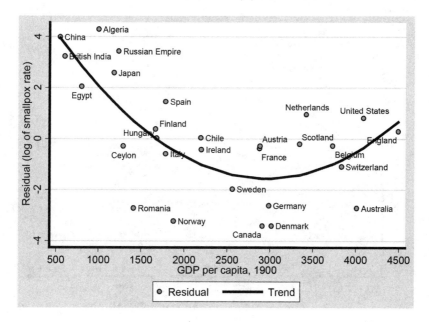

Figure 4.6b. Smallpox versus GDP after controlling for Catholicism.

the relationship between GDP per capita and mortality is usually negative: rich countries have the lowest mortality rates, poor countries the highest, and middle-income countries have middling disease rates. Given this pattern for other diseases, it is tempting to argue that, in some sense, smallpox mortality was too high in rich countries.[90] Yet if one considers the arguments developed in the book thus far, the U-shaped relationship between national income and smallpox mortality makes sense: the same institutional features that promoted economic growth simultaneously hindered efforts to implement mandatory vaccination programs. Indeed, if one looks closely at rich countries besides the United States, one finds evidence that they too possessed many of the same institutional features that hindered the implementation of effective smallpox vaccination programs here. Switzerland, for example, had a federalist system, where individual cantons held much power relative to the central government. Similarly, in England and Wales, local governments possessed much power in public health matters, and there were institutional protections of individual liberty, including a strong and independent judiciary, as in the United States.[91]

Perhaps the most powerful piece of international evidence for this line of thought comes from comparing the performance of the United States in combating disease at home and abroad in colonial settings. In mainland

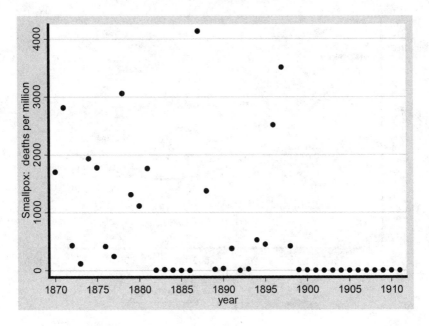

Figure 4.7. Smallpox in Havana, Cuba, 1870–1910.
(From Frederick L. Hoffman, "The Vital Statistics of Cuba," *The Insurance Monitor*, 1903, 23–25;
United States, Bureau of the Census, *Mortality Statistics* [various years].)

America, public health officials were fettered by constitutional concerns and
the preferences of voters, many of whom resented smallpox vaccination as
intrusive and unnecessary. By contrast, in colonial settings, American public
health officials were bound by no such constraints and, in fact, could make
use of a strong military force to compel vaccination—and compel they did.
For example, after acquiring Cuba and Puerto Rico in the Spanish-American
War (1899), the United States eradicated smallpox in Cuba and Puerto Rico
within five years. As figures 4.7 and 4.8 show, under Spanish domination,
smallpox ravaged both Havana and Puerto Rico, with rates varying between
five hundred and four thousand deaths per million; but within five years of
American acquisition, smallpox rates fell to almost nothing in both Havana
and Puerto Rico.

It is true that it took much longer (more than a decade longer) to bring
smallpox under control in the Philippines (also acquired by the United
States in the Spanish-American War), but that was because the Philippines
was a more rugged and geographically complex nation with a substantial
fraction of the population living in isolated villages. By contrast, serious
outbreaks of smallpox were still plaguing American cities in the 1930s and

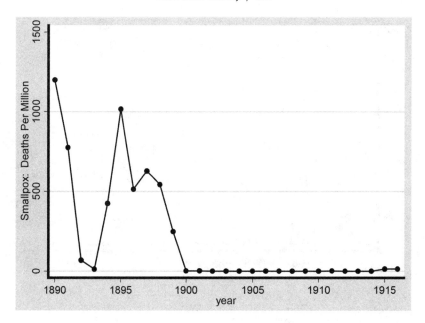

Figure 4.8. Smallpox in Puerto Rico, 1890–1915.
(Data from United States, Marine Hospital Service, *Public Health Reports*.)

40s, three decades after the American military had eliminated the disease in Cuba and Puerto Rico. Figure 4.9 puts the experience of mainland America into even sharper relief, plotting smallpox rates in Massachusetts alongside those in Puerto Rico; this comparison shows that, from the introduction of Jenner's vaccine, it took more than 110 years to eliminate smallpox in the State of Massachusetts, but only a few years to accomplish the same end in Cuba. This juxtaposition is especially revealing because Massachusetts was by most historical accounts at the vanguard of the American public health movement.[92]

Concluding Remarks

A simple graphical way to encapsulate the central points of this chapter is the aforementioned figure 4.6a, which shows a U-shaped relationship between GDP per capita and smallpox rates for a small sample of countries around 1900. The explanation offered for the uptick in smallpox rates in the richest countries was that these places were, like the United States, adopting institutions like federalism and a strong respect for individual rights that, while conducive to economic growth and political freedom, also interfered with

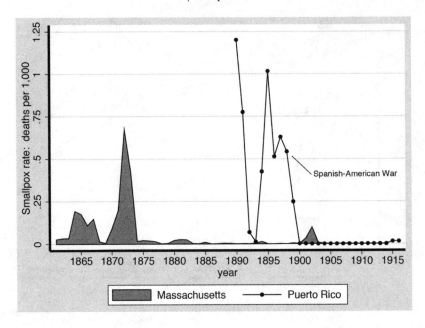

Figure 4.9. Smallpox in Massachusetts and Puerto Rico, 1850–1915.
(Data from United States, Marine Hospital Service, *Public Health Reports*; Massachusetts State
Board of Health, *Annual Reports* [various years].)

efforts to achieve universal vaccination. That said, the narratives in this chapter suggest that the American antipathy for coercive vaccination policies was rooted in far more than the Constitution; indeed, the Supreme Court validated mandatory vaccination in Massachusetts. What mattered most in this regard was American attitudes and a political system that appears to have allowed a small minority with intense opinions to overwhelm the preferences of a large majority whose preference for universal vaccination was less deeply held. To the extent that the Constitution hindered smallpox vaccination, this came about through two indirect mechanisms. The first of these was federalism, which, as explained in chapter 3, allowed individuals to sort into smaller communities of similarly minded individuals. The second mechanism was that the Constitution did impose hurdles on school officials and public health authorities requiring them to get express legislative authority before enacting and enforcing mandatory vaccination orders.

FIVE

The Palliative Effects of Property Rights

The American constitutional order shaped the country's battle against typhoid fever and waterborne diseases, and in the process helped drive the transition from high mortality to low in the United States. This story has two components. The first involves establishing a fundamental demographic point: that investments in public water systems had an enormous effect on human health beyond just eliminating typhoid fever. Water purification had broad health benefits in part because of its impact on gastroenteritis in infants, and in part because typhoid fever caused long-lasting and profound sequelae, which meant that when health authorities eliminated typhoid they not only got rid of that disease but also a host of other diseases and pathologies that otherwise would have attacked the survivors of typhoid.

The second part of the story is institutional, describing how various parts of the federal Constitution, state constitutions, and statutory law fostered investments in urban water systems and contributed to one of the most important public health initiatives in human history. In this way, the history documented in this chapter is more affirmative of American institutions than the history of smallpox documented in the last chapter. That said, there were aspects of the American constitutional order that, at least occasionally, hindered the efforts of municipal authorities to acquire and control water systems when private provision was found wanting.

The Causes, Symptoms, and Transmission of Typhoid Fever

During the late nineteenth and early twentieth centuries, the waterborne disease that posed the most serious threat to adult populations in America was typhoid fever—as of 1900, probably one out of every three Americans would have contracted typhoid at some point. Typhoid was caused by *Sal-*

monella typhi, a bacterium that could survive only in human hosts and lived in the intestinal tract. People typically contracted typhoid by drinking water contaminated by the fecal wastes of infected individuals. A common transmission might have gone something like this. The family of a typhoid victim dumped the patient's waste into a cesspool or privy vault. If the vault was too shallow or had leaks, it seeped into underground water sources. In turn, if these water sources were not adequately filtered, people who drew their water from them contracted typhoid. Typhoid rates in a given city or region were, therefore, highly correlated with the quality and extensiveness of water and sewerage systems.[1]

Although tainted drinking water was the most frequent mode of transmission, there were other modes of transmission. Typhoid could be spread by flies that had come in contact with infected human wastes. Shellfish from tainted rivers and lakes carried typhoid. If washed or sprinkled with tainted water, raw fruits and vegetables carried the typhoid bacillus. Milk became a carrier when it was put in containers cleaned with tainted water or when the individuals who milked the cow did not adequately wash before milking. Typhoid also spread through incidental, second-hand contact. Doctors, nurses, laundry-workers—anyone who came in contact with the wastes of an infected person—could carry typhoid bacilli on their hands and clothes. Caregivers sometimes unwittingly transferred those germs to the eating utensils in their own homes, infecting themselves and other family members.[2]

Once they entered the body, typhoid bacilli had a one- to three-week incubation period. During incubation, an infected individual experienced mild fatigue, loss of appetite, and minor muscle aches. After incubation, the victim experienced more severe symptoms: chills, coated tongue, nose bleeds, coughing, insomnia, nausea, and diarrhea. In its early stages, typhoid symptoms often resembled those of respiratory diseases, and pneumonia was often present. In nearly all cases, typhoid victims experienced severe fever. Body temperatures could reach as high as 105 degrees Fahrenheit. A week or so after incubation, rose-colored spots sometimes appeared on the patient's abdomen. For much of the nineteenth century, these rose-colored rashes were the only symptom doctors could use to identify typhoid definitively, but unfortunately in terms of promoting accurate diagnoses, these rashes appeared in only 5 to 20 percent of all cases.[3]

Three weeks after incubation, the disease was at its worst. The patient was delirious, emaciated, and often had blood-tinged stools. One in five typhoid victims experienced a gastrointestinal hemorrhage. Internal hemorrhaging resulted when typhoid perforated the intestinal wall and frequently continued on to attack the kidneys and liver. The risk of pulmonary complications, such as pneumonia and tuberculosis, was high at this time. The high fever associated with typhoid was so severe that about one-half of all victims experienced neuropsychiatric disorders at the peak of the disease. These disorders included encephalopathy (brain-swelling), nervous tremors and other Parkinson-like symptoms, abnormal behavior, babbling speech, confusion, and visual hallucinations. If, however, the patient survived all of this, the fever began to fall off and a long period of recovery set in. It could take as long as four months to fully recover. Surprisingly, given the severity of typhoid's symptoms, 90 to 95 percent of its victims survived.[4]

That typhoid killed only 5 to 10 percent of its victims might lead one to wonder just how significant this disease could have been for human health and longevity. But typhoid's low case fatality rate understates the disease's true impact, because when typhoid did not kill you quickly and directly, it killed you slowly and indirectly. A simple way to illustrate this point is by looking at the results of a study conducted by Louis I. Dublin, a statistician for the Metropolitan Life Insurance Company. In 1915, Dublin followed 1,574 typhoid survivors over a three-year period, using life-insurance records, and published his results. Comparing the mortality rates of typhoid survivors to the mortality rates of similarly-aged persons who had never suffered from typhoid, he found that during the first year after recovery, typhoid survivors were, on average, three times more likely to have died than those who had never been exposed to typhoid, and that in the second year after recovery, typhoid survivors were twice as likely to have died than others. By the third year after recovery, however, typhoid survivors did not face an elevated risk of mortality. The two biggest killers of the typhoid survivors were tuberculosis (39 percent of all deaths) and heart failure (23 percent). Other prominent killers included kidney failure (8 percent) and pneumonia (7 percent).[5]

From the Germ Theory of Disease to the
Mills-Reincke Phenomenon

For much of the nineteenth century, people believed typhoid arose spontaneously or spread through miasmas—poisonous atmospheres thought to rise from swamps, decaying matter, and filth. In 1840, William Budd challenged these ideas, showing that typhoid spread through water and food. Budd, an Englishman, recommended that European governments invest in public health infrastructure to halt the spread of typhoid. However, scientists who continued to espouse the idea that typhoid arose spontaneously or spread through miasmas vigorously attacked Budd and his new theory. Because of their attacks, Budd's recommendations were not soon implemented, and typhoid rates in Europe remained as high as five hundred deaths per hundred thousand persons. It took more than three decades for Budd's theories and recommendations to take hold in England. In 1875, the British government passed the Public Health Act and began improving its public health systems. Ten years later, typhoid rates in England had fallen by 50 percent.[6]

With the development of Budd's ideas in particular, and the germ theory of disease in general, public health officials in American and Europe came to agree: to control typhoid, cities needed, first and foremost, to assure the purity of drinking water through filtration and chlorination, and through sanitary sewage disposal. The experience of Pittsburgh, Pennsylvania, highlights the effectiveness of water filtration in controlling typhoid fever. Pittsburgh drew its water from the Allegheny and Monongahela Rivers. Upstream from the city, seventy-five municipalities dumped their raw and untreated sewage into the rivers, leaving Pittsburgh's typhoid rate higher than that of any other major US city. Pittsburgh held this dubious distinction throughout the late nineteenth century. Then, in 1899, Pittsburgh voters approved a bond issue for the construction of a water filtration plant. Unfortunately, political bickering delayed completion of the plant until 1907. Once the plant was in operation, though, typhoid rates improved, and by 1912, they equaled the average rate in America's five largest cities.[7]

As figure 5.1 shows, in the twenty years before the introduction of filtration, typhoid rates in Pittsburgh bounced around between 75 and 150 deaths per 100,000. Within two years, filtration had reduced typhoid rates in the city by roughly 75 percent. Subsequent improvements and extensions in the city's water supply brought typhoid rates down to around 6 deaths per 100,000 by 1920. This represented a reduction of about 95 percent from prefiltration levels. As impressive as the Pittsburgh example is, it understates the benefits of water filtration, because typhoid had large and general effects on human health; and eradicating typhoid affected mortality from a broad class of diseases and illnesses, including respiratory diseases, heart failure, and kidney failure. As shown by the data below, in most cities, public water filtration not only reduced deaths from typhoid fever but also deaths from a variety of diseases that one would not immediately consider waterborne or water-related.

The first observers to identify the negative correlation between non-typhoid death rates and water purification were Hiram F. Mills and J. J. Reincke. Mills and Reincke worked independently and had had no contact prior to

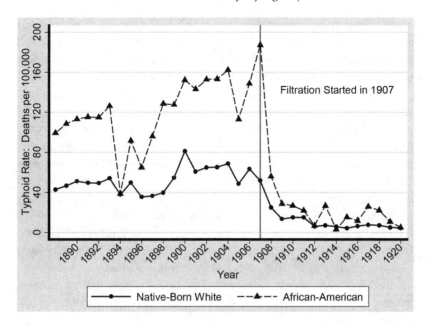

Figure 5.1. Typhoid fever in Pittsburgh, Pennsylvania.
(From Werner Troesken, *Water, Race, and Disease* [Cambridge, MA: MIT Press, 2004].)

their discoveries. During the late 1880s and early 90s, Mills worked as the chief engineer of the water company in Lawrence, Massachusetts, and served as an official at the Massachusetts State Board of Health. Reincke worked as a public health official in Hamburg, Germany, around the same period. Mills documented changes in the non-typhoid death rate following water filtration in both Lowell and Lawrence, Massachusetts, around 1893. Reincke documented similar changes taking place in Hamburg, also around 1893.[8]

The observations of Mills and Reincke were refined and extended in two papers, one by Allen Hazen and the other by William T. Sedgwick, a professor of biology at the Massachusetts Institute of Technology. Hazen and Sedgwick explored the Mills-Reincke phenomenon in cities outside Lawrence, Lowell, and Hamburg. These cities included Zurich, Switzerland; Albany, New York; Binghamton, New York; Watertown, New York; Newark, New Jersey; Jersey City, New Jersey; and Manchester, New Hampshire. Although Hazen and Sedgwick found that the size of the Mills-Reincke phenomenon varied from place to place, they concluded that, on average, for every one death from typhoid fever prevented by water filtration there would have been two to four deaths prevented from some other cause. Subsequent researchers documented the same phenomenon in Cincinnati, Boston, Baltimore, Pittsburgh, American military bases, and countless other cities and small towns. While some public health experts were skeptical of aspects of the Mills-Reincke phenomenon, they did not so much question the existence of the phenomenon, but rather its variability across time and space.[9]

The non-typhoid death rates that were the most responsive to improvements in water quality were infantile gastroenteritis (diarrhea), tuberculosis, pneumonia, influenza, bronchitis, heart disease, and kidney disease. Although other channels are possible, the available evidence suggests that these diseases improved with water filtration because typhoid was a virulent disease that left a person vulnerable to secondary infections, even if he or she survived its direct effects. Throughout the nineteenth and early twentieth centuries, it was common for an individual who survived the immediate effects of typhoid to succumb to pneumonia, tuberculosis, heart failure, kidney failure, meningitis, or some other ailment within a year or two of recovering from typhoid. Because of these sequelae, typhoid epidemics often had lingering effects, raising death rates from respiratory diseases, other infectious diseases, and heart and kidney failure years after the epidemic had subsided.

The experience of Chicago nicely illustrates the public health significance of the Mills-Reincke phenomenon. From the late-nineteenth century onward, Chicago's primary water source was Lake Michigan. Unfortunately, Lake Michigan was also frequently polluted with sewage, which carried disease-causing pathogens. This pollution occurred because, for much of the nineteenth century, the city dumped its sewage directly into the lake, or into the Chicago River, which flowed into the lake. Over the course of the nineteenth and early twentieth centuries, Chicago took three important steps (or collections of steps) in trying to prevent such fecal pollution from entering the city's water mains. The first collection of steps occurred in the years around 1870. In 1867, Chicago completed a two-mile tunnel under Lake Michigan, enabling it to build a water intake crib two miles away from the heavily polluted shoreline; in 1869, the city completed a water tower and pumping station; and in 1871, the city finished deepening the Illinois and Michigan Canal. By deepening this canal, the city at least temporarily solved the problem of sewage overflows contaminating the city's drinking water in Lake Michigan.[10]

The second set of steps occurred in or around 1893. At this time, the city completed the following projects: the Four-Mile water intake crib, the Sixty-eighth Street water intake crib, and the permanent closure of all shoreline sewage outlets.[11] The third regime change occurred around 1917, when the city opened the Wilson Avenue water intake crib and completed its citywide

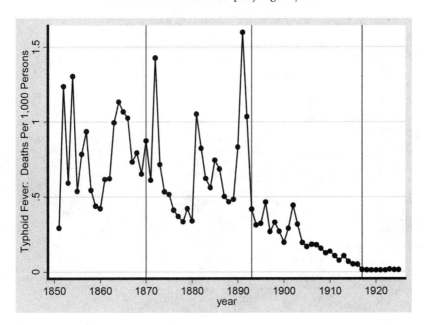

Figure 5.2. Typhoid fever in Chicago, 1850–1925.
(Data from Annual Reports of the Chicago Department of Health [various years]; Chicago Bureau of Public Efficiency, *The Water Works System of the City of Chicago* [n.p., 1917].)

chlorination of the public water supply.[12] The completion of these projects corresponded with sharp drops in the city's death rate from typhoid fever, as shown in figure 5.2, which plots typhoid rates in Chicago from 1853 through 1925. There are three vertical lines, each corresponding to the aforementioned technological improvements to promote water purity. Note in particular the dramatic effects of the Four-Mile and Sixty-eighth Street water-intake cribs and the closure of shoreline sewage outlets in 1893. Before 1893, typhoid rates averaged 0.73 deaths per thousand, and death rates were often as high as 1.0 to 1.5. After 1893, death rates never rose above 0.5, and shortly after the opening of the drainage canal in 1900, rates never rose above 0.25. The installation and extension of chlorination systems around 1917 drove down typhoid rates still further until rates were effectively 0 by the early 1920s.[13]

More surprising, but consistent with the evidence presented by Hiram F. Mills and J. J. Reincke in their original research, improvements in water quality were associated with large reductions in deaths from diseases other than typhoid fever, as shown in figure 5.3, which plots the total death rate.[14] As in figure 5.2, the vertical lines correspond to the three regime changes in the

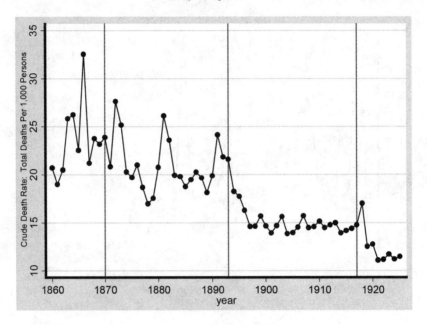

Figure 5.3. Total death rate in Chicago, 1860–1925.
(Data from Annual Reports of the Chicago Department of Health [various years]; Chicago
Bureau of Public Efficiency, *The Water Works System of the City of Chicago* [n.p., 1917].)

city's water supply. The patterns are striking. Although death rates appear to be trending downward almost from the start of the time-series, that trend is modest and highly variable.[15] There are three clear changes in trend in figure 5.3, all associated with improvements in the city's water supply. Note, in particular, that after 1893 the total death rate begins a sharp downward trend, and does not even remotely approach levels between twenty and twenty-five that were commonplace before 1893. By the late 1890s, death rates had fallen to around fifteen, where they stayed until 1917, when another sharp break in trend is observed, and death rates fall to around eleven. The year 1917, moreover, corresponds to the third step in improvements in the city's water supply: the completion of the water chlorination system.

How and why did improvements in Chicago's water supply affect diseases other than typhoid fever? Although other explanations are possible,[16] the available evidence suggests that by improving the local water supply, Chicago health authorities not only eliminated typhoid, they also eliminated its many sequelae.[17] To establish the viability of this explanation, one can explore the extent to which the death rates, at any given point in time, from tuberculosis, pneumonia, and the like, are correlated with typhoid rates at earlier points in time. The logic of the Mills-Reincke phenomenon suggests that lagged typhoid rates would have raised death rates from these other diseases, holding everything else constant. Formal statistical analyses confirm this logic.

Specifically, the logic of Mills-Reincke suggests that if typhoid rates were unusually high in year t, deaths from heart failure, kidney disease, and respiratory diseases would have been unusually high in years $t + 1$, $t + 2$, and $t + 3$. Conversely, if typhoid rates were unusually low in year t, deaths from heart failure, kidney disease, and respiratory diseases would have been unusually low in the subsequent three years. After estimating the relevant statistical models, the Chicago data suggest that for every one death prevented from typhoid fever, there were roughly seven deaths prevented from other causes.[18] A paper by David Cutler and Grant Miller suggests that Chicago's experience was not unusual: they find that in other cities water purification efforts also had large and diffuse health benefits, reducing not only deaths from typhoid and diarrheal diseases but overall death rates as well.[19]

In the introductory chapter, I described the broad contours of the American mortality transition. To briefly review, the data presented there indicated that between 1850 and 1950 life expectancy in the United States rose by 75 percent for whites and more than doubled for nonwhites. The Cutler and Miller paper suggests that roughly 60 percent of this increase can be attributed to improvements in urban water supplies. Or more concretely, over the course of one hundred years, improved water quality added another seventeen years of life for the average white American, and another twenty-two years of life for the average nonwhite American.[20] The Mills-Reincke phenomenon can help us understand why the eradication of typhoid could have had such profound effects, even though the case fatality rate from typhoid was low, and the vast majority of its victims survived. But understanding the Mills-Reincke phenomenon only gets us part of the way to understanding the role that water played in generating the American mortality transition. As explained in the introduction, a more fundamental question involves the legal and political institutions that supported the vast and historically unprecedented investments in infrastructure necessary to assure that broad cross-sections of the American population had access to drinking water that was clean and safe.

The Institutional Foundations of Urban Water Supplies

In this section, I describe how legal and political institutions shaped the provision of urban water supply and distribution in the United States. This description suggests that the institutions that mattered most were those dealing with the following two areas: access to credit on the part of local governments, and the transition from private to public ownership. Institutions related to credit mattered because urban water systems were expensive, and, when they were municipally owned and operated, required cities to borrow large amounts of money, mostly by issuing bonds.

Constitutional provisions at both the state and federal level facilitated efforts by cities to borrow money for water systems at low interest rates. These constitutional provisions promoted what economists call credible commitment: constitutional rules barred cities from making promises that they could not keep, and so when cities went to the debt market, creditors were more willing lend than they otherwise would have been. Institutions related to private and public ownership mattered because, over the course of the nineteenth and early twentieth centuries, the American water industry went from being dominated by private companies to being dominated by public ones. As the discussion below highlights, the choice between public and private provision of water was a choice between imperfect alternatives, and relative performance depended heavily on the institutional context. Private provision was the most reasonable alternative in some institutional settings, while public ownership was preferred in other settings.

Institutions and the Market for Municipal Debt

The number of urban waterworks in the United States grew rapidly over the course of the nineteenth century, from 45 systems in 1830 to 9,850 in 1924. This translates into an annual growth rate of just over 6.3 percent. At the start of this period, 80 percent of all waterworks were privately owned and operated; by the end of the period, only 30 percent of all urban water systems were private. Put another way, the number of publicly owned water systems in the United States grew from 9 in 1830 to 6,900 in 1924, while the number of privately owned systems grew from 36 to 2,950 over the same period. This translates into an annual growth rate of 7.3 percent for public systems, and 4.8 percent for private systems.[21] Data presented below suggest that over this long period, just under half of all public companies were private at some earlier point in time.

To pay for the construction of publicly owned water systems or to purchase existing private systems, cities rarely paid cash. Instead, they borrowed millions of dollars and engaged in one of the largest expansions in the size and scope of government observed in the history of the United States. Between 1843 and 1932, real municipal debt per capita rose tenfold, from

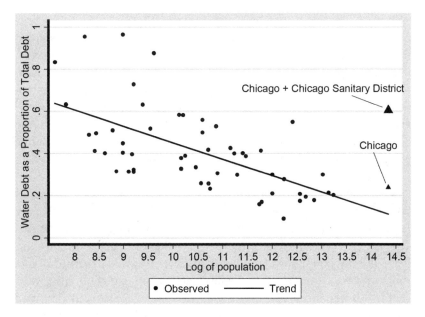

Figure 5.4. Water-related debt as a percentage of total debt for a sample of sixty-two
cities and towns, 1899.
(Data from *Commercial and Financial Chronicle, State and Local Supplement*, 1899.)

$265 per person to $2,660 (in constant 2000 dollars). After 1880, probably
the single most important driver of this increase was investment in public
water supplies. Indeed, by 1900, the available data (described below) suggest that for most cities and towns, borrowing related to water was the single
largest component of local borrowing, ranging from 20 to 60 percent of
total municipal debt.[22]

Figure 5.4 illustrates the situation more precisely. In the figure, the proportion of municipal debt associated with the local water supply in 1899 is
plotted against the log of population in the corresponding city. The sample
includes 62 US cities and towns. The smallest city in the sample is Celina,
Ohio, with a population around 2,000; the largest is Chicago, Illinois, with
a population just over 1.7 million in 1900. The distribution of population
is skewed, with a mean of 168,322, and a median population of 36,939.
For the mean city, the proportion of debt attributable to borrowing for local
water networks is 40 percent; for the median city, it is 42 percent. Notice that
there is a steep downward trend, with smaller cities borrowing the largest
proportion (usually around 60 percent but sometimes approaching 100 percent), and the typically sized city borrowing around 40 percent of its total

debt burden to finance the local water supply. While 40 percent is a large number, it is important to be clear that there are at least two reasons to think that these data significantly understate the level of municipal borrowing associated with water and the prevention of waterborne diseases. First, these data ignore spending on sanitary sewers, which, aside from roads, appear to have been the second largest component of municipal borrowing, and which were an important mechanism in the eradication of waterborne disease. Second, these data ignore borrowing for huge, water-related public works projects that were often treated independently of the normal water network.

Consider the case of Chicago. The data in figure 5.4 indicate that about 20 percent of all borrowing for the city was attributable to its local water network. Yet that figure ignores borrowing by the Chicago Sanitary District. The Sanitary District included Chicago and a couple of small towns that bordered the city, and it operated a canal and levee system that helped to prevent raw sewage from entering the lake and contaminating the city's water supply.[23] If one includes borrowing by the Sanitary District in Chicago's total debt burden, borrowing on investments related to water quality represented more than 60 percent of the city's debt. Similarly, when one looks at the large aqueducts and reservoirs built to supply water to major cities, the expenditures and debt associated with these investments were enormous.

The absolute and relative magnitude of spending on the Chicago Sanitary District is shown in table 5.1, which compares the costs of some of the largest public works projects in American history. Costs are reported in constant 2011 dollars. Notice that if one looks just at total costs, not per capita costs (costs spread across the relevant population) among the projects considered in table 5.1, the Transcontinental Railroad is larger than all the others. That said, aqueducts and other water-related projects for American cities were comparable in terms of expense to the Erie Canal, the Hoover Dam, and the Transcontinental Railroad.[24]

Municipal borrowing for these projects becomes far more impressive if one looks at their cost on a per capita basis. This is done in the second-to-last column of table 5.1, which divides the cost of the project by the population of the city, state, or the entire United States at the time the project was built. Considering project costs on a per capita basis is, for the purposes of the discussion here, probably the most appropriate metric, as the number of taxpayers varied greatly across municipalities, states, and the entire country. Once one divides the costs of the projects listed in the table by the population of the relevant constituency, borrowing for municipal water supplies and aqueducts far exceeds anything done by state and federal governments.

Table 5.1. Comparative costs of large public works projects in American history

Project	Built	Area served	Total cost (millions of constant 2011 dollars)	Population (millions)	Per capita cost (area)	Proportion of US GDP
Hoover Dam	1931–36	US	949	125	7.59	0.0008
Transcontinental Railroad	1863–69	US	1780	35	50.8	0.0013
Panama Canal	1902–13	US	751	92	8.16	0.0097
Erie Canal	1817–25	NY	172	1.4	122.8	0.0101
Erie Canal extension	1835–65	NY	911	2.4	379.5	0.0074
Chicago Sanitary District	1892–1910	Chicago	1110	1.7	652.9	0.0020
Catskill Aqueduct System	1907–24	NYC	1440	5	228.0	0.0024
Hetch Hetchy Reservoir	1914–34	SF	487	.560	869.6	0.0004
Old Croton Aqueduct	1838–43	NYC	336	.391	1052.9	0.0072
Owens River Valley Aqueduct	1908–13	LA	598	.319	1874.6	0.0008

Source: Data from the following sources: Stanley L. Engerman and Kenneth L. Sokoloff, "Digging the Dirt at Public Expense," in Corruption and Reform: Lessons from America's Economic History, ed. Edward L. Glaeser and Claudia Goldin (Chicago: University of Chicago Press, 2006), 95–124; Martin V. Melosi, The Sanitary City: Urban Infrastructure in America from Colonial Times to the Present (Baltimore, MD: Johns Hopkins University Press, 2000), 128–29, 376–77; Louis P. Cain, Sanitation Strategy for a Lakefront Metropolis (DeKalb: Northern Illinois University Press, 1977); Noel Mauer and Carlos Yu, The Big Ditch: How America Took, Built, Ran, and Ultimately Gave Away the Panama Canal (Princeton, NJ: Princeton University Press, 2011).

On a per capita basis, the four most expensive projects in this table are the Owens River Valley Water Aqueduct, which, in 2011 dollars, cost $1,874 per Los Angeles resident at the time of construction; the Old Croton Aqueduct, which cost $1,052 per resident of New York; the Hetch Hetchy reservoir and aqueduct, which cost $869 per San Francisco resident, based on an estimate of the city's 1924 population; and the Catskill Aqueduct System, which cost $822 per New York resident. On a per capita basis, the Owens River Valley Aqueduct cost twenty-three times more than the Panama Canal.

Once one thinks about the costs of these projects on a per capita basis, the fact that American municipalities were able to finance these projects is striking. But when one puts borrowing for water-related infrastructure in historical context, those costs become truly remarkable, because the story of how municipal governments came to be able to finance investments on such a massive scale begins with a story about municipal profligacy. During the mid-nineteenth century, city and state governments across the country issued millions of dollars in debt in an effort to attract railroads, canals, banks, and other large capital projects to their jurisdictions. In many cases, cities underwrote and guaranteed the debts of the railroads or made arrangements whereby they received a share ownership in the railroad in return for underwriting the railroad's bonds. When the railroads failed, which many of them did, city and state governments were left holding the bag, and themselves had to declare bankruptcy.[25]

This insolvency undermined the market for state and municipal debt: lenders grew wary of the promises of borrowers who had already demonstrated their inability to keep their financial house in order and repay their loans. Describing conditions during the mid-nineteenth century, Howard Beebe explained that the "issuance of so-called 'bonus bonds' to aid the construction of new railroads [and] the establishment of manufacturing and other industrial plants" had been made "by communities with more ambition than sound judgment." The default and repudiation of the bonus bonds generated a "very decided prejudice" in the "minds of intelligent investors" and the "market for municipal bonds" was "thereby restricted."[26]

Yet fifty years later, the municipal bond market could be described in very different terms, especially with regard to bonds for municipal waterworks. In *The Principles of Bond Investment*, Lawrence Chamberlain provided an overview of the American bond market during the early 1900s. After surveying all types of bonds issued by public and private entities, Chamberlain concluded that "municipal water bonds as a class are a premier security because of the ease and certainty of their support and ultimate payment." According

to Chamberlain, during bankruptcy proceedings for municipalities, water bonds had "fared better" than other municipal debt obligations. Chamberlain's assessment of the conditions for municipal water bonds during the early 1900s stands in stark contrast to how municipal bonds of all sorts were viewed during the mid-nineteenth century, when, as noted above, they were viewed with prejudice by most informed investors. Certainly, they would not have been considered a "premier security." What happened to transform the market for municipal bonds, especially those related to water?[27]

In the wake of the excesses of local lending during the railroad boom, state constitutions across the country were rewritten so as to assure lenders that state and local governments would not repeat the mistakes of the past and underwrite risky projects that should never have been subsidized by taxpayers in the first place. To appreciate the significance of these constitutional changes for local governments and municipal borrowing, one needs to understand that municipalities were creatures of state governments; they derived their powers from the state. More precisely, like private corporations, municipal corporations were granted their authority and privileges through state charters. These charters defined a wide array of powers, including the power to regulate the services provided and the rates charged by privately owned public utilities; the authority to own and operate municipal enterprises; and the power to regulate how much debt cities could take on and for what purposes.[28]

Municipalities were not free to break these rules; if they did, taxpayers and bondholders or any other party with standing could sue and have the city enjoined from undertaking behavior not authorized under the state constitution.[29] As a result, if the state limited a city's debt to two million dollars, the city could borrow no more, and anyone considering lending to the city would have known this. In this way, a city's ability to overextend itself was limited by the institutional setting. Without such institutions, a city's promise to potential lenders that it would not overextend itself—and, say, borrow in excess of two million dollars—would have lacked credibility. Potential lenders, in turn, would have demanded compensation for that increased risk in the form of higher interest rates.[30]

A few examples from state constitutions illustrate how the excesses of municipal indebtedness during the mid-nineteenth century railroad boom gave rise to institutional changes that would make low-cost, municipal borrowing for waterworks possible. These examples highlight how institutions were fundamental in the creation of American waterworks and, in turn, helped drive the American mortality transition. More precisely, the institutional history that follows demonstrates the ways in which state constitutions and legislative measures allowed municipalities to make credible promises about their ability to repay large loans. These promises or, as defined above, credible commitments helped assure potential lenders and creditors that American municipalities were good credit risks, and this, in turn, lowered the cost of borrowing and facilitated the construction of waterworks.

The first example involves municipal debt limits. First, municipal debt limits constrained the ability of municipal governments to overextend themselves. Debt limits were often tied to a given municipality's tax base and ability to raise the revenue necessary to fund and service debt. Limits were also placed on the ability of a municipality to fund certain projects, such as underwriting private projects.[31] Recognizing that water and sewer were unusual and were especially important to the health and welfare of any urban area, many state constitutions separated debt for water networks from debt for other sources. This limited borrowing for less pressing urban matters but gave cities and towns plenty of room to borrow for an essential public service at reasonable cost.[32]

The Supreme Court of South Dakota explained the broader rationale for constitutional exemptions for water debt. According to the court, "The existence of a large municipal debt does not render an adequate water supply less necessary or beneficial." On the contrary, in the court's opinion, "the ability to provide pure water for domestic uses may become absolutely essential to procurement and retention of a population sufficient to meet existing municipal obligations." The logic of this last clause, though counterintuitive on first reading, is not implausible or unreasonable: by issuing more debt to build and maintain public water systems, a city having difficulty meeting its other debt obligations might actually improve its financial standing, because an adequate water supply could help promote local population growth and thereby bolster property taxes. By the same token, letting a waterworks fall into disrepair because the city in question could not borrow further to improve or maintain the works might generate outmigration and a contraction in the local tax base.[33]

Another common constitutional provision protecting the holders of water bonds were those mandating the establishment of sinking funds. Through sinking funds, every year cities took some of the proceeds of the operation of waterworks and set them aside to create interest-bearing accounts that would guarantee sufficient funds to meet obligations on payments of principal and interest related to the waterworks. Although there were problems associated with sinking funds, which are discussed in detail in a later section, when properly administered, they helped assure that money would be available for cities to meet their debts, water-related and otherwise. In the process, sinking funds also would have lowered interest and borrowing costs, because creditors would have gained greater confidence in the capacity of the town to repay its loans.[34]

Sinking funds remained a popular and at least partially effective means of protecting creditors throughout the late nineteenth and early twentieth centuries. According to the United States Census, as of 1906, there were 158 cities with a population of thirty thousand or more. Of these, 140 (89 percent) had one or more sinking funds established to help city officials meet their obligations for water-related debt and other municipal projects. Among the 15 cities with populations greater than three hundred thousand, the typical city had three sinking funds established. New York, for example, had ten funds; Chicago and Buffalo each had eight funds; Cleveland had five; and Detroit had four. For cities with populations between one and three hundred thousand, the typical city had two separate sinking funds established. Most smaller cities with less elaborate debt structures had one or fewer funds.[35]

Another institutional mechanism that protected bondholders from default and thereby reduced borrowing costs for cities was the specific bond tax. Fifteen states had constitutional provisions that required municipalities to pass irrevocable ordinances creating a tax levy sufficient to pay the interest and retire the principal on all municipal debts incurred.[36] According to Chamberlain's authoritative overview of the American bond market in the early 1900s, specific bond taxes "greatly enhanced" the "security" of municipal bonds. Chamberlain, moreover, saw specific bond taxes as far more protective of the interest of bondholders than sinking funds, largely because such funds were liable to misappropriation, unwise investment, and suspension. Specific bond taxes, by contrast, had no such weaknesses. They relied primarily on the taxing power of the municipality, which the city itself could not abrogate: once granted police powers by the state, municipal corporations could not contract those powers away, though they might choose not to exercise them.[37] Even in states without constitutional mandates for specific bond taxes, it was not uncommon for policymakers to use ordinary legislation to require municipalities to employ specific bond taxes.[38]

As explained in chapter 3, following the Glorious Revolution in late seventeenth-century England, institutional constraints were placed on the British monarchy. These constraints made it difficult for the king to renege on his loans and promises, and, in so doing, made his promises to repay creditors more believable. Creditors, in turn, grew much more willing to lend. As a result of these institutional changes, interest rates in England fell, and government borrowing increased by a factor of sixteen within a few decades' time. What makes this history so compelling, and the reason economic historians return to it so frequently, is that the institutional constraints that grew out of the Glorious Revolution effectively undid a long history of financial profligacy on the part of the king, a profligacy that had left the world unwilling to lend England any more money.[39]

The story of American municipalities appears to have been much the same, but with an added demographic twist. In particular, the excesses of the financial borrowing during the canal and railroad booms left potential creditors chastened and unwilling to lend to American municipalities, unless they were compensated by high interest rates.[40] Had state constitutions not been altered to address this unwillingness, municipalities would have had a difficult time raising the money to finance the investments in water that were so important in bringing about the American mortality transition.[41] Not unlike the financial history of the Glorious Revolution, constraints placed on the behavior and borrowing capacity of municipalities facilitated efforts to finance the construction and operation of public water and sewer systems.

The Standard Explanation for the Rise of Municipal Ownership in the Water Industry

As explained above, over the course of the nineteenth and early twentieth centuries, there was tremendous growth in the relative and absolute frequency of municipal ownership in the water industry. The standard explanation for the growth of municipal ownership is that private provision was a failure. According to the standard logic, private enterprises distributing pure water generated large positive externalities by reducing the risk of epidemic diseases such as typhoid fever and by reducing the risk of conflagrations like the Great Chicago Fire. If externalities were substantial, and private companies found it harder to internalize them than public enterprises, this could account for the rapid rise of public ownership. In this section, I argue that the standard argument is shallow and ideologically driven. The efficiency characteristics of private provision, and public provision for that matter, were the result of the underlying legal and political institutions. But before developing my argument and critiquing the prevailing understanding, I would first like to give the standard argument some historical structure and content.

According to Progressive Era reformers, municipal water companies were more likely than private companies to make socially beneficial but presumably unprofitable investments in water purification and typhoid eradication because they were guided by political rather than economic motives.[42] An engineer and champion of municipal ownership, R. E. McDonnell, argued that private companies did not have a financial incentive to provide adequate service and filtration: "The task of treating the supply and protecting it from pollution and contamination calls for a greater and greater investment in the modern waterworks system. With this great investment, it is impossible to charge enough for the product to pay the expected dividends of the average utility owner." In this setting, the private enterprise would have had no choice but to curtail service. As McDonnell wrote, "the private company is thus faced with an alternative of curtailing either dividends or service. With first allegiance to its stockholders and itself, it has but one choice."[43]

In contrast to the motives of private companies, those of municipal companies were pure. "The governing motive of a municipally owned water utility," McDonnell wrote, "is to furnish an adequate supply of pure, clear and acceptable water to the citizens at the lowest cost possible. The first allegiance of the municipal utility is to its citizens or its customers. There is no watered stock. There are no stockholders clamoring for dividends." In its 1898 biennial report, the North Carolina Board of Health used similar logic to explain why public companies charged lower rates than private companies:

The readers of this report will doubtless be struck by the high price charged for water, especially to small consumers, which, of course, includes all the poorer classes. In several instances a minimum consumption amounting to $12 per annum is required, which is practically prohibitory to the poor. We have no control over the price charged, but we feel it our duty to say that high-priced water is not in the interest of public health. Pure water in abundance, at a price within reach of all, is one of the most powerful agencies for promoting the health of any community. It is for this reason that we believe so strongly in municipal ownership.

The board went on to explain that public water companies were more likely to respond to the needs of the poor than were private companies because the former were governed by non-economic motives: "We can not expect those who have invested their money in such enterprises for the purpose of securing dividends to look at the matter from a [public health] point of view—they have a right both in law and equity to make such charges as will ensure them a reasonable return on their investment. But when the water works are owned by the people as a whole, the object of the management will not be dividends but health, comfort, beauty, and safety." [44]

While the notion that public firms were animated solely by such noble motives strains credulity, baser political incentives might also have led public water companies to behave differently than private companies. For example, public firms might have won votes or maximized the employment of patronage workers by installing mains and providing service in areas that private companies deemed unprofitable. Whatever their motivation, it appears that public water companies generally did charge lower rates than private companies. A large survey conducted at the end of the nineteenth century found that the rates charged by public water companies were, on average, 24 percent lower than the rates charged by private companies.[45] Formal econometric studies comparing the rates of public and private utility companies corroborate these findings: publicly owned utilities tend to charge significantly lower rates than privately owned utilities.[46] Similarly, if one looks at water prices before and after public acquisition, there is evidence that rates fell sharply with municipalization. For example, in the years leading up to the municipalization of the water supply in Omaha, Nebraska, water rates rose more than 10 percent over the course of five years, and fell by 35 percent in the seven years following the public takeover.[47]

Because municipal enterprises charged lower prices and were (at least in the minds of Progressive Era reformers) more likely to invest in water filtration, reformers predicted that typhoid rates would fall with public ownership. McDonnell, for example, argued that "water purification has practically eliminated typhoid epidemics [and] records show that the greatest strides in this phase of service have been made under municipal ownership." An administrator in Kansas City explained that "old timers shuddered" when they recalled the days when the city's private water company distributed raw, untreated water from the Missouri River. Only after municipalization in 1909 did the city begin filtering its water supply.[48]

Advocates of public ownership frequently cited the experience of Duluth, Minnesota, to highlight the benefits of municipalization. In Duluth, "Typhoid" Truelson launched his political career by blaming typhoid epidemics during the 1880s and early 1890s on the ineptitude of the city's private water company. Truelson promised voters that, if elected mayor, he would acquire the company at a reasonable price, take the necessary steps to purify the water, and eliminate typhoid. After winning the election, Truelson acquired the waterworks in 1896 and oversaw improvements in the city's water and sewer system.[49] The results were dramatic. Before 1896, typhoid rates had averaged 186 deaths per hundred thousand and exhibited a mild upward trend. As figure 5.5 shows, municipalization reversed this trend, with typhoid rates falling by more than 60 percent; after 1896, typhoid rates in the city averaged around 61 deaths per hundred thousand. Although this rate was still high by national standards, relative to the era of private ownership it represented a significant reduction.[50]

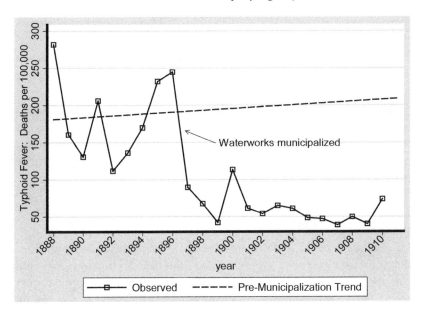

Figure 5.5. Typhoid rates in Duluth, Minnesota, 1888–1910.
(Data from United States, Bureau of the Census, *Mortality Statistics* [various years]; George C. Whipple, *Typhoid Fever: Its Causation, Transmission, and Prevention* [New York: John Wiley & Sons, 1908], 375.)

Reformers also frequently pointed to a study conducted by the National Civic Federation to show that public ownership reduced typhoid rates. The federation found that typhoid rates in Chicago, Cleveland, and Syracuse were less than half the rates in Indianapolis and New Haven. Chicago, Cleveland, and Syracuse had publicly owned water companies, but those in Indianapolis and New Haven were privately owned. To the National Civic Federation, a group dedicated to furthering the cause of municipal ownership, the import of this finding was clear: public ownership improved water quality and reduced typhoid rates. Only if one believed that people in Chicago and Cleveland boiled their water more than people in Indianapolis and New Haven could anything but public ownership have caused typhoid rates to be lower in these cities. And this, the federation claimed, was highly unlikely.[51]

Although there are good reasons to question these arguments, reformers seemed to have a point. Preventing typhoid required water companies to make at least two large investments: extending main service into all areas of the city, rich and poor alike, and building filtration plants. Chlorination systems required much smaller investments, but to eradicate typhoid, all three of these steps were needed. Filtering and chlorinating water would not have benefited the poor much if their neighborhoods lacked adequate main service. Beyond this, preventing typhoid was a public good. When a water company installed filters, initiated chlorination, and extended main service, it reduced the risk that typhoid would break out, and this benefited every person in the city, whether or not that person purchased the company's water. In this setting, conventional economic logic predicts that neither consumers nor producers would invest sufficiently in disease-prevention efforts, because they would not be able to internalize all of the gains in disease reductions.[52]

On the Incentives of Private Firms to Filter Water Supplies

Progressive Era reformers were wrong when they suggested that private firms did not have incentives to invest in water filtration and quality. First, and perhaps foremost, there was a clear market-based incentive: a company that regularly sold water tainted with disease would have had fewer customers than one that sold water that was pure and disease-free. Second, two institutions—municipal franchises and the common law—created incentives for private water companies to invest in water filters and take steps to eradicate typhoid. As explained earlier, municipal franchises were contracts between cities and water companies. Franchises granted water companies the rights they needed to use public streets and alleys to lay mains and the rights to access nearby water sources. These rights sometimes included the power of eminent domain, and allowed companies to seize private property to install their distribution systems. Also, franchises often included provisions guaranteeing companies monopoly status. In return for these rights, water companies consented to a variety of measures designed to protect cities and their residents.[53]

Franchises typically set standards regarding water pressure; main size, weight, and composition; water rates; taxes; the speed with which companies were to install mains; and standards for quality and health. Sometimes franchises established vague standards for water quality and filtration, merely stating that the company had to provide clean and wholesome water, suitable for domestic use. At other times, franchises explicitly dictated the types of filters companies were to install and the quality of the water they were to provide. Franchises also included stiff punishments if the water company failed to comply with the terms of the franchise. For example, the franchises of water companies in Topeka, Kansas, and Birmingham, Alabama, expressly stated that if the water company in question "failed to comply with any of the provisions" of the franchise it would "forfeit" its rights to operate in the city. But even in the absence of such draconian actions, cities were able to influence the performance of the water company in terms of disease prevention through later legislative actions and by withholding payment for such things as fire hydrant rentals.[54]

In addition to franchise contracts, another constraint arose from private individuals, who often sued water companies for damages arising from typhoid epidemics. How the courts responded to such suits influenced the degree to which private companies invested in water filtration and typhoid prevention. The more likely the courts were to hold water companies liable for typhoid epidemics, the more likely those companies were to invest in water filtration systems. According to one authority, water companies owed their customers "the duty of exercising reasonable care and diligence in providing pure and wholesome water free from contamination." But what constituted "reasonable care and diligence"? By 1920, the courts had established two rules. First, water companies could not use ignorance as an excuse. It was incumbent upon companies to test their water for disease-causing impurities. Second, if water companies discovered dangerous bacteria, like typhoid, they had to purify the water, or at the very least notify their customers of the dangers associated with drinking their water.[55]

How effective were economic incentives, franchise contracts, and the courts in encouraging private firms to invest in water filtration? The data described below suggest that they were very effective: private firms were 2.5 times more likely than public firms to invest in water filters. In 1899, the federal government surveyed 1,034 water companies, about 30 percent of all water companies then operating in the United States.[56] For each company, the survey provides information about the following: whether the company was public or private; when, if ever, the company had changed ownership (i.e., when it switched from private to public or from public to private); if the company had invested in a filtration system; the company's water source (e.g., river, lake, or underground well); and when the company built its plant and distribution system. The survey provides only limited information about the size of each water company: it ranks all of the companies in terms of how much water they sold but does not report the exact level of sales or output. Unfortunately, the survey includes no information about location or any other information that might reveal the precise identity of a company.[57]

Of the 375 private water companies in the sample, 19 percent had water filters. Of the 659 public companies in the sample, only 6 percent had filters. This simple comparison of means survives a formal statistical analysis.[58]

How does one reconcile this observation with the standard argument that private firms had no incentive to invest in water filters? How too does one reconcile this with the history of Duluth and Kansas City, where there is strong evidence that switching from private to public provision of water was followed by improved investment and sharp reductions in typhoid rates? The answer begins with a simple observation that private ownership worked best in situations where property rights were secure, where private companies were confident that their expensive investments in distribution and filtration systems would not be expropriated by municipal governments.

So long as private companies felt that, even if they were taken over by municipal authorities, they would receive adequate compensation for their capital stock without extensive and costly litigation, they invested appropriately. On the other hand, when institutional protections against opportunistic behavior on the part of municipal authorities were limited, private companies were reluctant to commit fully to the city; their investment choices were therefore made with trepidation and tentativeness. Yet it was that same trepidation that gave cities a reason to take the companies over and operate them in a way that assured adequate investment in water mains and filters. In short, once the threat of an opportunistic municipal takeover became substantial, that threat was self-fulfilling; the optimal response of a private company in that context was to pull back significantly on its investments in mains and filtration systems, which virtually guaranteed that the forces pushing for municipalization would succeed.[59]

Institutions and the Specter of Municipalization

In this section, I describe the legal and political processes that surrounded efforts by municipal authorities to take over private water companies. Among other things, this description helps explain why private water companies were reluctant to invest in mains and filters without assurances that the municipalization process would be short-lived and fair. Table 5.2 presents a state-by-state breakdown of the number of private water companies as of 1897 and the number and percentage of these companies that were taken over by municipal authorities between 1897 and 1915. For the overall United States, of the 726 private water companies operating in 1897, 258, or 45 percent, were municipalized over the eighteen-year period. However, table 5.2 also highlights the fact that there was a great deal of cross-state variation in the number of municipalizations. In a few states, such as Nevada and West Virginia, none of the private water companies operating in 1897 were municipalized by 1915. In others, such as Alabama, Colorado,

Table 5.2. State-level municipalization patterns for private water companies, 1897–1915

State	Number of private water companies in 1897	municipalized by 1915	(%)	State	Number of private water companies in 1897	municipalized by 1915	(%)
Alabama	11	8	(72.7)	Nebraska	6	6	(100.0)
Arizona	3	2	(66.7)	Nevada	5	0	(0.00)
Arkansas	9	3	(33.3)	New Hampshire	10	7	(70.0)
California	39	13	(33.3)	New Jersey	27	7	(25.9)
Colorado	12	7	(58.3)	New Mexico	5	2	(40.0)
Connecticut	27	4	(14.8)	New York	58	18	(31.0)
Florida	8	4	(50.0)	North Carolina	9	6	(66.7)
Georgia	6	5	(83.3)	Ohio	23	4	(17.4)
Idaho	6	2	(33.3)	Oklahoma	2	2	(1.00)
Illinois	27	5	(18.5)	Oregon	12	5	(41.7)
Indiana	27	3	(11.1)	Pennsylvania	81	6	(7.4)
Iowa	26	13	(50.0)	Rhode Island	5	1	(20.0)
Kansas	33	25	(75.8)	South Carolina	8	4	(50.0)
Kentucky	19	1	(5.3)	South Dakota	7	4	(57.1)
Louisiana	5	2	(40.0)	Tennessee	8	4	(50.0)
Maine	30	5	(16.7)	Texas	28	12	(42.9)
Maryland	10	4	(40.0)	Utah	1	1	(100.0)
Massachusetts	23	9	(39.1)	Vermont	4	2	(50.0)
Michigan	19	11	(57.9)	Virginia	5	3	(60.0)
Minnesota	6	4	(66.7)	Washington	9	4	(44.4)
Mississippi	6	5	(83.3)	West Virginia	5	0	(0.00)
Missouri	24	10	(41.7)	Wisconsin	22	11	(50.0)
Montana	9	4	(44.4)	Wyoming	1	0	(0.00)
				United States	726	258	(44.8)

Georgia, Kansas, and Mississippi, as many as 84 percent of all private companies operating in 1897 were municipalized by 1915.[60]

Efforts to municipalize private water companies frequently resulted in litigation; roughly 40 percent of all municipalization proceedings ended in litigation.[61] Three interrelated factors explain the frequency of litigation. First, there was a bilateral monopoly problem: typically the exchange of water systems involved only one buyer and one seller, the city and the private water company. In a bilateral monopoly setting, there are no outside options to discipline either the buyer or the seller. If the buyer sets an unreasonably low price, there are no outside bidders to drive the price back up to more reasonable market levels; alternatively, if the seller sets a ridiculously high price, there are no other sellers waiting in the wings, ready to offer the product at a lower price. Second, the capital exchanged was long-lived and specific to place and purpose: companies could not pick up their mains and water filters and move to another city, nor could they sell them for some other purpose. They were tied to the city and its water industry. Third, the city had the power to regulate and tax; the water company did not. Unequal regulatory strength and specific capital left the water company vulnerable to opportunistic behavior on the part of local politicians. Simply put, city authorities could use their power to regulate and tax to reduce the company's selling price and acquire the assets in a fire sale.[62]

Cities employed a wide range of strategies in an effort to get private water companies to reduce their asking prices for their plants and distribution systems. Some cities lobbied for and secured passage of state laws allowing them to acquire water companies through the power of eminent domain.[63] Other cities used their regulatory powers to undermine the value of private enterprises. For example, in 1900 in Knoxville, Tennessee, the city council passed an ordinance requiring the water company to cut its rates by 25 percent. The company sued for injunctive relief. Challenging the rate ordinance on several grounds, the company suggested that the ordinance was part of a larger scheme to acquire its capital at bargain rates. Although the courts ultimately rejected this argument, the city initiated proceedings to acquire the company three years later.[64]

In Kansas City, local politicians used a tortured interpretation of a phrase in a private water company's franchise as a pretext for seizing the company's plant and distribution system without offering any compensation whatsoever.[65] Although the city ultimately lost, the details of the episode are instructive and help explain why the private water company might have been reluctant to invest fully in the city. On October 27, 1873, the city council of Kansas City, Missouri, granted a twenty-year franchise to the National Waterworks Company. In the franchise, the city reserved the right to purchase, at its option, the company's plant and distribution system. The franchise also stated that if after twenty years the city had neither purchased the company nor renewed the company's franchise, the city would, at that time, have to purchase the company's plant and distribution system. If the city and company could not agree on a price, the circuit court or other court of record would decide a "fair and equitable" price. Finally, the franchise stipulated that "if upon examination" it was "found that such works" were "not in all respects in good condition, and of first-class and sound materials, and in every way efficient, then the city" was not "required to purchase the same at any time nor at any price."[66]

After twenty years, Kansas City had not renewed the company's franchise nor had it purchased the company's plant and distribution system. City authorities intended to simply take the company's works, without paying any compensation, when the franchise expired on April 30, 1894. Not surprisingly, National Waterworks sued, asking that the courts compel the city to pay for its plant. The city launched a countersuit. It claimed that the company had not, as required by franchise, built a first-class waterworks. A complex and protracted legal battle followed, but on the company's central claim—that the franchise compelled the city to purchase its plant and distribution system—the courts sided with the company.[67]

In several cities and towns, local authorities sued to have the franchises of private water companies revoked. In these suits, the cities claimed that the conduct of the water company in question was so outrageous that its rights to operate in the city should be forfeited, or that the state should dissolve the company.[68] For example, in Topeka, Kansas, the city used the water company's refusal to extend mains into particular areas of the city as grounds for revoking the company' franchise and right to operate in the city.[69] Although the courts in Kansas ultimately blocked Topeka officials from revoking the company's franchise, cities and towns elsewhere in the state were successful in their efforts to rescind the operating rights of private water companies for failure to perform.[70] Revocation left the plant and distribution systems of the affected water companies worthless to the investors and owners of the companies, because the capital could not be resold or redeployed for any purpose except distributing water. That said, once the companies had abandoned their fixed investments, city officials in the affected towns were free to simply take the plants and mains for free and begin operating them on the city's behalf.

The most common strategy employed by cities to get private companies to reduce their asking price was to construct public waterworks to compete with the private companies. All concerned, including the United States Supreme Court, recognized that competition from "the city may be far more destructive than that of a private company" because the city could conduct its "business without regard to profit" and "resort to public taxation to make up for losses."[71] A handful of state and federal justices even believed that competition from municipal waterworks violated private water companies' rights to substantive due process, in effect, depriving private companies of their property without "just compensation or due process of law." In a scathing dissent to a decision by the New York Supreme Court that allowed a municipal water company to enter into competition with a private company, Justice Bartlett wrote, "It is obvious that the municipal water company is in no legal sense the ordinary competitor of the old company, but is armed with powers that will inevitably drive the latter from the field, and its bondholders and stockholders be subjected to a total loss of all capital invested." According to Bartlett, this "is not competition; it is annihilation."[72]

Private water companies anticipated such problems and often demanded provisions in their franchises limiting the authority of local governments to regulate, tax, and construct competing enterprises. For private water companies, though, the problem with such contractual provisions is that they were often unenforceable or interpreted in unforeseeable ways. The courts ruled, for example, that as corporations chartered by the state, cities could not contract away their powers to regulate and tax, regardless of what the franchises they granted to private water companies said. Hence, if a state legislature empowered a local government with the authority to regulate water rates, the municipality could not forsake that power in a contract; only the state could revoke such power. The courts, moreover, were bound to interpret ambiguous or unclear franchise provisions against the franchisee (the private water company) and in favor of the local government.[73]

In some states, private water companies were protected against municipal entry by required-purchase laws. These laws compelled towns to buy private water companies already in operation before they built their own waterworks. At least two state courts viewed required-purchase laws as mechanisms to promote private investment and development of the water industry in general. Upholding a required-purchase law in Pennsylvania, the state supreme court explained that "in its beginnings" a municipality is "perhaps not so financially strong, or its debt limit may approach the constitutional limit so closely that it cannot borrow." Yet the municipality's "low financial condition" did not render "less urgent the necessity of water supply." In such a setting, the town could obtain a reliable water supply in "but one way" and that was by contracting with a private enterprise with the "money" and the willingness "to invest [its] private capital in the construction of waterworks."

According to the court, the Pennsylvania "legislature knew that capital would not be invested in such an enterprise if in the future it were liable to confiscation by competition with a public enterprise operated from a municipal treasury capable of replenishment from the pocket of the taxpayer."[74] Consistent with the court's interpretation, the state's required-purchase law was passed in 1784, at a time when municipal credit markets were poorly developed, and when Meadville (the town at the heart of the case) was small with limited financial means. Other state courts, while less explicit in explaining the historical context in which required-purchase laws were passed, expressed the same basic idea: that the possibility of competition from a municipal enterprise would have spelled financial doom for private corporations and thereby discouraged private investment.[75] In this way, required-purchase laws fostered the early development of the American water industry, particularly in smaller cities and towns.[76]

When statutory and contractual measures failed to insulate private water companies from unwanted competition and regulation, they turned to other strategies for protection. Specifically, there is anecdotal evidence that private water companies facing a high-risk municipal takeover in the immediate future often refused to extend water mains or build water filtration systems without additional promises from city authorities that they would not be taken over or would, at least, be adequately compensated if taken over. For example, in Akron, Ohio, during the early 1900s, the local water company refused to build a water filtration plant until the city promised that it would renew its franchise, which was set to expire in a few years. Akron officials later used the company's refusal as a pretext to initiate proceedings to municipalize the private water company.[77] The same scenario played itself out in Billings, Montana, a few years later.[78]

Municipal Ownership in the Long Run

In the discussion above, I argued that the failure of private provision was best understood as a response to ill-defined institutions and property rights. A parallel argument can be made about the failures of municipal ownership over the long run, because while municipal ownership often worked quite well in the short run, evidence presented below suggests that its long-run performance is less impressive. I argue that the failures of municipal ownership over the long term can be understood, at least in part, as the result of institutional failures. Two court cases from Massachusetts help to illuminate the underlying problems.

The first case involves the Town of Salem. In 1864, the Massachusetts legislature passed a law authorizing Salem to build a waterworks at "the cost of a million dollars or more." The thirteenth section of this law stated explicitly that Salem was to set rates for water sufficiently high so "as to provide annually, if practicable, from the net income and receipts . . . for the payment of the interest, and not less than one per cent of the principal of the 'City of Salem water loan.'" This section further mandated that the "net surplus income . . . shall be set apart as a sinking fund, and applied solely to the principal and interest of the [debt] until [it] is fully paid and discharged." Soon after completing the waterworks, however, Salem chose not to establish any sort of sinking fund and instead devised a plan to "distribute water free to all" of the city's "inhabitants" and "businesses." In response, the state attorney general filed suit to revoke Salem's franchise to operate a waterworks because the city had violated the terms of its franchise, which clearly stated it was to charge sufficient rates to cover its operating expenses and capital costs, or least try to set rates in that range. In its opinion, the Massachusetts Supreme Court conceded that Salem had violated the terms of its franchise, but held that revocation of the franchise was far too steep a penalty.[79]

The second case involves the Town of Fall River. In 1874, Fall River passed an ordinance establishing a sinking fund. Under the terms of the sinking fund, all revenues the city collected from its water company were to be paid to the city treasurer and "placed by him to the credit of the water company." The ordinance prohibited the city from using the revenues for anything other than the operation and maintenance of the waterworks and payment of the interest and principal on the city's water debt. In contrast to the Salem example, in Fall River the sinking fund was aimed primarily at assuring that funds would be available in the future to improve and maintain the capital stock, particularly water mains. Initially, revenues from the waterworks were not sufficient to cover all of these expenses, and taxes had to be raised to make up for the shortfall. Over time, however, revenue from the waterworks increased, and soon a large surplus had accumulated in the sinking fund.

By 1907, so much money was in the fund that the Fall River city council passed an ordinance ordering the treasurer to transfer money from the waterworks sinking fund into the city's general fund. The city council passed this ordinance over the mayor's veto and the objections of the city treasurer, who both saw the measure as financially imprudent and a violation of state laws mandating that cities maintain sinking funds for water-related debts. When the treasurer and the mayor refused to transfer the funds even after the ordinance had been passed, the city council sued asking the courts for a writ of mandamus to compel performance. The Massachusetts Supreme

Court issued the writ, ruling that how the sinking fund was managed was a local matter not subject to state supervision.[80]

These cases illustrate two fundamental points. The first point is that the institutions that supported and fostered responsible financial stewardship of municipal waterworks were malleable, and their effectiveness depended on how the courts interpreted and enforced the relevant laws. Second, local politicians often faced strong incentives to shift resources away from the long-term health and viability of water systems (e.g., paying off the principal on loans) toward more short-term goals (e.g., immediate reductions in rates for consumers). This phenomenon is by no means unique to the history of Salem and Fall River, Massachusetts. On the contrary, if one looks at the crumbling infrastructure of municipally owned water and sewer systems in the United States today, there is ample evidence to suggest that failure to maintain capital stocks is a serious and pervasive problem, and that problem is by no means unique to the United States. Underinvestment in long-term capital is a problem that plagues municipally owned waterworks the world over, and it has serious public health consequences, especially among the poorest children.[81]

If one looks closely at the incentives faced by local politicians, their decision to trade off lower water rates today for less investment and financial security in the long term makes sense. Local politicians face short electoral cycles, usually no more than a few years' time. Given this, who does the politician want to satisfy: the consumer clamoring for lower water rates today; or the consumer twenty or thirty years from now demanding a water system free from water main breaks and disruptions in service? Any politician concerned with winning reelection would focus on the former. The political incentives to focus on the short term are only heightened by the fact that Americans are a highly mobile people and always have been.[82] The odds are that most voters will not live in the same city for more than five or ten years. It makes sense for those mobile voters to value immediate reductions in water rates more than long-term investments in the capital stock that pay off twenty or thirty years down the road, because they probably will not be around long enough to enjoy that payoff.

A potential solution to this problem would be to have investment decisions in water and sewer mains taken away from local politicians and given to federal authorities. Because most voters move from city to city, but not from country to country, shifting political control to the federal level would foster a less parochial attitude toward investment in the infrastructure of water and sewer systems, and counteract the adverse effects of mobility for long-term investment decisions.

To see the argument more clearly, imagine a country with only two cities, city A and city B. Assume voters move between cities but not out of the country. Now consider two alternative scenarios involving (*a*) decentralized and (*b*) centralized governance over water and sewer investments. In the first scenario, assume first that taxes and spending on water-related infrastructure are administered at a local level. In that setting, mobile voters in city A are likely to oppose any tax levy that might go to funding long-term investments in the city's water and sewer systems because they might not be around long enough to enjoy the fruits of those investments. In the second scenario, assume that taxes and spending on water and sewers are administered at the federal level, and federal officials decide how to allocate spending across cities. As long as mobile voters find the intercity allocation mechanism fair and reasonable, they are more likely to favor tax levies that would go to funding long-term investments in infrastructure because, while they do not know which city they will be in, they do know they still will be in the country, in one or another of the cities, and will enjoy the fruits of any long-term investment.

An alternative solution to the problem of chronic underinvestment in maintaining long-term capital stocks is to create a local agency to oversee the capital stock. If properly constructed and administered, this agency can be insulated against short-term political pressures to set rates too low or pay patronage workers too much. In most settings, this is done by having officials appointed, and not elected, and by having their appointed terms exceed the electoral cycle. These are the same arrangements that make federal judges and the Federal Reserve Board independent from politics. A third possible solution is private ownership. If private companies have secure property rights and are confident that their capital will not be expropriated, theory suggests they would balance the trade-offs between prices today and long-term investments in an economically efficient and rational manner. Simply put, in a world with secure property rights, the private company can be confident of internalizing the gains of long-term investments sometime in the future. It does not matter to them if one voter moves out and another moves in, so long as both are willing to pay for their services.

Conclusions

This chapter has developed four central points. First, because typhoid had a low case fatality rate but damaging sequelae, it typically killed its victims slowly and indirectly, often through secondary infections (e.g., tuberculosis and pneumonia), or through cardiac disease and kidney failure. Hence, when cities cleaned up their public water supplies and eradicated typhoid fever, they not only reduced deaths rates from typhoid but also death rates from a whole series of secondary afflictions that followed typhoid. Second, the largest reductions in human mortality observed in recorded history occurred between 1850 and 1950. About 60 percent of those reductions can be attributed to the development of clean and adequate public water supplies, which eradicated not only typhoid but also its many sequelae. Third, when considered in the aggregate, investments in urban water systems were perhaps the largest, and certainly among the largest, public investments in American history; and on a per capita basis, they clearly were the largest. Fourth, to finance these investments, cities had to make credible commitments to borrowers that they would repay the loans, or they had to assure private water companies investing in their cities that they would not abuse them after the mains had been installed. These commitments were made possible by provisions in state and federal constitutions that protected private property rights and fostered capital markets.

SIX

Empire, Federalism, and the Surprising Fall of Yellow Fever

Yellow fever ravaged American cities throughout the seventeenth, eighteenth, and nineteenth centuries. For example, between 1817 and 1819, yellow fever killed 15 percent of the population in New Orleans. Just north, in Shreveport, a yellow fever epidemic in 1853 killed one-quarter of the population. In 1878, a yellow fever epidemic in Memphis killed one out of every eight city residents. The available data suggest that case fatality rates during these epidemics ranged from 70 to 90 percent.[1] To put these numbers in perspective, more people died in the Memphis epidemic of 1878 than in the Chicago fire, the San Francisco earthquake, and the Johnstown flood combined.[2] During the great influenza pandemic of 1918, Camden, New Jersey, had the highest death rate of any major American city: the flu killed one out of every eighty Camden residents, or 1.2 percent of the local population. By contrast, the death rates from yellow fever in Memphis and Shreveport exceeded the death rate from the flu in Camden by a factor of ten or more.[3]

Despite their magnitude, these statistics are not especially surprising. Any country that traded with the Caribbean and other tropical places with large mosquito populations would have been struck by severe yellow fever epidemics from time to time. What makes the American experience intriguing is that yellow fever largely disappeared from the United States before most scientists and policymakers fully understood what caused and transmitted the disease—full understanding of how the disease was transmitted did not arrive until the early 1900s.[4] Yet decades earlier, yellow fever had already started to fade away, and by the late 1890s it had had largely disappeared from the American South. In northern cities like Philadelphia and New York, which had been plagued by severe yellow fever epidemics throughout the eighteenth and early nineteenth centuries, yellow fever had largely disappeared before the onset of the Civil War in 1861.

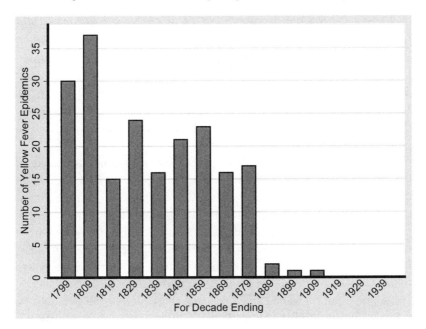

Figure 6.1. Yellow fever in major American cities by decade, 1799–1939.
(From "On the Natural History and Distribution of Yellow Fever in the United States, from
A.D. 1688 to A.D. 1874," paper presented at the American Public Health Association,
November 12, 1873. Reprinted in the *Annual Report of the Marine Hospital Service*, 1873; *Public
Health Reports* (various years, various volumes).

The sharp decline in yellow fever that occurred prior to the early 1900s
is shown in figure 6.1, which plots the number of yellow fever epidemics
occurring in major cities by decade from the end of the eighteenth century
up to the end of the 1930s. Yellow fever was at its peak in the United States
between 1790 and 1810, when there were thirty to thirty-seven epidemics
per decade. From 1810 to 1879, serious outbreaks of yellow fever declined,
with large American cities experiencing between fifteen and twenty-five
epidemics per decade. But after 1880, the disease almost completely disappeared: there were only two epidemics during the 1880s and one during
the 1890s, and by historical standards these three epidemics were relatively
minor events.

In this chapter, I argue that the rise and fall of yellow fever in the United
States was the result of a constellation of American political institutions and
ideologies. While it is true that, even during the colonial era, rapidly growing port cities, such as New York, Philadelphia, and Charleston, had been
vulnerable to yellow fever, that vulnerability was codified with the ratifica-

tion of the Constitution in 1789. I say that the Constitution codified this vulnerability because it gave a formal legal structure to ideologies, natural conditions (see chapter 2 on the significance of port cities), and informal arrangements that probably would have rendered the United States vulnerable to yellow fever even in the absence of explicit constitutional structures. These ideologies and informal arrangements include the American commitment to commerce and antipathy toward centralized authority and federal power, particularly among Southerners.[5]

The institutional history of yellow fever is one of internal contradiction. On the one hand, American legal and political institutions heightened the intensity and frequency of yellow fever epidemics during the early 1800s; on the other hand, however, those same institutions laid the foundation for the eradication of the disease during the late 1800s and early 1900s. One can see this paradox in the ways the Constitution helped shape the American quest for foreign trade, particularly with the West Indies and other areas where yellow fever was endemic. As I show later in this chapter, during the early 1800s, the quest for trade helped generate yellow fever epidemics, but by the late 1800s and early 1900s, that same quest helped eradicate the disease. One can also see this paradox in the ways economic and mercantile interests influenced public health policies related to the control of yellow fever. While businesses and merchants typically (but not always) lobbied against policies such as quarantines that combated yellow fever by slowing or interfering with trade, those same interest groups often used their influence to secure public investments that improved human health and welfare generally, even if those investments had no direct effect on yellow fever.

And one can see the paradox at work in the context of federalism, whereby much of the authority for combating yellow fever was vested with state and local officials, as opposed to the federal government. On the one hand, because state and local politicians were elected only by the citizens in their respective districts, their primary concern was the well-being of those citizens; the well-being of citizens in neighboring and nearby jurisdictions did not merit much, if any, consideration. As a consequence, when state and local governments formulated policies to combat and control yellow fever, they did not temper or alter those policies even when citizens in neighboring jurisdictions were adversely affected. This sort of parochialism could generate dysfunctional conflicts across jurisdictions that were inimical to both public health and social welfare more broadly construed. On the other hand, by vesting control in state and local authorities, federalism gave rise to a diversity of approaches to disease control, which were often well suited to the idiosyncratic conditions of particular states and municipalities.

A Brief History of Yellow Fever in the United States

As its name implies, yellow fever impaired liver function (resulting in jaundice) and caused a high fever. Other symptoms included headache, restlessness, chills, and nausea. For those who survived, the disease reached its peak three or four days after the onset of symptoms. For those who did not, death usually came after a week of suffering. One or two days before death, the patient's kidneys would shut down and urine output would cease. Profuse internal hemorrhaging resulted in blackened vomit, and bleeding from the gums, nose, mouth, and even old bruises. In an era of limited medical understanding, medical treatments for the disease ranged from the benign to the malignant. On the latter end of the spectrum, some physicians continued to use poisons such as antimony and mercury, as well as bleeding and ice-cold baths to treat the sick. On the other end of the spectrum, homeopaths used bed rest, cool baths, various herbal mixtures, and diet in an effort to check the disease. Life insurance companies at this time were reported to have offered their customers discounts if they would limit themselves to homeopathic treatments. An effective vaccine to prevent the spread of the yellow fever virus was not developed until the twentieth century.[6]

An individual's susceptibility to yellow fever depended on his or her race, age, and migrant status. After thousands of years of repeated exposure, Africans developed a resistance to the disease, which persons of European extraction did not possess. In contrast to other epidemic diseases of the nineteenth century, yellow fever hit older age groups harder than younger ones—according to most observers, yellow fever tended "to be quite mild" in young children. As to migrant status, yellow fever was called "Stranger's Disease" in New Orleans because it affected newly arrived immigrant groups more than long-time city residents who had been acclimated to the disease. The importance of migrant status helps explain why the United States, which during the nineteenth century was largely a nation of immigrants from Northern Europe with limited exposure to yellow fever, was particularly vulnerable to the disease. The country's expanding economy and openness to immigration guaranteed that when the disease struck there would be a large population of individuals with no prior exposure or immunity status.[7]

Although the Cuban physician Carlos Finlay had identified the *Aedes aegypti* as the mosquito that spread yellow fever in 1881, it was not until the early 1900s that Walter Reed, through a series of experiments, convinced the rest of the world that Finlay was correct.[8] The peculiar characteristics of the *A. aegypti* help explain why yellow fever existed almost exclusively in cities and towns and was largely unknown in rural areas. Sometimes referred to as a "cistern mosquito," A. *aegypti* is a small and gray-backed insect common throughout the American South and the Caribbean. It breeds in fresh water sources that are clear and relatively free of organic activity such as cisterns, metal gutters, and buckets. Such man-made containers are attractive, in part, because the mosquitoes can cement their eggs to a stable and flat surface. By the same token, historians often claimed that the A. *aegypti* avoided marshes, swamps, lakes, and water sources otherwise polluted with mud, urine, and feces. A. *aegypti* flourishes in temperatures between 70 and 90 degrees Fahrenheit; its activities begin to slow when temperatures dip below 70, and it will not feed when temperatures are below 60. It becomes inert at temperatures below 50 degrees.[9]

Because it was spread by the mosquito, the incidence of yellow fever was highly correlated with climate and geography. This correlation was highlighted in 1873 by J. M. Toner, the president of the American Medical Association, in a lengthy paper titled "On the Natural History and Distribution of Yellow Fever in the United States." Culling articles from every medical journal and government report that he could find, Toner documented as many outbreaks of yellow fever as possible that occurred in the United States from 1668 through the early 1870s.[10] More than a century later, Toner's paper remains the most complete record historians have of yellow fever epidemics in the United States prior to 1875. According to Toner, there were at least 723 epidemics of yellow fever in 229 cities and towns. With few exceptions, these towns were below 500 feet above sea level, and were coastal, bordering rivers, large bayous, the Atlantic Ocean, or the Gulf of Mexico. Although yellow fever bore disproportionately on places in the American South, Toner's data indicate that northern cities were not exempt from the disease.

Based on data presented in Toner's original paper, table 6.1 highlights these patterns in greater detail. More than half of all yellow fever epidemics took place in four states: Louisiana (23 percent of all epidemics); New York (12 percent); Texas (10 percent); and South Carolina (9 percent). Moreover within these states, epidemics were concentrated in large cities that served as major seaports. No city in the United States was as susceptible to yellow fever as was New Orleans. Although New York, New York, and Charleston, South Carolina, were a close second and third, by the early nineteenth century New Orleans had, by far, the worst yellow fever problem of any city in the United States. Toner's data indicate that yellow fever had largely disappeared from New York by 1805, and after 1800 the epidemics in Charleston were almost all fairly minor events. By contrast, between 1790 and 1860, there were no fewer than twenty-nine epidemics in New Orleans. Such

Table 6.1. Yellow fever in the United States, 1688–1874

	Frequency of epidemics		Intrastate concentration			
State	No.	Percentage of U.S. total*	No. of cities struck	Worst city	No. of epidemics	Percentage of state total
Alabama	45	6	11	Mobile	28	62
Arkansas	6	1	6	—	—	—
Connecticut	15	2	9	New Haven	6	40
Delaware	5	1	4	Wilmington	2	40
Florida	56	8	13	Pensacola	22	39
Georgia	13	2	4	Savannah	9	69
Illinois	1	0	1	Cairo	1	100
Louisiana	166	23	43	New Orleans	66	40
Maryland	15	2	2	Baltimore	14	93
Massachusetts	16	2	6	Boston	10	63
Mississippi	55	8	20	Natchez	13	24
Missouri	3	0	2	Saint Louis	2	66
New Hampshire	1	0	1	Portsmouth	1	100
New Jersey	5	1	5	—	—	—
New York	84	12	17	New York City	62	74
North Carolina	11	2	5	Wilmington	4	18
Ohio	3	0	2	Cincinnati	2	66
Pennsylvania	43	6	9	Philadelphia	34	79
Rhode Island	12	2	5	Providence	5	42
South Carolina	64	9	7	Charleston	52	81
Tennessee	4	1	1	Memphis	4	100
Texas	72	10	41	Galveston	10	14
Virginia	28	4	10	Norfolk	18	64

Source: American Public Health Association (November 12, 1873), "On the Natural History and Distribution of Yellow Fever in the United States, from A.D. 1668 to A.D. 1874"; reprinted from the *Annual Report of the Marine Hospital Service* (Washington, DC: Government Printing Office, 1873), 18–36.

* US total is 723 epidemics from 1668 through 1873.

epidemics routinely killed between 2 and 8 percent of the local population within a few months time, and in two particularly severe epidemics, death rates reached 10–15 percent.

Outside of New York State, the diffusion of yellow fever was greatest in the Southern states. In Alabama, eleven different cities were afflicted, at one point or another, by the disease, though more than half of the epidemics in the state occurred in Mobile. In Florida, thirteen cities were struck, with three cities—Saint Augustine, Key West, and Pensacola—bearing the brunt of the outbreaks. In Louisiana, yellow fever erupted in forty-three different cities and towns. Aside from New Orleans, the state's most vulnerable towns were Alexandria, Baton Rouge, Shreveport, Thibodeaux, and Washington. In Mississippi, yellow fever was also widespread, affecting twenty different localities. Natchez, where yellow fever struck most often, accounted for only 24 percent of the outbreaks observed in the state. Yellow fever was most diffuse, however, in Texas, where outbreaks occurred in at least forty-one places. The two Texas cities with the most frequent visitations from yellow fever were Galveston and Houston, which together account for only 28 percent of all outbreaks in the state.

Yellow Fever and International Trade

Many nineteenth-century observers believed that yellow fever was not endemic to the United States, but was instead introduced by foreign trade, particularly trade with the Caribbean and more tropical climates. An article published in 1873 in the *Medical Times and Gazette* argued that yellow fever did not "originate in United States territory," but was "introduced to it by vessels from foreign ports, following the great routes of travel and trade." As evidence for this position, the *Gazette* pointed to Natchez, Mississippi, which had never been "visited by yellow fever before steamboats commenced their trips on the Mississippi River in 1819." But "after that year the town was ravaged by the disease whenever it prevailed in New Orleans, and never at any other time." Similarly, Vidalia, Louisiana, had never experienced a yellow fever outbreak "previous to 1853, in which year, for the first time, steamboats stopped" there.[11] Along the same lines, during the Civil War, Union Army blockades caused trade and boat traffic to divert to previously little-used ports or ports normally dedicated only to domestic commerce, causing yellow fever to erupt in places where it had never appeared before.[12]

Aside from the examples offered by the *Medical Times and Gazette*, a number of other pieces of evidence point to the significance of trade in spreading yellow fever. In the aforementioned article by Toner, it is clear that all significant epidemics were located in large, coastal cities that served as major seaports, such as New York, Charleston, South Carolina, and New Orleans. In addition, yellow fever was highly sporadic. It would disappear for years and then erupt suddenly, killing hundreds or thousands of people within a few months time. For example, in Memphis, Tennessee, for the half-century preceding 1878, the only deaths in the city from yellow fever occurred in 1853, 1855, 1867, and 1873, and the number of deaths from these epidemics was far fewer than the number in the 1878 epidemic.[13] Similarly, in Savannah, Georgia, yellow fever struck in 1820, 1854, and 1876; in the intervening years, no one in the city perished from the disease.[14] That yellow fever would vanish for years, or even decades at a time, and then erupt with sudden ferocity suggests that the disease was not indigenous to Southern cities, but was instead introduced by migration and trade.

Furthermore, when these sporadic epidemics broke out, local physicians repeatedly traced the source of the outbreak to ships from foreign ports, particularly the Caribbean. In a Congressional inquiry made during the 1878 yellow fever epidemic, investigators concluded "that in all countries outside of the West Indies, . . . yellow fever is an exotic disease; and in all [such countries] its introduction can be traced, either directly or indirectly, to the West Indies."[15] Decades later, after it was well known that the disease was spread by mosquitoes, public health officials in the United States began investigating ships arriving from foreign ports for evidence that they were carrying the *Aedes agypti*, the mosquito that carries yellow fever. Their research indicated that mosquitoes were not uncommon, and that they could indeed survive the voyage from ports in the Caribbean and South America. In one example, the two-masted sailing ship *John H. Crandon* was inspected at a Gulf Coast quarantine station after a twenty-two day journey from Vera Cruz, Mexico, a port where yellow fever was endemic. Larvae were found in the ship's ballast tanks, and all during the voyage to the United States mosquitoes were in abundance. There was "a constant buzz" in the ships forecastle, and anyone entering was "sure to be attacked by several mosquitoes." By the time it arrived at the American port, "a veritable plague" of *agypti* inhabited the boat.[16]

By the same token, when foreign trade stopped, so too did the yellow fever epidemics. The clearest example of this comes from New Orleans during the Civil War and the Union occupation after the war. As figure 6.2 shows, with the start of the Civil War, total trade (imports plus exports) passing through the Port of New Orleans fell from $202 million (constant 1860 dollars) in 1860 to zero by 1862 and remained at $4 to $7 million (2 to 3 percent of its prewar level) until the end of the war in 1865. As late as 1870, trade in New Orleans had only recovered to 60 percent of its prewar

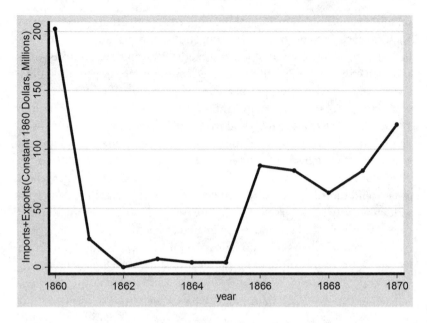

Figure 6.2. Total trade (imports plus exports) into the Port of New Orleans
(in constant 1860 dollars).
(Data from United States, *Annual Reports of Commerce and Navigation* [various years].)

levels. This reduction in trade was historically unprecedented in terms of its depth and length, and with it came a historically unprecedented disruption from yellow fever epidemics in the city.

It was, moreover, not just during the Civil War that disruptions in trade with the Atlantic world led to the sudden disappearance of yellow fever. Writing in 1842, John W. Monette explained that this pattern was observed during the Revolutionary War, the War of 1812, and the embargo leading up to the War of 1812.[17] By the same token, yellow fever was unknown in Europe until Columbus made contact with the Americas, after which the disease began striking ports in Spain, Portugal, and all along "the south shore of the Mediterranean Sea."[18]

Yellow Fever, Tariffs, and the Constitution

Given the centrality of trade in the propagation and spread of yellow fever, tariffs on foreign trade and the rise of American imperialism toward the end of the nineteenth century helped shape the American experience with yellow fever. As for the tariff, the United States was not born committed to

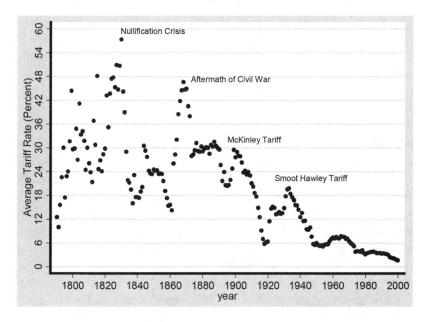

Figure 6.3. Average tariff rates in the United States, 1800–2000.
(Data from *Historical Statistics of the United States*; see chap. 1, n. 21.)

the principle of free trade or even low federal taxes. On the contrary, the founders believed that "taxes on imports" were "the only sure source of revenue" for the federal government, and throughout the first half of the nineteenth century, revenue from the tariff constituted roughly 85 percent of all government revenues. Only after the Civil War did the proportion of federal revenue derived from the tariff drop; between 1865 and 1900, about 52 percent of all federal revenues came from taxes on foreign trade.[19]

In part because tariff revenues represented such a large proportion of total government revenue, tariff rates were quite high, in both an absolute and a relative sense. Figure 6.3 plots the average tariff rates in the United States over the past two hundred years. During the antebellum period, tariff rates averaged between 20 and 30 percent, though there were intervals where the average tariff rate neared 60 percent.[20] After the 1875, the average tariff rate fell steadily until the late twentieth century, where it lingers at around 2 or 3 percent. Notice that, by the standards of the early 1800s, even tariff schedules that are notorious for their high rates (i.e., the McKinley Tariff during the 1890s and the Smoot-Hawley Tariff at the start of the Great Depression) appear relatively low.

The early reliance on tariffs and excise taxes on domestic goods grew out of the fact that under the Articles of Confederation the national government had no power to tax. Instead, the national government was dependent on the individual states for contributions, leaving it destitute and powerless in relation to the states. Advocates of the new Constitution saw tariffs and import duties as a means of rectifying this imbalance and increasing the revenue-raising power of the federal government relative to the states. As Hamilton explained in *Federalist Papers* 12, a "nation cannot long exist without revenue. Destitute of this essential support, it must resign its independence, and sink into the degraded condition of a province."[21] And if revenue were not drawn from commerce, particularly foreign commerce, Hamilton saw only one realistic alternative: a tax on land, which (for reasons explained below) Hamilton believed would prove politically unpopular and very difficult administer. By the same token, Hamilton argued that a system whereby states taxed foreign commerce individually was unworkable and expensive.[22] The need for federal revenue and the expedience of federal collection and enforcement of tariffs on international trade were, therefore, an integral part of the argument for inserting the Commerce Clause (Article 1, Section 8) into the federal Constitution, which, as explained in chapter 3, gave the federal government the authority to tax and regulate international trade.

For the Founders, the case for using tariffs to raise revenues had both practical and ideological components. On the practical side, tariffs were in their view, the easiest of all taxes to implement and collect, especially at the early stages of political development. On the ideological side, Hamilton favored tariffs because they were self-limiting in the following sense: if the tax rate was set too high, demand for the product would drop and so too would government revenue. "It is a single advantage of taxes on articles of consumption, that they contain in their own nature a security against excess. They prescribe their own limit; which cannot be exceeded without defeating the end proposed, . . . that is, an extension of the revenue. . . . [Because] if duties are too high, they lessen the consumption; the collection is eluded; and the product of the treasury is not so great as when they are confined within proper and moderate bounds."[23]

The logic of Hamilton's early variant on the Laffer Curve was that people who aspired to limited government should use tariffs and taxes on domestic consumption to constrain the taxing power of the state.[24] Or, as Hamilton wrote, "This forms a complete barrier against any material oppression of the citizens, by taxes of this class, and is itself a natural limitation of the power of imposing them."[25]

Because tariffs constituted such a large portion of federal revenue and because average tariff rates were so high during the nineteenth century, one is

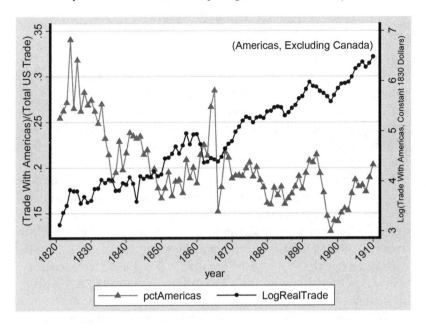

Figure 6.4. Total trade with the Americas (excluding Canada).
(Data from *Historical Statistics of the United States*; see chap. 1, n. 21.)

tempted to conclude that the tariff during this era inhibited trade and therefore the transmission of yellow fever. Put another way, one might hypothesize that, absent the tariff, yellow fever rates in American ports and cities would have been even worse. That, however, would be a mistake because, as the data below suggest, in the long run it appears that American trade policy promoted trade with yellow-fever regions. Indeed, one advantage the Founders saw from embracing tariffs is that they could be used strategically to promote trade with particular regions. Hamilton was particularly fond of this idea, arguing that through high tariffs and "other prohibitory regulations," the United States could oblige "foreign countries to bid against each other for the privileges our markets." Hamilton held out special hope that American navigation laws would prompt Britain to relax its tariff laws, and enable American businesses and consumers to "enjoy the commerce of the West Indies," just as they had during the colonial period.[26]

If one looks at the broader history of trade in the Atlantic world, and not just the West Indies, Hamilton's aspirations for American trade policies appear to have been realized. Over the course of nineteenth century, the United States developed robust trade relationships with countries throughout the Caribbean and South America. As figure 6.4 shows, total trade (imports plus exports) with the Americas (including the Caribbean) grew nearly thirtyfold between 1820 and 1910, slightly slower than growth in overall international trade but an impressive increase nevertheless. There is no question that these trade relationships benefited American business interests that exported. As early as 1804, one can find writers arguing that demand for American food-stuffs in the Spanish Caribbean, particularly Cuba, was central to the pros-perity of the Southern United States.[27] A downside of increased trade with these regions, however, was that it brought with it repeated yellow fever epidemics.

The rapid increase in trade was, at least in part, facilitated by American legal and political institutions.[28] The central element of this institutional architecture was the Commerce Clause, which prevented the states from regulating foreign trade and vested that authority solely in the federal gov-ernment. This created a uniform national trade policy, as opposed to the fragmented one that had persisted under the Articles of Confederation.[29] Moreover, soon after adoption of the Constitution, the First Congress passed legislation granting "a 10 percent discount from the duties on all goods imported in American vessels, and the same law reduced the duties on tea imported from Europe, India, and China . . . so as to build up the direct trade between the United States and China."[30] Later, a navy was created to protect American merchants and ship owners from the depredations of the Barbary pirates and others who might prey on shipping and otherwise inter-fere with foreign trade.[31] Some observers have also argued that the Monroe Doctrine—which stated that any intervention by European powers in the politics of the Americas could be interpreted as an act of war against the United States—was promulgated in part to promote and foster trade with the Caribbean and South America.[32]

Yellow Fever and America's Quest for Empire

As explained in chapter 3, the Constitution granted the federal government more power than it had possessed under the Articles of Confederation but nevertheless circumscribed its realm and in many cases rendered it deferen-tial and secondary to the power of state (and sometimes even local) govern-ments. In practical terms, this meant that the federal government was more powerful acting abroad and in areas of foreign policy than it was at home dealing with domestic concerns. This general proposition was no less true in the case of yellow fever: only when the federal government was untethered from the ideological and institutional constraints that governed its behav-ior within US borders was it able to confront the disease with full force. It

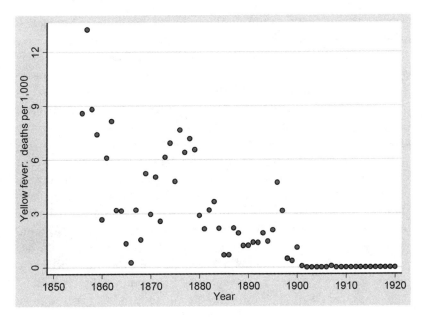

Figure 6.5. Yellow fever in Havana, Cuba, 1850–1920.
(From George Miller Sternberg, *Report on the Etiology and Prevention of Yellow Fever* [Washington, DC: Government Printing Office, 1890], 39; United States Public Health Service, *Public Health Reports* [various years, various volumes].)

was, therefore, no accident that the federal government realized its greatest effectiveness in combating yellow fever not through a domestic agency, but through its military. In particular, when Walter Reed conducted his experiments establishing that yellow fever was spread by a mosquito, he did so as an agent of the US Army and in the context of an increasingly belligerent and imperialist foreign policy. Moreover, when the United States eradicated yellow fever from Havana, Cuba, its success there flowed from its military strength and its willingness to impose stringent police measures that would never have been accepted within its own borders.

The United States came to launch a vigorous antimosquito campaign in Havana in the immediate aftermath of the Spanish-American War and as part of its broader occupation of Cuba. The effects of this campaign were impressive in the both the short and the long run. As figure 6.5 shows, under Spanish domination (pre-1899), the death rate from yellow fever in Havana varied between three and nine deaths per thousand. But within two years, the United States military had reduced the death rate to zero. Furthermore, even after the American withdrawal from Cuba, yellow fever rates in Havana remained at or near zero for decades. This occurred because the new

Cuban Republic continued to effectively control the mosquito population in Havana. Among public health officials in the United States, eradicating yellow fever from Havana was seen as a huge accomplishment and one that would protect the United States from future epidemics for a long time to come. Given its proximity to the United States and the heavy volume of trade between Havana and ports in the American South, Havana was often portrayed as the single most important foreign source of yellow fever outbreaks in the United States, though that claim is questionable.[33]

The architect of the US program to eradicate yellow fever in Havana was William C. Gorgas, a colonel and physician in the US Army. Reflecting on the significance of yellow fever eradication in Cuba for ports in the Southern United States, Gorgas explained that "for two centuries the United States had been . . . scourged with yellow fever, which had generally been imported from Havana." In an effort to prevent this importation, by the late nineteenth century, various states and cities along the Gulf Coast began imposing "cast iron commercial" quarantines every summer, disrupting commerce and trade with the West Indies. For this reason, Gorgas and other observers believed that if yellow fever could be banished from Havana in particular, and Cuba in general, "yellow fever would cease to be a menace" to the Southern United States, and trade and commerce might continue through the summer months unabated. In developing this line of thought, Gorgas makes clear that the United States had not only a strong public-health rationale for getting rid of yellow fever in Havana—doing so would reduce the incidence of the disease in the United States—but a strong economic incentive as well. By getting rid of yellow fever in Havana and other sources of infection in the Atlantic world, American states would no longer need to maintain costly quarantines every summer and regularly divert and slow foreign trade.[34]

To appreciate just how belligerent and aggressive the United States was in matters regarding yellow fever in Cuba, consider the following question: Why did Cuban authorities continue the antimosquito initiatives launched by the American military when the extant scholarly literature suggests that every other aspect of the Cuban public health system was in poor to abysmal shape in the years before 1940? Part of the answer surely involves the Platt Amendment, which was appended to the new Cuban constitution at the behest of the US military. Under the Platt Amendment, the United States secured the right to reinvade Cuba if yellow fever were to return to the island. And return they did. In 1905, after a relatively minor yellow fever epidemic broke out in New Orleans, US troops returned to Cuba to quash whatever disease-carrying mosquito populations might remain on the island.[35]

There is, moreover, circumstantial evidence to suggest that it was not only in Cuba where Americans intimidated foreign governments to launch aggressive anti–yellow fever campaigns or at least to cooperate with the United States government. Consider the experiences of Vera Cruz, Mexico, and Rio de Janeiro, Brazil. Like Havana, these two cities traded heavily with ports in the American South, and both had severe yellow fever problems that were said to have spilled over and caused yellow fever epidemics in Florida, Louisiana, Texas, Alabama, and elsewhere in the South.[36] Quarantine stations operating during the early 1900s found that roughly half of all ships detained with passengers infected with yellow fever originated from the Port of Vera Cruz.[37] During the early 1900s, Brazilian and Mexican authorities initiated mosquito control measures that were highly successful. The death rate from yellow fever in Vera Cruz fell from an average of 8.9 deaths per thousand in the years before treatment (1903) to 0.234 in the years afterward, a reduction of 97 percent. A similar result can be observed in Rio de Janeiro, where Brazilian authorities reduced the death rate from around 3.5 deaths per thousand before 1904 to near zero in the years following the antimosquito intervention.[38] Because these ports were so heavily involved in trade with ports in the American South, reductions in the frequency and intensity of yellow fever epidemics probably would have contributed to reductions in yellow fever in the United States.

At least two aspects of American foreign policy appear to have helped motivate Brazil and Mexico to address the yellow fever problems in Rio and Vera Cruz. First, government officials recognized that high rates of yellow fever in their ports induced quarantines and trade restrictions in the United States, and these were seen as real obstacles to economic progress. The role that trade restrictions played in helping to drive public health initiatives in Mexico can be seen in a short address made by Dr. Eduardo Liceaga, who oversaw the highly successful campaign to eradicate yellow fever from Vera Cruz. Liceaga was lauded by the American military as one of the "brilliant products of the Western Hemisphere," in part because he managed to bring yellow fever under control in the midst of the Mexican Revolution.[39] In his address to the Third International Conference of the American Republics in 1907, Liceaga argued that for "four centuries" the "legendary and fatal focus" of yellow fever had rendered the gulf coast of Mexico "a terror of our neighbors." But Liceaga hoped that when the "fearful scourge of yellow fever" had disappeared from the Mexican territory, the United States and other neighboring countries would remove their restrictions on "trade and free communication." He concluded his address with a plea that all countries in the Americas treat one another as "brothers" who did not conduct their sanitary policies without due regard for their neighbors but at the same time did not "isolate" one another and "allowed" their brother's goods "free transportation."[40]

Second, while domestic officials in Rio and Vera Cruz were the ones who successfully eliminated yellow fever from both places, if one looks at the broader historical context in which those campaigns took place, it is reasonable to suggest that the threat of American military intervention likely played some motivational role. In particular, both campaigns took place in the wake of the Spanish-American War and the passage of the Platt Amendment. Both campaigns also took place soon after President Roosevelt announced the so-called Roosevelt Corollary, whereby the United States reserved the right to invade countries throughout South America if they should default on their debts to European powers. Ostensibly this was done because European militaries were regularly visiting places in South America to secure payment of foreign debts and Roosevelt saw their presence as a possible threat to the United States and its broader regional interests. The United States, it should be noted, did on occasion use gunboat diplomacy to get South American countries to meet their debt payments to European governments.[41]

Although there was no stated policy like the Roosevelt Corollary in relation to yellow fever, there were episodes in which the United States did invade and intervene in the affairs of foreign countries when unsanitary conditions were thought to pose a serious health risk to the United States. Aside from the American return to Cuba in 1905, for example, in 1914, the United States sent a military expedition from Galveston, Texas, to Vera Cruz, Mexico. The marines involved were charged solely with taking over the public health responsibilities of the city and preventing the outbreak of epidemic diseases, particularly those spread by mosquitoes.[42]

The Federal Government at Home and Abroad: A Brief Comparison

At this juncture, it is useful to juxtapose the behavior of the federal government abroad to its behavior at home. Specifically, imagine that the United States military had imposed the same threats and belligerence on, say, New Orleans or the State of Louisiana that it had imposed on Cuba through the Platt Amendment. This is not idle speculation. As the narrative below demonstrates, during the nineteenth century, authorities in New Orleans and Louisiana repeatedly objected to the anti–yellow fever policies of the federal government. And in stark contrast to Cuba, when Louisiana challenged the federal government, Louisiana usually won. Why did the federal government act with such belligerence abroad but with such timidity at home? A simple but unsustainable answer is that the Constitution directly forbade the United States from pursuing more aggressive anti–yellow fever policies at home.

In this regard, one might argue that the Commerce Clause forbade the federal government from interfering in matters of intrastate trade, and yellow fever was an intrastate matter. The difficulty, of course, is that yellow fever clearly was not confined by state borders, and it heavily affected interstate trade; even during the nineteenth century, the courts held that the federal government had the power to intervene. As the discussion of *Morgan's Steamship Company v. Louisiana Board of Health* in chapter 3 emphasized, the Constitution expressly allowed the federal government to intervene in cross-border trade flows to prevent the spread of yellow fever; it was only that legislatures at both the state and federal level seemed to agree that the control of yellow fever, no matter what its proclivity to cross state and national borders, should be left to the states.

Moreover, although there were historical moments when the nation as a whole seemed to coalesce around the idea that federal intervention was necessary to combat yellow fever effectively, those moments were fleeting, limited by the ideologies and practical imperatives that sustained the American commitment to states' rights. Consider the short and unhappy life of the National Board of Health. The National Board of Health was created in March, 1879, following the 1878 epidemic that devastated Memphis and the broader Mississippi Valley. At that moment there was a broad national consensus that the prevention of future epidemics required a federal agency with the power to implement a truly national quarantine system that would isolate and disinfect ships carrying yellow fever from any port where the disease was present.

Despite the fact that the system of state and local quarantines that had preceded the National Board of Health was considered a failure, the board existed for only four years; the system of state and local quarantines survived. As explained below, the national board's undoing stemmed, in large part, from the refusal of the Louisiana State Board of Health to cooperate with federal authorities. What is particularly telling about the demise of the National Board of Health is that, while it enjoyed middling to strong support among health boards in nearly all states, it only took strong opposition from a single state (Louisiana) to undermine federal intervention. That says a lot about the relative status of state and federal health authorities during the nineteenth century.[43]

The Political Economy of Quarantines

For centuries, port cities in Europe had used commercial quarantines in an effort to prevent the plague and, later, yellow fever. During the seventeenth and eighteenth centuries, as the slave trade and intercourse with the West Indies rose, port cities in the American colonies followed the same course and also began using commercial quarantines to prevent yellow fever. By the nineteenth century, commercial quarantines were a standard mode of yellow fever prevention in port cities throughout the United States.[44]

The exact form and penetrability of such quarantines varied over space and time. In a typical commercial quarantine, ships carrying cargo and crew that gave evidence of sickness were not allowed to dock but were isolated off shore at nearby islands or anchored at sea. Isolated, the boat and cargo underwent a thorough cleansing and disinfection process that could go on for days, weeks, or even months, which imposed heavy costs on ships carrying perishable goods. During isolation, it was standard protocol to forbid the captain and crew from going ashore and intermingling with the general population, although sick individuals were, on occasion, removed to isolation hospitals. The strictest and most impenetrable quarantines approached autarky in their effect, leading to a complete suspension of trade with infected ports and regions.[45]

Ironically, the strictest and most oppressive quarantines were probably less effective than more lenient measures in protecting cities, and even when strict quarantines were successful in forestalling epidemics, they could levy a heavy toll on both short- and long-term economic development. From a disease-prevention standpoint, strict and burdensome quarantines often failed because they induced evasion strategies and merely diverted trade and migration to neighboring ports. As one observer during the nineteenth century explained the situation, "Passengers who are excluded from landing" at a quarantined port would not "debar themselves" of the "privileges of freely traveling from place to place." Instead, they would "quietly evade the law by shipping" to a nearby place "that dispenses with the restrictions." They would then, traveling via "land routes" or local coastwise transportation networks, make their way back to the port city that originally denied them entry. With their bags and diseases in tow, they would thus render an ostensibly impenetrable quarantine "of no avail as a sanitary measure."[46] As explained below, to assure compliance with quarantine measures and prevent evasion, cities had to enact policies that were minimally invasive but judiciously enforced.

Because shotgun quarantines could be so costly and counterproductive, many contemporary observers advocated more reasonable quarantine measures that were not unduly burdensome. While public health officials at the time sometimes dismissed these so-called reasonable or rational quarantines as ineffective shams foisted on cities by commercial interests, there is evidence to suggest that, over the long term, they could be highly effective in identifying and isolating disease-carrying ships. This is well illustrated by two quarantine laws adopted by New York in 1805 and 1806. According to John Griscom, the city's quarantine policies only "took a definite shape" and started to be enforced with "vigor" with the passage of these laws. The 1805 legislation prohibited ships with infected individuals on board from coming "within 300 yards of the Island of New York." The 1806 law restricted any ships arriving from the West Indies or the Mississippi River to a four-day detention at an offshore quarantine to establish that the boat was disease-free. In addition, the crews of these ships were prohibited from "intercourse" with the City of New York, except under the regulations of the city's chief health officer. To minimize its effects on commerce, the law only affected vessels arriving at New York between June and October, the months when yellow fever was a legitimate concern.[47]

The passage of these laws was associated with a significant reduction in the frequency and intensity of yellow fever epidemics. Before 1806, yellow fever was a regular visitor to New York City; between 1700 and 1806, it struck roughly once every four years. By contrast, after 1806, yellow fever struck the city proper only once every sixteen years: there were minor epidemics in 1822, 1856, and 1873, but all other cases were successfully confined to the city's quarantine hospital.[48] Put another way, in all but three years, all infected vessels were successfully interdicted; and in every single year after 1806, quarantine officers discovered ships carrying sailors sick with yellow fever, and presumably many of those same boats were carrying the mosquitoes that made the sailors sick—recall the discussion above citing evidence from the 1900s that the *Aedes agypti* could survive for extended periods of time on boats.[49] What is significant about quarantine procedures like those observed in New York is that, even though officials during the early 1800s did not comprehend that the disease was spread by a mosquito, those procedures, if judiciously enforced and respected, had the potential to actually forestall outbreaks of yellow fever.[50] Indeed, press reports suggest that routine quarantine and inspection measures in many cities regularly identified and isolated cases of yellow fever and prevented ships potentially carrying infected mosquitoes from entering port.[51]

Several interrelated factors prevented cities like New York from adopting more draconian quarantine measures. The first was the threat of trade diversion. If New York set quarantine policies and interdiction procedures that were excessively onerous, they would have diverted trade to nearby ports with less severe regulations, undermining trade prospects in both the short and long term. To the extent that trade was associated with tax revenues and economic activities that the local government valued, this would have limited the city's desire to set highly stringent quarantine measures.[52] Along the same lines, if they imposed undue costs on vessels they interdicted, any boat getting close to the Port of New York that considered itself at risk of getting quarantined (i.e., any boat that was carrying a cargo or crew infected by a potentially serious disease) would have diverted and unloaded its cargo at a smaller, nearby port in New Jersey. If this happened, there was always the risk that the infected cargo or crew (or both) would make their way back to New York by land and end up infecting the city anyway.

Policymakers in New York appear to have been aware of these risks and sought to keep their inspection and isolation procedures as bearable as possible while still maintaining adequate disease protection. As a result, when a captain was fairly certain his ship would be detained for a few days because it was carrying an infected crew member or cargo, he would be willing to bear that cost for the benefit of landing directly in New York—if the detention ran far longer than a few days, his willingness to bear the cost of detention would have diminished. Consequently, reasonable and minimally invasive quarantine procedures would have been more likely to be effective over the long haul, especially from a broader regional perspective, than were more draconian policies, which simply induced shippers to engage in diversion and evasion strategies.

Underlying the quarantine policies of city governments were the lobbying efforts of businesses and merchants, who usually opposed strict quarantine measures because they believed quarantines were ineffective in preventing the spread of disease, and because they saw costs associated with strictly enforced quarantines as excessive. In this way, a strong and politically active business and merchant class probably fostered a more rational and effective system of local quarantines.[53] This point has been developed by the legal historian Herbert Hovenkamp in another context; Hovenkamp argues that the support of business groups for a particular policy or regulation does not necessarily imply that the policy is inefficient or contrary to the broader public interest.[54] In the case of quarantines, the optimal policy probably was not what many business groups wanted—which was no quarantine at all—but it also probably was not what many public health officials wanted either—which was often the strictest quarantine imaginable.[55] Hence, allowing business groups to express their preferences and influence policy would have had a moderating influence on the most extreme public health officials and helped promote a more moderate position between health officials and the business community.

Having described how business and mercantile interests could serve as a moderating force and help promote more reasonable and effective quarantine policies, it is equally important to consider two possible pathways through which those same interests could set in motion degenerate political processes, and in the long run, undermine effective public health policies. To do this, I appeal to two general models well known to economists and political scientists. The first model employs the logic of the race-to-the-bottom: in an effort to attract more commerce and trade to their ports, cities would constantly undercut one another in terms of their quarantine measures. Over the long run, the never-ending quest for trade would lead cities to abandon their quarantines altogether. Although the historical evidence considered below fails to offer much support for the race-to-the-bottom framework, it is nevertheless useful to consider it and confront it with data, both because so many historical observers subscribed to it, and because it remains a popular way of thinking.[56]

The second model employs the logic of strategic trade. According to this view, cities and ports used quarantines just as American states had used tariffs under the Articles of Confederation, imposing trade barriers to disrupt and channel regional trade flows in ways that benefited the city (or state) in question but harmed the broader region. Quarantines, in this rubric, were nothing more than trade wars masquerading as public health initiatives. Like the race-to-the-bottom, the inexorable result of the strategic trade model of quarantines is that all cities end up enacting policies that, while individually rational in the short run, are socially pathological in the long run.

One of the first observers to give intellectual and historical structure to the race-to-the-bottom argument was William Wragg, a public health official from Charleston, South Carolina. In a paper presented at the Third National Quarantine and Sanitary Convention in 1859, Wragg argued that neighboring cities, much like firms in a cartel trying to collude on prices, faced strong incentives to undercut one another in terms of their quarantine policies: "As soon as one city sets in operation a stringent law, by the action of which the trade of infected or suspected ports is hampered, its neighbor has only to follow an opposite policy, and the result is a gain corresponding in amount to the loss sustained by the first." In the city with the stricter quarantine, the loss in trade imposed political as well as pecuniary costs, as local politicians saw their support among the business community fall, and as the relative status of the city declined. The loss in trade, Wragg believed, rendered "it difficult for the authorities of any city to face the opposition raised by interested parties," who not only saw "their gains cut off" but had to endure "the mortification of knowing that" all those losses were going "into the coffers of their less scrupulous neighbors."[57]

Moreover, the undercutting city not only harmed the quarantining city by stealing away some of its trade; it also hurt that city by giving those who would prefer to evade the strict quarantine a friendlier landing point from which they could make their way to the quarantined city over land or via a coastwise trade not subject to interdiction. This only compounded the incentive of the strict city to abandon its course and start loosening up on its quarantine as well. After all, if its quarantine was going to be blown anyway by infected individuals making their way into the city through the back door, why bother with the expense and loss of commerce associated with the quarantine? By this logic, the constant battle for commerce was inescapable and would, in the long run, lead all cities to abandon their quarantine policies. "Prompted by the stimulus of rivalry," Wragg wrote, neighboring cities could not "withstand the temptation held out to them to undermine the commerce of each other, by acts which result directly in the destruction of all quarantine restrictions." The unfortunate irony of this logic is that all cities would be made better off if they somehow could constrain themselves from entering the race in the first place; if they could somehow cooperate on their quarantine policies.[58]

Wragg suggested what is now a fairly conventional solution to the race-to-the-bottom problem: he advocated having the Congress pass a federal law that mandated equal and uniform quarantine laws across the United States. Although Wragg made this recommendation in reference to quarantine laws, the same basic proposal is made today in relation to a host of public policies, including labor standards, the minimum wage, welfare policies, and environmental regulations. Such mandated uniformity would have forestalled the race-to-the-bottom process, because no matter how strong their temptation to do otherwise, federal law would have prevented city governments from compromising their obligation to protect the public health in an effort to garner more commerce and trade. Furthermore, once laws were made uniform, there would no longer be any incentive to evade quarantines by moving to a port with weaker laws, because ships would be subject to the same quarantine policy at every port. As a result, compliance with quarantines should have risen after the laws were made uniform across all ports.[59]

Wragg mistakenly believed that the Constitution was the primary obstacle to his plan. Reading the case law, he argued that the Constitution granted Congress "no direct and general power" over health-related quarantine laws, even if those laws did affect interstate commerce. Instead, he claimed, the case law left no doubt that quarantines were "the subject of state legislation." Elsewhere, he wrote that "throughout" the "whole" of this law, it was "evident that the authority of the States to enact quarantine laws" was "fully recognized" by the courts. He claimed that, by contrast, the courts regularly enjoined efforts by the federal government to aid in "the execution of such laws." Quoting liberally from *Gibbons v. Ogden*, one of the early Marshall Court opinions on the Commerce Clause, Wragg made reference, for example, to the British situation, in which the Crown and Parliament possessed the power to regulate commerce, but London enacted its own health laws. In Wragg's view, the same structure applied in the American context: the federal government possessed the sole power to regulate interstate commerce, but state and local governments reserved the right to intervene in matters of public health and other matters relating to police powers.[60]

At least two pieces of evidence suggest that Wragg was mistaken in this assessment. First, the creation of National Board of Health in 1879 clearly demonstrates that Congress believed that it had the authority to create a national agency with the authority to oversee and manage quarantine policies throughout the United States. It is true that the powers of the National Board of Health were attenuated and circumscribed in the sense that it could only regulate purely interstate matters, but as the discussion below emphasizes, the board's failure to successfully confront recalcitrant state officials had more to do with a strong ideological commitment to states' rights, personality conflicts between state and federal officials, and partisan political concerns. The Constitution was, at most, a secondary concern.[61]

Second, the *Morgan Steamship* decision discussed in chapter 3 indicates that the Supreme Court interpreted the Commerce Clause as granting the federal government the authority to establish national quarantine laws; the Court argued, however, that legislatures in the United States had decided that it was a matter best left to the states under their police powers. Other Supreme Court decisions, it should be pointed out, went even further than *Morgan Steamship* and forbade states from interfering with interstate trade even if there were a legitimate public health rationale for that interference.[62] All of this suggests that any decision to limit the federal government's authority to create and oversee a national quarantine system to prevent yellow fever was the product of ideology and political preferences, not Constitutional law.

But the central difficulty with Wragg's analysis has nothing to do with Constitutional interpretation or case law; the problem is that his race-to-the-bottom framework suggests that cities would have rarely adopted and maintained commercial quarantines of any sort. Yet if one looks at the broad sweep of American history, from the seventeenth century to the beginning of the twentieth century, commercial quarantines were by no means rare, and in the midst of particularly severe epidemics, such as the 1878 epidemic, they were frequently adopted in port cities in both the North and the South.[63] Moreover, if one looks closely at the frequency and structure of quarantines, one might just as easily argue that cities were establishing quarantines too frequently and too harshly. In particular, the evidence discussed in the next section suggests that at least some Southern cities instituted quarantines ostensibly to protect themselves from yellow fever when, in fact, there was absolutely no legitimate threat from the disease.

Imperfect Information and the Excessive Quarantining of New Orleans

The proximate causes of excessive quarantining were twofold. First, as suggested by strategic trade models and recent historical work, cities often used quarantines not to protect public health but as a thinly veiled means of imposing tariffs and interfering with interstate trade in ways that benefited the city and harmed its rivals.[64] In her authoritative history of yellow fever in the United States, Margaret Humphreys describes how port cities throughout the South imposed quarantines against New Orleans on "the barest whisper" that yellow fever was present and sometimes refused to remove those quarantines even when it "had been conclusively demonstrated" that there was no yellow fever in the city. These quarantines, she concludes, were "conducted much to the benefit of shipping lines" that serviced port cities competing with New Orleans, such as Galveston and Mobile.[65]

The second cause of excessive quarantining was an inadequate system of disease reporting. The complex role that poor disease reporting played in generating unnecessary quarantines is illustrated by a battle between the Sanitary Council of the Mississippi Valley and the Louisiana State Board of Health. Created in the wake of the 1878 yellow fever epidemic, the Sanitary Council of the Mississippi Valley was a combination of representatives from state and local boards of health from across the South and even as far north as Illinois. The Sanitary Council was especially concerned with the failure of the Louisiana State Board of Health to report cases of yellow fever in New Orleans accurately and promptly. Among other state and local health boards, Louisiana had what appears to have been a well-deserved reputation for concealing yellow fever cases out of fear that other cities might impose quarantines against goods shipped from New Orleans.[66] New Orleans was a focus of concern not only because of its unreliable reporting of disease but also because it was seen as an entrepôt of disease, particularly for other cities along the Mississippi River. As one observer saw it, experience had "amply proved that New Orleans" was "pre-eminently liable" to "receive and disseminate" the "infection of yellow fever" because of the amount of shipping it handled—it was the fifth largest port in United States—and because it was "probably unsurpassed" in the amount of river traffic it handled.[67]

In light of all the concern about yellow fever in New Orleans, the Louisiana State Board of Health had to repeatedly issue public resolutions and proclamations asking the press to not report on rumors of yellow fever in the city but only on cases certified as true by Louisiana health officials.[68] No one, including the popular press, put any credence in such pleas. On the contrary, every statement issued by the Louisiana Board of Health minimizing the threat of yellow fever in New Orleans was viewed as unreliable and tainted by commercial interests. The Sanitary Council went so far as to issue counter proclamations along the following lines: "Our people habitually view with distrust all announcements and sanitary acts of local boards, when those acts and announcements are of a character to affect the commercial interests of the locality directly concerned. . . . And . . . there is unfortunately a want of confidence with regard to the prompt furnishing of information by the health authorities of New Orleans with referenced to infectious and contagious disease."[69]

The Sanitary Council proposed a simple and reasonable solution to this problem. It suggested that the recently created National Board of Health have an agent in New Orleans examine all suspected cases of yellow fever in the city. The National Board would then have been in charge of certifying that the city was free from yellow fever. Because the National Board represented much broader geographic interests, and it was not unduly concerned with the commerce of the city, its pronouncements would have been credible, but state and local authorities in New Orleans refused to participate in that arrangement in any meaningful way.

The refusal of New Orleans to cooperate with this broader regional initiative adversely affected both disease-prevention efforts and commerce. In terms of disease prevention, when health officials in New Orleans did not immediately and accurately report cases of yellow fever, they made it harder to identify the specific ship or ships that were carrying infected passengers (and mosquitoes). This, in turn, undermined the ability of other cities to effectively and efficiently identify infected ships and left those cities much more vulnerable to yellow fever. For example, during the 1878 yellow fever epidemic, New Orleans failed to report cases of yellow fever aboard the tow boat *John D. Porter* while it was operating and docked in the city. That same boat was later identified as carrying yellow fever to ports upstream and causing "great additional devastation."[70]

In terms of commerce, absent reliable and trustworthy information, health officials in other states and cities often had no choice but to respond to the slightest hint of yellow fever in New Orleans by interdicting ships arriving from that city. If they failed to do otherwise, and yellow fever broke out in their jurisdiction, they risked incurring a heavy political penalty from voters harmed by the ensuing epidemic. This undoubtedly led some cities to incur the costs of imposing quarantines when such quarantines were unnecessary, and it is certainly possible that New Orleans had to endure more externally imposed quarantines against it because of its refusal to cooperate with the Sanitary Council.

In justifying its plea for independent reporting, the Sanitary Council also suggested that this was the only way to prevent "premature and unnecessary restrictions on commercial and personal intercourse with New Orleans." Put another way, to the extent that rumormongering about yellow fever undercut trade coming out of New Orleans, it might well have been in the commercial interest of the city to assure accurate and reliable reporting of disease. Consistent with this view is the fact that both the New Orleans Chamber of Commerce and New Orleans Auxiliary Sanitary Association (a group dominated by wealthy merchants and industrialists in the city) lobbied heavily, but in vain, to get the Louisiana State Board of Health to cooperate with the Sanitary Council's proposal for independent reporting of yellow fever.[71]

The history of the New Orleans Auxiliary Sanitary Association undercuts arguments like those of William Wragg, which suggest that business and commerce always acted in ways that were inimical to the public health. In this context, it was the business community that lobbied for accurate and independent disease reporting and promoted rational and effective approaches to disease control; they were only stymied in their efforts by parochial political concerns and turf battles. As Margaret Humphreys explains, it was the obstinacy of state and local public health officials in New Orleans, motivated more by personal animosity and resentment than concerns over public health, that undermined regional cooperation and a more credible system of disease reporting in New Orleans. Humphreys gives particular attention to the personality of Joseph Jones, the president of the Louisiana State Board of Health. She suggests that his refusal to cooperate with the National Board of Health stemmed at least in part from the board's rescinding a job offer it had made to him earlier in his career.[72]

Yellow Fever and the Commercial Origins of Sanitation:
Two Case Studies

The previous sections described how, at least in some situations (e.g., New York's quarantine measures) the lobbying efforts of businesses and merchants moderated for the better the quarantine policies of local governments. Another way in which the lobbying of business groups encouraged more reasonable and effective public health policies, especially those related to yellow fever, grew out of the expediency and intuitive appeal of sanitation. Business groups, drawing from a vocal contingent in the medical community, argued that the best way to prevent yellow fever was through improved sanitation.

Before going too far down this road, I should emphasize that when businesses argued that good sanitation could prevent yellow fever, they were wrong: yellow fever was not like typhoid, typhus, tuberculosis, or other diseases associated with poor sanitation; it was not spread by water tainted with fecal matter; or the bad air of crowded, dilapidated tenements; or the rats and bugs that inhabited piles of trash; or the horse manure that littered city streets during the early 1800s.[73] Without question, cleaning up urban wastes would have addressed a whole panoply of infectious and sanitation-related diseases, but unless such measures significantly reduced mosquito populations, there is little, if any, scientific basis for believing that they would have had any impact on yellow fever. Nevertheless, business and mercantile groups during the late nineteenth century were often vocal supporters of improved sanitation generally, because they saw it as means of promoting long-term economic development. Clean, healthy cities, the argument went, would attract more migrants, industry, and trade than disease-ridden places.[74]

How yellow fever intersected with efforts to promote regional economic development through improved sanitation is well illustrated by the experiences of Memphis, Tennessee, and New Orleans. Accordingly, short case studies of both cities follow. The case study of Memphis shows how severe yellow fever epidemics, particularly when they were associated with perceptions that they were caused by poor sanitary conditions in a city, could impair long-term economic growth. But Memphis also illustrates how, in an effort to counteract those perceptions and become more attractive to migrants, cities made large investments in sanitation that probably did not affect yellow fever rates but had large public health benefits in relation to other diseases. At the heart of the case study of New Orleans is a famous court battle: the *Slaughterhouse Cases*. The *Slaughterhouse Cases* grew out of an effort to relocate and centralize the slaughtering of animals in New Orleans so that the disposal of dead animal carcasses and other related wastes would no longer defile the city's drinking water. Although this effort might well have been tainted by economic interests—the centralization of slaughtering in New Orleans probably gave a monopoly, or at least significant market power, to politically connected business groups—the available evidence suggests that the law had large public health benefits.

Case Study One: Memphis, Tennessee

After the Civil War, probably the single most important event in nineteenth-century Memphis was the yellow fever epidemic that struck the city in 1878. Killing one of every eight Memphis residents, this was among the worst epidemics (from any disease) to ever strike an American city. As the epidemic raged in the summer of 1878, one-third of the black population and two-thirds of the white population fled the city. Of the blacks that remained in the city, 80 percent contracted yellow fever; of these, 10 percent died. Of the whites that remained in the city, 98 percent contracted the disease; of these, 70 percent died. Only five years earlier, in 1873, a combined epidemic of yellow fever and cholera killed at least two thousand Memphis residents, about 5 percent of the local population. Nor were these the first epidemics in the city. The year Memphis was chartered, it was afflicted by smallpox, and in the years to follow there were repeated visitations of smallpox, cholera, dysentery, influenza, and yellow fever. Although it is difficult to know whether Memphis was really any worse than any other developing American city in terms of disease, there was a widespread belief that it was. Even the city's own newspaper conceded that "all visitors" saw Memphis as "the filthiest and most deathly appearing town in the Union."[75]

Memphis certainly seemed an unhealthy place. Lying only 260 feet above sea level, the city was surrounded by swamps, with a miserable bayou that ran through the city and served as a sort of all-purpose sewer. The city's climate (hot and wet) seemed conducive to the proliferation of miasmatic poisons. There were only a few miles of private sewers, and most residents dumped their waste in cesspools, privy vaults, or in open ditches; there was no system of storm water drainage or public garbage disposal; and, except for a small, poorly run private company, there was no public water supply. In 1880, a government investigation found evidence that 72 percent of the city's private wells were contaminated by human waste; hundreds of buildings in the city had standing water in their basements or cellars from two to eighteen inches deep; and the few city streets that were not dirt were made of rotting wood that emitted a foul smell.[76]

When the yellow fever epidemic of 1878 erupted, most observers could not help believing that all of this filth had something to do with it. In response, officials in Memphis launched a massive campaign to cleanse the city of disease-causing fomites and poisons. In the midst of the epidemic, officials hired teams of people (largely African American, given their elevated immunity status and relatively dire economic circumstances) to empty all privy vaults and disinfect them with carbolic acid. The wastes of yellow fever victims were then to be treated with acid and disposed of into impervious containers; the towels, blankets, sheets, curtains, furniture, and mattresses of yellow fever victims were washed with carbolic acid; when these items were too soiled to be cleaned, they were burned. Hundreds of houses so unsanitary that they were suspected of harboring poisons were burned; mail entering and leaving the city was fumigated; trains and boats entering and leaving the city were quarantined, as were their passengers; refugee camps were set up outside the city; cannons and large fires were set off at night to disinfect the air.[77]

By the time the epidemic subsided in the winter of 1879, the city was bankrupt. After revoking the city's charter, the state also stripped Memphis of its name. The city was now referred to as "The Taxing District of Shelby County," and would not be rechartered as a city until 1891. Compounding these difficulties was population flight and a subsequent drop in real estate values. After the epidemics of 1873 and 1878, people fled the city en masse. On January 1, 1880, the population of the city formerly known as Memphis stood at 30,659—three-quarters of its population in 1870 (40,226).[78] Figure 6.6 depicts the cumulative effects of the epidemics of 1873 and 1878 on population growth in Memphis. Two series are plotted, one for observed population levels and one for predicted levels based on the rate of growth realized between 1850 and 1870. The predicted population levels indicate that Memphis was well below its expected population in 1880 by around 23,500 (40 percent below its expected level), but the predicted series also suggests that the city had recovered from the 1873 and 1878 epidemics by 1890.

These data and observations prompt the question: Why was the city's population in 1880 40 percent lower than that predicted by historical trends? Excess deaths from yellow fever (and cholera) only partially account for the deficit. The data above indicate the population of Memphis in 1880 was roughly 23,500 lower than it would have been in the absence of the epidemics of 1873 and 1878. The epidemics, however, killed only about seven thousand individuals, just under one-third of the population deficit, leaving two-thirds of the deficit unexplained. This suggests that most of the population deficit in 1880 is explained by reductions in fertility and, more

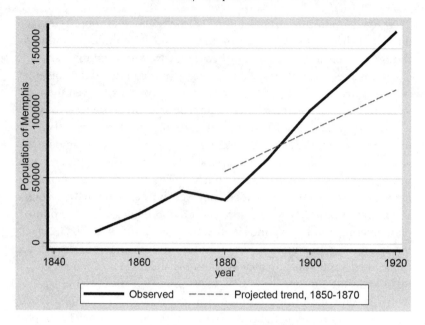

Figure 6.6. Population of Memphis, 1850–1920.
(Data from United States Census [various years, various volumes].)

importantly, lost in-migration. Memphis was having such difficulty attracting white migrants that it was forced to integrate its police force.[79]

Summarizing the city's bleak economic state in the aftermath of the yellow fever, Margaret Humphreys argues that businesses and merchants believed the city's only hope for revival was to be found in sanitary reform.
"Especially after the return of yellow fever in 1879, Memphis' case seemed
hopeless to many," but "from such gloom," Humphreys writes, "arose the
mercantile drive to rejuvenate the city with sanitary reform." Business interests in Memphis enjoyed the support of the city's major newspaper, the *Daily
Appeal*, whose editors believed that "good hygiene makes good business"
and that "a good sanitary condition is one of the best advertisements a city
can have." For the businesses and merchants advocating for sanitary reform,
the city's most glaring problem was the absence of a public sewer system.
As stated earlier, without public sewers, Memphis residents used cesspools
and privy vaults to dispose of fecal matter. This, in turn, left the ground
"saturated with human waste" and the air reeking with an awful stench.
Sanitary reformers were especially concerned with the Bayou Gayoso, a
swampy creek that ran through city but was really little more than an open
sewer.[80]

Accordingly, by 1880, the city had begun work on a vast sewer system that, when completed, would service the entire city. In the first year of construction alone, twenty-five miles of sewer mains were laid, and by 1884, there were forty miles of sewer mains in the city. The new sewer system was associated with reductions in overall mortality and waterborne disease rates. Between 1884 and 1895, the total mortality rate (deaths from all causes per hundred thousand persons) for both blacks and whites in Memphis fell by about 50 percent, and the difference between black and white death rates fell by about 70 percent. Looking exclusively at waterborne diseases (cholera, diarrhea, and typhoid), the diseases most likely to have responded to the construction of sanitary sewers, the same conclusion emerges: black and white waterborne disease rates both fell by about 70 percent between the early 1880s and the mid-1890s.[81]

How exactly these new sewers would have affected yellow fever is unclear. On the one hand, it is possible that the new sewers improved city drainage and that this destroyed breeding grounds for the *Aedes agypti*. On the other hand, because the *Aedes agypti* did not breed in stagnant pools of muddy water but preferred to breed in cisterns of relatively clean water, it seems unlikely that a new sewer system would have had much an effect on yellow fever in Memphis. Moreover, while it is true that epidemics of yellow fever never returned to Memphis after 1879, yellow fever also became much less frequent throughout the United States. (See figure 6.1 and discussion in the introduction.)

Case Study Two: New Orleans

In 1869, the Louisiana State Legislature passed the law now commonly referred to as the Slaughterhouse Monopoly Act. The act included four major provisions. First, the law chartered the Crescent City Live-Stock Landing and Slaughterhouse Company. Under the company's charter, it was to be located south of the city, on the west side of the Mississippi River, opposite to the city. Second, the company was to enjoy a geographically defined monopoly over all butchering and slaughtering in the city. No meat could be butchered or slaughtered anywhere else in the city or Jefferson Parish. After the law was passed, any butcher operating somewhere else in the city had to move his operations to the Crescent City slaughterhouse and the slaughterhouse was required by law to rent that butcher space. Third, under the law, the Crescent City slaughterhouse was subject to state inspection. The law dictated that the governor "shall appoint a competent person . . . to examine all animals . . . to ascertain whether they are sound and fit for human food." Animals not certified as sound, could not be slaughtered for sale at the Crescent City slaughterhouse or anywhere else in the city. Fourth, the Act established the rates and fees that the Crescent City slaughterhouse was to charge participating butchers, and it established fines and punishments should the new company violate any of the terms of its charter. This last aspect of the law has led some legal scholars to argue that the act did not create a monopoly but a price-regulated public utility that was legally mandated to provide space to any butcher who wanted to operate in the city.[82]

Before the passage of the Slaughterhouse Monopoly Act, there were hundreds, or perhaps thousands, of butchers in New Orleans, nearly all them working along the shoreline upstream from the city. They worked close to the river because running water was essential to the slaughtering and butchering process. Running water was used to flush off carcasses, to keep vermin and insects away, and to dispose of animal entrails and wastes, most of which was flushed back into the Mississippi River. Quoting liberally from an investigation conducted by the Louisiana state legislature, Herbert Hovenkamp described the "immense quantity of filth and offal" that was dumped into the river, which "if not prejudicial to health" was "certainly very revolting." So much animal waste was being dumped into the Mississippi that when the river was low, it was not "uncommon to see intestines and portions of putrefied animal matter." Because the Mississippi River was the city's primary water source and because most of the entrails and "putrefied animal matter" were "lodged around" or got "sucked into" the city's water pipes, this situation posed, in Hovenkamp's words, a "monumental" public health problem.[83] On its face, the Slaughterhouse Monopoly Act represented a perfectly reasonable nineteenth-century solution to this problem: move all slaughtering to the southern tip of the city so that the animal wastes would be flushed into the Gulf, not into the city water supply. Indeed in Britain and France during this period, one of the primary motivations for centralizing the location of slaughterhouses was to protect municipal water supplies.[84]

The Slaughterhouse Monopoly Act grew, in part, out of the fear that conditions surrounding the slaughtering industry in New Orleans might play a role in the generation of yellow fever. In particular, in the popular nineteenth-century mind, there was a deeply held belief that rotting animal carcasses and other sources of effluvia were contributing factors in the propagation of yellow fever. Even those who believed yellow fever was not indigenous to New Orleans but was imported through trade believed that the city's unsanitary conditions heightened its vulnerability to the disease; absent unsanitary conditions, the argument went, the disease would not have been able to take hold. In the words of one nineteenth-century observer, "experienced yellow fever physicians" regularly declared that "filth in every form—from the of-fal of the slaughterhouse to human excreta—is the nidus on which yellow fever feeds and propagates, and by which it is sustained and perpetuated."[85] An English physician writing during the 1840s argued that slaughterhouses produced a "narcotic poison" he described as malaria.[86]

Along the same lines, a medical observer in New Orleans described how a "vast number of physicians . . . have adopted the belief that filth and offal accumulating in [New Orleans] are the causes of yellow fever."[87] That concerns about epidemic diseases like yellow fever helped motivate passage of the Slaughterhouse Monopoly Act is also illustrated by the fact that in the legislative record, the act had a longer and more accurate name: "An Act to Protect the Health of the City of New Orleans, to Locate the Stock Yards and the Slaughter Houses, and to Incorporate the Crescent City Live Stock Landing and Slaughter House Company."

Today there is no scientific basis for believing that yellow fever was directly connected to slaughtering or the disposal of animal entrails and offal into the Mississippi River: the mosquitoes that caused yellow fever did not breed in the carcasses of dead animals, as did some other insects; nor was the *Aedes agypti* attracted to muddy and turbid water, as were other mosquitoes. Instead as already noted, the yellow fever mosquito was drawn to water cisterns where the water was clear, and the smooth sides of the vessel served as an attractive place to attach their eggs. This suggests, at most, an indirect connection between yellow fever and slaughterhouse conditions: if cleaning up the river prompted city residents to abandon their cisterns for water from the public system, that process would have destroyed an important breeding ground for the *Aedes agypti* and given the city some modicum of protection when new mosquitoes were introduced through foreign trade with the West Indies and other places where yellow fever was endemic. This might help explain a correlation mentioned repeatedly by historians writing about the slaughterhouse situation in New Orleans: yellow fever epidemics became much less frequent and severe after the act was passed. That said, given the dearth of scientific evidence that better disposal of animal carcasses can affect mosquito populations, any proposed connection between reductions in yellow fever and the Slaughterhouse Act is speculative at best.

Whatever its effects on yellow fever, the formation of the Crescent City Slaughterhouse was associated with a dramatic improvement in overall mortality in New Orleans, as shown in figure 6.7, which plots the crude death rate in the city from 1810 through 1920. In the years leading up to the Civil War, the crude death rate in the city rose from around fifty deaths per thousand persons to sixty, an increase of 20 percent. But with Union occupation,

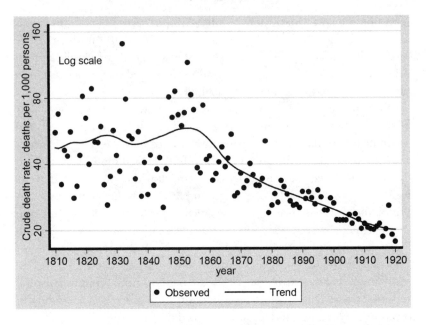

Figure 6.7. The crude death rate in New Orleans, 1810–1920.
(From Michael R. Haines, "The Urban Mortality Transition in the United States, 1800–1940,"
NBER Historical Paper No. 134, July 2001 [Cambridge, MA: National Bureau of Economic
Research, 2005].)

sanitary conditions in the city were improved, and the trade with the West Indies was brought to an almost complete stop. Better sanitation and the break in foreign trade reversed this upward trend—a trend that had been going on for nearly half a century—and there was a sudden and discrete shift downward in mortality rates from around sixty deaths per thousand to less than forty, a reduction of roughly 30 percent.

A continuation of the Union policies that had helped reduce death rates in the city, the passage of the Slaughterhouse Monopoly Act was followed by a secular decline in the crude death rate. Between 1869 and 1920, the crude death rate in New Orleans plummeted from around fifty deaths per thousand to twenty, a drop of 60 percent. Relative to other major cities in the United States, New Orleans went from having among the very highest death rates in the country to a middling death rate.

One can interpret what happened in New Orleans as evidence of the power of the federal government to address public health problems in the context of war and looser constitutional restrictions. In particular, during the Civil War, the federal government was acting as an occupying force; it cared little for democracy or the individual rights of a rebel population with which it was at war. It simply imposed a sort of martial law for public health on the city, and in so doing was able to accomplish in a few years what New Orleans politicians could not accomplish for over half a century: ram good sanitation and commercial quarantine down the throats of a resistant population. By the same token, the Slaughterhouse Monopoly Act probably would not have been passed in the absence of federal power. The act was passed by a Republican legislature dominated by northern carpetbaggers and African American legislators who were elected to the state government only because of Reconstruction and a military threat that, for the first time in the history of the United States, gave African Americans full access to the ballot box. Only after Reconstruction ended in 1877 were blacks disenfranchised once again and denied the same political rights that they had been denied as slaves.

Despite the sustained improvements in the city's health status that followed its passage, the Slaughterhouse Monopoly Act remained a source of anger and resentment among the white elite in New Orleans for years, or perhaps even decades. The city's white elite did not oppose the public health aspect of the law—even the law's harshest critics had to admit that getting offal and rotting animal carcasses out of the city's water supply was probably good idea.[88] Instead, they repeatedly lamented the fact that the law created a spatially defined monopoly that would make it impossible to slaughter, or even keep, cattle or other animals anywhere in the city without authorization. This would, the critics contended, interfere with all sorts of markets and economic activities. For one, the supply of fresh milk would be interrupted because cows could no longer be kept in the city.[89]

Probably the most enduring claim made by critics of the law is that the Slaughterhouse Monopoly Act was secured through bribery and corruption. According to this argument, the owners and operators of the Crescent City Slaughterhouse bribed key politicians in the state government to pass the law. They wrapped law in the rubric of public health only to fool the public; the real motivation was to grant a narrow special interest group a means of extracting rents from an otherwise competitive industry. It is, however, not clear how seriously historians today should take this claim. The notion that passage of the act was secured through bribery can be traced back to a group of racially biased historians writing during the early 1900s, who wanted to discredit not only the legislators who passed the measure (most of whom were either blacks or northern carpetbaggers) but also the larger program of Reconstruction.[90]

Soon after passage of the Slaughterhouse Monopoly Act, the law was challenged in court by the Butchers Benevolent Association (BBA), a combination of hundreds of butchers in the city. The BBA claimed that the act was an unconstitutional violation of their Fourteenth Amendment rights to equal protection and due process. According to the BBA, the operation of the Crescent City Slaughterhouse granted one group of butchers special privileges while it deprived others of their right to pursue a gainful occupation. The BBA argued that the new slaughterhouse law would restrict entry and make it harder for some butchers to operate in the city. Those who were lucky enough or who had close political ties to the operators of the new slaughterhouse would presumably gain from the reduction in competition, but those displaced would lose even more. In this way, at least to the thinking of the BBA, the Slaughterhouse Monopoly Act was discriminatory and unequal in its effects; it favored some butchers but denied those same benefits to the butchers who were members of the BBA. According to counsel for the BBA, the act was the product of "legislative partiality" that enriched the seventeen persons who owned the Crescent City Slaughterhouse but deprived "a thousand other" butchers the means by which they earned "their daily bread."[91]

In a now famous decision, the United States Supreme Court ruled against the BBA by a narrow margin, holding that the Slaughterhouse Monopoly Act was a legitimate exercise of the state's police powers. Quoting prior authority, the Court wrote,

> Unwholesome trades, slaughter-houses, [and other] operations offensive to the senses . . . may all be interdicted by law, in the midst of dense masses of population, on the general and rational principle, that every person ought so to use his property as not injure his neighbors; and private interests must be made subservient to the general interests of the community. This is called the police power [and] upon it depends the social order, the life and health of the citizen, the comfort of . . . a thickly populated community, the enjoyment of private and social life, and the beneficial use of property.[92]

Moreover, when the Court looked specifically at the Slaughterhouse Monopoly Act and how it would work in New Orleans, it saw a measure whose provisions were "appropriate," "stringent," and "effectual." The Court wrote, "It cannot be denied that the statute under consideration is aptly framed to remove from the densely populated part of the city, the noxious slaughterhouses, and large and offensive collections of animals . . . incident to slaughtering . . . and locate them where the convenience, health, and comfort of the people require."[93]

The Supreme Court also rejected the primary complaint of the BBA— that the law would deprive them of their ability to butcher and slaughter meat in the city. As the Court saw it, the Slaughterhouse Act did not deprive anyone of such a right. On the contrary, the act mandated that the Crescent City Slaughterhouse provide space to any butcher who requested it and was willing to pay the relevant fee, which was the same for everyone. Moreover, the Crescent City corporation would face a stiff fine if it failed to comply with this provision.[94]

The most coercive and anticompetitive element in the act was that it dictated where butchers had to operate, but it did not expressly dictate who might engage in the industry. There would still be hundreds of individual butchers operating at the new slaughterhouse. As the Court explained, the statute "defines these localities [where butchers can operate] and forbids slaughtering in any other. It does not, as has been asserted, prevent the butcher from doing his own slaughtering." Moreover, the Court continued, "the Slaughter-House Company is required, under a heavy penalty, to permit any person who wishes to slaughter in their houses; and they are bound to make ample provision for the convenience of all the slaughtering for the entire city." In this way, "the butcher" was still permitted "to slaughter, to prepare, and to sell his own meats." The only change was that he was now "required to slaughter at a specified place and to pay a reasonable compensation for the use of the accommodations furnished him at that place." While the Court conceded that the "wisdom of the monopoly [over land] granted by the legislature" might have been "open to question," it did not accept the BBA's "the assertion that [their] butchers" were "deprived of the right to labor in their occupation."[95]

Although most legal scholars decry the Constitutional interpretations that undergirded *Slaughterhouse* decision,[96] in practical terms the decision to uphold a law creating a single public slaughterhouse was conventional and hardly surprising by nineteenth-century standards. There was a long history in Continental Europe, the United States, and England of state and local laws governing the location of markets and economic activity, particularly when those markets and activities involved offensive trades and nuisances, and as offensive trades go, slaughtering was fairly high on the offensive list—a nineteenth-century commentator described slaughterhouses as nuisances of the worst class. Slaughterhouses in Britain had long been subject to common law rules governing nuisances and loathsome trades. These rules dictated that firms or individuals engaged in processes that produced nuisances and adversely affected neighboring properties could be held liable for damages, or enjoined from continuing the harmful activities, if successfully challenged in courts of equity.[97]

In the American context, slaughterhouse regulations at a municipal level dated all the way back to the seventeenth century, and such regulations were not uncommon in large cities by the early nineteenth century. For example, a Milwaukee ordinance restricted all slaughtering to a specific site in the city, while San Francisco simply banned slaughtering within the city limits. Similarly, in New York, state courts enjoined the construction of new slaughterhouses and upheld municipal actions that restrained the operations of slaughterhouses that had long been in operation. Indeed, as early as 1826, a state court in New York suggested that it was common knowledge that cities had the power to regulate the location of nuisances and offensive trades such as slaughtering. In 1865, New Jersey passed legislation banning slaughterhouses and other offensive and noisome trades along one area of the Hudson River. Following passage of this law, the New Jersey attorney general secured an injunction against the New Jersey Stock Yard Company, putting an end to the company's most offensive practices and operations.[98]

Concluding Remarks

This chapter has described the rise and fall of yellow fever in the United States. The American vulnerability to yellow fever grew out of its commitment to commerce, particularly trade with the West Indies, and the development of large port cities like New Orleans, which appear to have been the entrepôts through which yellow fever mosquitoes gained entry into the United States. The decline of yellow fever is a more complicated and surprising story. The federal government was an aggressive and highly effective actor abroad in reigning in yellow fever. Once it was discovered that yellow fever was spread by the *Aedes agypti* mosquito, the US military inspired, or bullied, its trading partners in Latin America to pursue mosquito eradication policies that had spillover benefits for the United States. At home, however, the federal government was much weaker, and throughout the nineteenth century showed great deference to state governments in the formation and implementation of commercial quarantines. This deference grew out of a constitutional and ideological commitment to federalism and states' rights.

Much of the chapter was dedicated to understanding the political economy of commercial quarantines. Because quarantines were typically administered by city governments, and not the federal government, they were vulnerable to two types of problems: the race to the bottom and strategic trade. Although critics of American quarantine policies like William Wragg emphasized the race-to-the-bottom problem, the experience of New Orleans suggests that commercially strategic quarantines were a more serious concern. In part because New Orleans failed to cooperate in accurately reporting outbreaks of yellow fever in its jurisdiction, rival port cities were quick to impose commercial quarantines in an effort to capture some the trade that had belonged to New Orleans.

Perhaps the most surprising element of the history of yellow fever prevention in the United States is how the business community, in its efforts to oppose strict and autarkic quarantines, lobbied for stronger sanitation measures in cities like New Orleans and Memphis. The results were investments in projects such as a massive new sewer system in Memphis and a slaughterhouse monopoly in New Orleans that protected the local water supply from pollution. While it is doubtful that either of these measures had any substantive effect on yellow fever rates in either city, the available data indicate they brought large public health benefits more generally. The Memphis sewer system and the Slaughterhouse Monopoly Act in New Orleans were both associated with large reductions in overall mortality.

Finally, the history of Memphis and New Orleans illustrates a potential benefit to a federalist or decentralized approach to disease prevention: experimentation. When the cause of a disease is unknown, each city can tailor its own response to the disease and identify optimal responses. While neither Memphis nor New Orleans discovered that the mosquito caused yellow fever, the responses of both cities ended up addressing other public health problems. The result was a general decline in death rates in both cities, even though the policies in question likely did little to combat yellow fever.

SEVEN

Concluding Remarks

In the opening chapters, I argued that America had high smallpox rates not *despite* being rich and free, but precisely *because* it was rich and free. More generally, I argued that the same Constitutional provisions that promoted riches and freedom in the United States also shaped, for better and for worse, the American disease environment. In this conclusion, I would like to return to these ideas, not to reaffirm them but to expand on them and discuss their sources and limits. Toward that end, note that when economists and political scientists write about the Constitutional principles that fostered economic growth and political freedom, they typically focus on three broad areas: property rights, individual liberty, and federalism.

Property rights were important for economic growth because they fostered innovation and investment in fixed capital stock that firms would have been reluctant to undertake if they were faced with the risk of expropriation. It has also been argued by Milton Friedman and Richard Pipes that property rights are, in and of themselves, an important form of political freedom.[1] In the usual discussions of protections of individual liberty, emphasis is often given to the Bill of Rights, but legal historians also argue for the fundamental importance of the Fourteenth Amendment, which, as the preceding discussion suggests, influenced both economic outcomes and disease-prevention efforts. Of these three areas, federalism has had perhaps the most pervasive effect on American society, generating a highly localized approach to governance that has discouraged unduly onerous business regulations and promoted the optimal provision of local public goods (for those without external effects).

Whatever its effects on economic development and political freedom, federalism nicely illustrates how the Constitution influenced public health outcomes in both positive and negative ways. On the positive side, it is likely that federalism hastened the construction of public water systems because of interjurisdiction competition for taxpayers and residents. As explained in chapter 5, communities with public water systems that offered residents a pure and easily accessible supply of water were attractive places to locate. In addition, through demonstration effects, early adopters of new technologies, such as water filtration, highlighted the benefits and large social returns of these technologies to neighboring cities that were slower and would have been otherwise reluctant to adopt. In a more centralized system, demonstration effects are less likely, and recalcitrant jurisdictions can slow the adoption of new technologies, even among places that favor quick investment.

On the other hand, the same forces of interjurisdictional sorting and competition that gave rise to early investment in water systems probably also hindered efforts to achieve universal smallpox vaccination in the United States. In particular, the patterns described in chapter 4 suggest that anti-vaccinationists sorted into jurisdictions that adopted noncompulsory vaccination policies, while in a more centralized system, federal authorities would have adopted stronger policies that appealed to the majority of national voters. Outside the United States, this process of devolution, with states adopting looser policies than federal authorities, can be seen in the history of Switzerland. In 1882, Switzerland passed a federal law that made vaccination compulsory in all cantons, but this was undone by a series of local referenda that gradually made vaccination optional in several cantons, with the result that smallpox rates increased in those same cantons.[2] Further evidence that federalist approaches to public health can be dysfunctional emerges from the history of yellow fever and typhoid fever, where regional and interpersonal rivalries prompted officials to adopt policies that might have been rational from a purely individual or city level, but were clearly suboptimal at a larger, regional level (see chapters 5 and 6).

It is common to think of private property rights as an obstacle to public health. Why? Because regulations promoting public health often restrict how property is used. In this way, one might argue that strictly enforced private property rights would not allow cities to shut down offensive trades such as slaughterhouses, the processing of offal, or pig farms in residential neighborhoods. While there would be plenty to quibble with in such an argument (e.g., what about the property rights of the neighbors?), the analysis in chapter 5 shows how property rights, at least in the case of public water systems, can also have large and positive effects on the provision of public health. Property rights for private water companies encouraged entrepreneurs to invest in expensive water mains and filtration systems at times when cities where financially strapped. Similarly, protections for private bondholders made it possible for cities to borrow money at low interest rates to finance the construction of large and expensive public water systems, aqueducts, and sewers. Such property rights for water-related investments were especially important, because access to pure water explains roughly 60 percent of the increase in human life expectancy that occurred between 1850 and 1950.

As explained in chapter 3, the Fourteenth Amendment is perhaps the single most important element in the Federal Constitution in terms of protecting individual rights and liberties from the encroachments of the state and majoritarian legislatures. It is no surprise, then, that popular thinking about the Fourteenth Amendment and broader notions of individual rights played a central role in the implementation of public vaccination programs for smallpox during the nineteenth and twentieth centuries. Although the available evidence suggests that vaccination with cowpox was a highly effective and reasonably safe means of protecting people from smallpox, there was a relatively small community of individuals who vigorously opposed vaccination under *all* circumstances, and a larger community who would only undergo vaccination if there were an epidemic. In litigation surrounding mandatory vaccination laws, individuals who dissented regularly appealed to the Fourteenth Amendment. Although the courts routinely rejected such appeals and gave the state and local government broad powers to enforce mandatory vaccination orders, popular thinking about the Fourteenth Amendment and individual rights more generally helped animate opposition movements like those of Lora Little's in Portland, Oregon. In this way, it was not just the Constitution that mattered but popular thinking *about* the Constitution, as well as broader ideological beliefs regarding personal liberty, medicine, and social obligation.

While I have focused on the Constitution and American history, the arguments developed here are not unique to the United States. They have broader relevance, and can be applied to other countries. Stated in its most general form, the central argument of *The Pox of Liberty* is that political institutions shape government responses to epidemic diseases and thereby influence disease environments. This, in turn, suggests that when we look at international variation in disease rates, we should not only consider the effects of geography and climate, but also the impact of politics and political institutions. Why is it, for example, that waterborne diseases continue to linger in some parts of the world, but in other places such diseases were eradicated more than a century ago? Undoubtedly, poverty and economic deprivation explain part of the story, but it would be a worthy endeavor to consider the role that political institutions play as well. Perhaps if politicians in disease-ridden places faced different incentives and different constraints on their behavior, they would be able to find constructive responses to the diseases that afflict their constituents. Perhaps demonstrating governmental capacity to deal with diseases would, in turn, promote greater faith in the state and facilitate efforts to raise revenues and cement the state's legitimacy among the citizenry. All of this is worthy of further consideration, something I hope to do in my next book.

NOTES

PREFACE

1. See Gilberto Hochman, "Priority, Invisibility and Eradication: The History of Small-pox and the Brazilian Public Health Agenda," *Medical History* 53.2 (2009): 229–52; and A. W. Hedrich, "Changes in the Incidence and Fatality of Smallpox in Recent Decades," *Public Health Reports* 51.14 (1936): 363–84.
2. See chapter 3 for a full discussion of federalism, the Contract Clause, and the work of Barry Weingast.
3. See chapter 5 for a detailed discussion of the health effects of pure water and the associated documentation.

CHAPTER ONE

1. Andrew A. Bruce, "Judicial Buncombe in North Dakota and Other States," *Central Law Journal* 88. 9 (1919): 155. See, more generally, Herbert L. Meschke and Ted Smith, "Judicial Values: The Justice Robinson Experience," *North Dakota Law Review* 82.1 (2006): 25–48.
2. Max Radin, "The Good Judge of Chateau-Thierry and His American Counterpart," *California Law Review* 10.4 (1922): 300–10.
3. Samuel Williston, "The Progress of the Law, 1919–1920," *Harvard Law Review* 34.7 (May 1921): 741–67.
4. Bruce, "Judicial Buncombe," 155.
5. This case was orchestrated and pushed by anti-vaccination activists such as Lora Little. See Robert D. Johnston, *The Radical Middle Class: Populist Democracy and the Question of Capitalism in Progressive Era Portland, Oregon* (Princeton, NJ: Princeton University Press, 2002), 209–12.
6. Rhea v. Board of Education of Devils Lake, 41 N.D. 449 (1919), 458. It is notable that more than two decades before the North Dakota decision, the United States Supreme confronted a very similar case involving a mandatory smallpox vaccination order in Massachusetts. In that case, however, the Supreme Court upheld the mandatory vaccination order. Had Robinson and others on the North Dakota court followed the precedent of the Supreme Court, they would have arrived at a ruling very different from the one they issued and upheld the school board's policy. See Jacobson v. Massachusetts, 197 U.S. 11 (1905). This case will be discussed in chapter 4.
7. *Rhea*, 41 N.D. 449 at 458.

8. Ibid. at 457–58.

9. See James P. Leake, "The Essentials of Smallpox Vaccination," *Public Health Reports* 36.33 (1921): 1975–89; and Samuel W. Abbott, "Progress in Public Hygiene," *Boston Medical and Surgical Journal* 146.18 (1902): 465–67. For further data and documentation of the claims made in this paragraph, see chapter 3.

10. *Mosher's Magazine*, July 1902, 248–49.

11. Ibid.

12. Writing in 1920, in the wake of a series of legal developments that undermined his cause, Anderson claimed that there had "never been a time in the history of the United States" when it was more important to keep in mind the words "eternal vigilance is the price of liberty." To Anderson's way of the thinking, the liberty of all Americans was in peril: mandatory vaccination was but the opening wedge in a larger, state-sponsored assault on medical freedom and individual choice in health care. See Harry B. Anderson, *State Medicine: A Menace to Democracy* (New York: Citizen's Medical Reference Bureau, 1920).

13. J. T. Biggs, *Leicester: Sanitation Versus Vaccination. Its Vital Statistics Compared with Those of Other Towns, the Army, Navy, Japan, and England and Wales* (London: National Anti-Vaccination League, 1912), 109–10. For recent histories that put the Leicester protests in a broader European context, see Peter Baldwin, *Contagion and State in Europe, 1830–1930* (Cambridge: Cambridge University Press, 2005), 245–354; and Nadja Durbach, *Bodily Matters: The Anti-Vaccination Movement in England, 1853–1907* (Durham, NC: Duke University Press, 2005), 50, 61–63, 111, and 122.

14. *Mosher's Magazine*, July 1902, 248–49.

15. Ibid.

16. William R. Fisher, "Some Popular Objections to Vaccination," *St. Louis Clinique* 17.1 (1904): 54–55.

17. For the history of antisterilization laws and the American eugenics movement, see Buck v. Bell, 274 U.S. 200 (1927); Paul A. Lombardo, "Three Generations, No Idiots: New Light on *Buck v. Bell*," *New York University Law Review* 60.2 (1985): 30–121; Robert J. Cynkar, *"Buck v. Bell*: 'Felt Necessities' v. Fundamental Values," *Columbia Law Review* 81.7 (1981): 1418–61; Edwin Black, *War Against the Weak: Eugenics and America's Campaign to Create a Master Race* (New York: Dialogue Press, 2012).

18. See, for example, the discussion in chapter 3 of plague vaccination and the Chinese in San Francisco.

19. Although this topic is discussed in detail in chapter 5 on the development of urban water supplies, see, more generally, Jon C. Teaford, *The Unheralded Triumph: City Government in America, 1870–1900* (Baltimore, MD: Johns Hopkins University Press, 1984).

20. See Michael Haines, "The Urban Mortality Transition in the United States, 1800–1940," Historical Paper 134 (Cambridge, MA: National Bureau of Economic Research, 2001). Haines argues that mortality in cities begins to show sustained improvement only after 1870. A shorter version of Haines's working paper was later published under the same title in *Annales de Demographie Historique* 1.10 (2001): 33–64. See also James C. Riley, *Rising Life Expectancy: A Global History* (Cambridge: Cambridge University Press, 2001).

21. These data are from the *Historical Statistics of the United States, Earliest Times to the Present: Millennial Edition*, ed. Susan B. Carter, Scott Sigmund Gartner, Michael R. Haines, Alan L. Olmstead, Richard Sutch, and Gavin Wright, 5 vols. (New York: Cambridge University Press, 2006), table Ab644–655. This database is also published

online (http://hsus.cambridge.org/HSUSWeb/index.do) and was accessed through the University of Pittsburgh's online catalogue.

22. Ibid.

23. Between 1850 and 1950, life expectancy for whites increased by around half a percent per year (.0054778); after 1950, life expectancy increased at a rate of just under a quarter of a percent per year (.0023691). For nonwhites, the contrast is even greater: nonwhite life expectancy increased three times faster from 1850 to1950 than during the subsequent period. Specifically, between 1850 and 1950, life expectancy for nonwhites increased by just under 1 percent per year (.0091572); after 1950 life expectancy for nonwhites grew at an annual rate of .0032396 (data calculated from the *Historical Statistics of the United States*). For a full discussion of how improvements in public water supplies helped narrow the gap between black and white life expectancies, see Werner Troesken, *Water, Race, and Disease* (Cambridge, MA: MIT Press, 2004): esp. 1–8.

24. Probably around half of all deaths in 1850 occurred in children under the age of five; by 1950, well under a quarter of all deaths occurred in children under the age of five. In 1850, between 20 and 30 percent of all newborns perished in the first year of life; one hundred years later, only 2.5 to 3.5 percent of all infants died. See *Historical Statistics of the United States* (Millennial Edition Online).

25. This paragraph draws heavily from the data in Joseph P. Ferrie and Werner Troesken, "Death and the City: Chicago's Mortality Transition, 1850–1925," Working Paper 11427 (Cambridge, MA: National Bureau of Economic Research, 2005). See also Robert William Fogel, *The Escape from Hunger and Premature Death, 1700–2100* (Cambridge: Cambridge University Press, 2004); Herbert S. Klein, *A Population History of the United States* (Cambridge: Cambridge University Press, 2012); and Michael R. Haines and Richard H. Steckel, *A Population History of North America* (Cambridge: Cambridge University Press, 2000).

26. For evidence and a review of the broader literature on the origins of the mortality transition, see Fogel, *Escape from Hunger*.

27. See, for example, Simon Szreter, "Economic Growth, Disruption, Deprivation, Disease, and Death: On the Importance of the Politics of Public Health for Development," *Population and Development Review* 23.4 (1997): 693–728.

28. See Troesken, *Water, Race, and Disease*, and Werner Troesken, "The Limits of Jim Crow: Race and the Provision of Water and Sewerage Services in American Cities, 1880–1925," *Journal of Economic History* 62.3 (2002): 734–72.

29. Chapter 5 presents documentation and evidence for the observations made in this paragraph.

30. On the overall returns to investments in public health, see Edward Meeker, "The Social Rate of Return on Investments in Public Health, 1880–1910," *Journal of Economic History* 34.2 (1974): 392–421.

31. David M. Cutler and Grant Miller, "The Role of Public Health Improvements in Health Advances: The Twentieth Century," *Demography* 42.1 (2005): 1–22.

32. Joseph P. Ferrie and Werner Troesken, "Water and Chicago's Mortality Transition, 1850–1925," *Explorations in Economic History* 45.1 (2008): 553–75.

CHAPTER TWO

1. Tocqueville defines a township as follows: "The township of New England is midway between the district [canton] and the township [commune] of France. It generally numbers two to three thousand inhabitants; it is therefore not so extensive that all

its inhabitants do not have nearly the same interests and, on the other hand, it is sufficiently populated so that one is always sure of finding within it the elements of good administration." Quoted from Alexis de Tocqueville, *Democracy in America*, ed. and trans. Harvey C. Mansfield and Delba Winthrop (Chicago: University of Chicago Press, 2000), 58. Hereafter this work is cited as *DIA*. For my purposes, the technical definition of township given here is secondary to what I call the ideology of the township, a collection of beliefs that I describe below regarding the most effective ways to govern that emerged in townships.

2. It is important to note, however, that there were scientific discoveries before the advent of the germ theory that seemed to justify strong, state-based interventions in the disease environment. Perhaps the best known example of this is John Snow's work on cholera in London, which would eventually help rationalize improvements in the London water system. See, generally, Steven Johnson, *The Ghost Map: The Story of London's Most Terrifying Epidemic—and How It Changed Science, Cities, and the Modern World* (New York: Riverhead Press, 2007).

3. See, generally, Alberto Alesina, Reza Baqir, and William Easterly, "Public Goods and Ethnic Divisions," *Quarterly Journal of Economics* 114.4 (1999): 1243–84; and John O. Ledyard, "Public Goods: A Survey of Experimental Research," in *The Handbook of Experimental Economics*, ed. John H. Kagel and Alvin E. Roth (Princeton, NJ: Princeton University Press, 1995), 111–96.

4. Describing conditions in Pittsburgh, Joel Tarr writes, "While the Board of Health tried to mandate household connections to the sewers, both homeowners and landlords of rental buildings resisted, and retained their old privy vaults and cesspools. Even working-class homeowners often avoided connections with the sewer system because of costs, preferring to invest in other forms of home improvement." See Joel Tarr, *The Search for the Ultimate Sink: Urban Pollution in Historical Perspective* (Akron, OH: University of Akron Press, 1996), 93.

5. See, for example, Health Department v. Rector, 145 N.Y. 32 (1895); and Harrington v. City of Providence, 20 R.I. 233 (1897).

6. Tocqueville, *DIA*, 40. "The sovereignty of the people in the township is therefore not only an old state, but a primitive state," according to Tocqueville, one that served "as the very bosom" of New England's "political life" (*DIA*, 62, 65).

7. William Blackstone, *Commentaries on the Laws of England in Four Books*, with Commentary by Thomas Cooley, 3rd ed., revised (Chicago: Callaghan, 1884), 469–73; repr. by The Lawbook Exchange (Clark, NJ: 2003.)

8. Quotations in this paragraph are from Tocqueville, *DIA*, 40, 60, 62, 54, and 62, respectively.

9. The "institutions of a township," were therefore, "to freedom what primary schools [were] to science" (ibid., 57).

10. Ibid.

11. "The inhabitant of New England is attached to his township because it is strong and independent; he is interested in it because he cooperates in directing it; he loves it because he has nothing to complain of in his lot; he places his ambition and his future in it; he mingles in each of the incidents of township life: in this restricted sphere that is within his reach he tries to govern society; he habituates himself to the forms without which freedom proceeds only through revolutions, permeates himself with their spirit, gets a taste for order, understands the harmony of powers, and *finally assembles clear and practical ideas on the nature of his duties as well as the extent of his rights*" [my emphasis] (ibid.).

12. While state governments legislated on such social matters, it was the township that implemented the policy or project, raised and collected the money to finance it, and appointed the relevant boards and agencies (ibid., 62–63).

13. Some readers have suggested that Tocqueville's statements here are misleading and that it was not until the late nineteenth century that townships began keeping records of births, deaths, and marriages.

14. Tocqueville, *DIA*, 41–42. There is, however, a legal irony to Tocqueville's argument that should be noted. While he describes the township as a primal institution, upon which all political authority was built, townships were themselves creatures of higher state authorities. Like private corporations, they were chartered by state legislatures, and they derived all of their powers from state governments. As a consequence, townships would have had no legal authority were it not for the state legislatures that chartered them. See, generally, John F. Dillon, *Commentaries of the Law of Municipal Corporations*, vols. 1 and 2 (Boston: Little, Brown, 1881).

15. For a full medical history of smallpox and smallpox vaccination, see chapter 4.

16. *Independent Whig*, Newburyport, Massachusetts, 3 May 1810, 1.

17. *Farmer's Cabinet*, Amherst, Massachusetts, 24 January 1824, 3.

18. Through variolation, a practitioner would take the scabs of an individual with a mild case of smallpox and then grind those scabs into a powder. The patient would then inhale the powder and, in most cases, develop a mild, nonlethal case of smallpox. There was, however, a great deal of opposition to this practice because of the possibility of infections spreading to healthy individuals and because the person undergoing the procedure sometimes died as a result. See Elizabeth C. Tandy, "Local Quarantine and Inoculation for Smallpox in the American Colonies, 1620–1775," *American Journal of Public Health* 13.3 (1923): 203–7; Edward Huth, "Quantitative Evidence for Judgements on the Efficacy of Inoculation for the Prevention of Smallpox: England and New England in the 1700s," *Journal of the Royal Society of Medicine* 99 (May 2006): 262–66; and Larry Stewart, "The Edge of Utility: Slaves and Smallpox in the Early Eighteenth Century," *Medical History* 29.1 (1985): 29, 54–70.

19. This article was reprinted in the *Middlesex Gazette*, Middletown, Connecticut, 1 January 1824, 4.

20. *Connecticut Gazette*, New London, Connecticut, 14 November 1810, 2.

21. "In many respects," the reporter claimed,

    we are surpassed by the superior wealth and enterprise of the town of Providence; let us not be far behind them in the work of humanity. They have discharged a solemn duty by enforcing a general vaccination once in two years: are we not equally liable to disease; and can we be insensible to the advantages of a preventive? I may say, can it be a matter of indifference to us whether life is preserved by a prompt attention to the only remedy—or is sacrificed by a criminal neglect? Would it not be prudent for the town of Newport to adopt a system which will ensure safety? Is not a general [vaccination] necessary—is it not expedient? Citizens of Newport answer this question." (*Rhode-Island Republican*, Newport, Rhode Island, 3 April 1822, 2).

22. *City Gazette*, Charleston, South Carolina, 21 February 1924, 2.

23. *Farmer's Cabinet*, Amherst, New Hampshire, 7 February 1824, 3. What is meant by the word *hospital* here is subject to interpretation. In this context it might have meant something much closer to the modern notion of hospice, where an individual is given supportive care until death, but there is no presumption of offering a cure.

24. In rendering this opinion, the court cited a New Jersey law providing that "any town may appoint an agent for vaccination, who may vaccinate all persons at the expense of the town, who have not had the small pox, and shall receive a suitable compensation therefor, to be paid by the selectmen" (Wilkinson v. Albany, 28 N.H. 9 [1853]). Similarly, in 1837 in Perth Amboy, New Jersey, a ship with thirty-six passengers sick with smallpox and typhus docked at the local port. A local physician was hired by a city official to board the ship and care for the passengers. The city, however, refused to compensate the physician when he presented them with his bill; the city claimed that the official who had hired the physician was not authorized to make such an arrangement. The New Jersey Supreme Court flatly rejected the city's claim and ordered that the physician be paid, citing state legislation that "bound" the city to pay for relief in these circumstances. See The Inhabitants of the Township of Perth Amboy Adsm. Charles M. Smith, 19 N.J.L. 52 (1842). For a nearly identical case from Ohio, see Trustees of Cincinnati Township, Hamilton County v. Aaron Ogden, 5 Ohio 23 (1831).

25. All quotations in this paragraph are from the *Baltimore Patriot,* 14 February 1822, 1.

26. The argument follows:

> But does he run risk of committing this crime [of suicide] by neglecting vaccination? Most certainly he does, if it may be incurred by a neglect of those very means of preserving life, which God himself has appointed. We are under no greater obligation to defend ourselves against one of the numerous ministers of human destruction, than another; and it is as much our duty to employ the various methods, by which the evils of life are prevented, as those, by which they are remedied. Conscience will not fail to upbraid that person, who, in the arms of a mortal disease, has this reflection upon his mind that he might have avoided it, by following the kind direction of Providence." (*Salem Gazette,* 27 December 1811, 3)

27. *Baltimore Patriot and Mercantile Advertiser,* 12 May 1824, 2.

28. Dan Hazen v. David Strong, 2 Vt. 427 (1830).

29. Ibid.

30. A reviewer for the University of Chicago Press has suggested that the Hazen case reveals the problem of herd immunity. The claim is that when many people are vaccinated or otherwise immune, the incentive to undergo vaccination is reduced for the simple reason that there is a relatively low risk of a smallpox epidemic. Indeed, this was the same logic employed by Justice Robinson in his decision striking down a mandatory vaccination order issued by a North Dakota school board. I return to this issue in chapter 4.

31. Herbert Hovenkamp, *Enterprise and American Law, 1836–1937* (Cambridge, MA: Harvard University Press, 1991), 171–206.

32. See the discussion of *Potts v. Breen* and *Jacobson* in chapter 4.

33. Tocqueville, *DIA,* 526, 387.

34. A critical reader might argue that the Commerce Clause, the Takings Clause of the Fifth Amendment, and the Contract Clause were not about promoting commerce but about protecting individual rights. It is true that all of these clauses and provisions were aimed, at least in part, at promoting individual rights. That said, even if promoting individual rights were their primary aim, they ultimately had a significant effect on commerce. Moreover, if one looks at the *Federalist Papers,* it is hard not to believe that protecting commerce was a central aim of these provisions. See *Federalist Papers* 42, where Madison discusses the importance of the Commerce Clause in

protecting interstate commerce (Alexander Hamilton, John Jay, and James Madison, *The Federalist Papers: The Gideon Edition*, ed. George Carey and James McClellan [Indianapolis, IN: Liberty Fund, 2012]; hereafter cited as *FP* (with page references to the Liberty Fund edition).

35. Hamilton, Jay, and Madison, *FP*, 55.
36. Ibid., 164.
37. Tocqueville, *DIA*, 390.
38. In *Federalist Papers* 12, Hamilton wrote, "It is, therefore, evident, that one national government would be able, at much less expense, to extend the duties on imports, beyond comparison further, than would be practicable to the states separately, or to any partial confederacies" (*FP*, 58–59).
39. Tocqueville, *DIA*, 369.
40. See the discussion of the *Slaughterhouse Cases* and sanitation in New Orleans in chapter 6.
41. Critical readers might argue that Reconstruction was a military measure imposed on conquered territories, not an expansion of federal power. To the extent that this military measure was, in fact, exercised by the federal government, the argument strikes me as an exercise in semantics.
42. I emphasize the word *gradually* in the last sentence. It took decades for complete disenfranchisement to occur. For a detailed analysis of the origins and consequences of black disenfranchisement, see Daniel B. Jones, Werner Troesken, and Randall P. Walsh, "A Poll Tax by Any Other Name: The Political Economy of Disenfranchisement," Working Paper 18612 (Cambridge, MA: National Bureau of Economic Research, 2012).
43. Although it is overstating to suggest that the Fourteenth Amendment revolutionized the Constitution, it was a fundamentally important addition that helped to define more clearly the rights of the individual in relation to the state. See, generally, Michael P. Zuckert, "Completing the Constitution: The Fourteenth Amendment and Constitutional Rights," *Publius* 22.2 (1992): 69–91; Akhil Reed Amar, "The Bill of Rights and the Fourteenth Amendment," *Yale Law Journal* 101.6 (1992): 1193–1284; and Herbert Hovenkamp, "The Political Economy of Substantive Due Process," *Stanford Law Review* 40.2 (1988): 379–447.
44. See, Joshua Rosenbloom, "One Market or Many? Labor Market Integration in the Late-Nineteenth Century United States," *Journal of Economic History* 50.1 (1990): 85–107; David W. Galenson, "Economic Opportunity on the Urban Frontier: Nativity, Work, and Wealth in Early Chicago," *Journal of Economic History* 51.3 (1991): 581–603; Jeremy Atack, Fred Bateman, and Robert A. Margo, "Skill Intensity and Rising Wage Dispersion in Nineteenth-Century American Manufacturing," *Journal of Economic History* 64.1 (2004): 172–92.
45. Increases like these were by no means limited to New York, or even other large American cities. Throughout the Western world, disease and death rates in cities worsened with the onset of industrialization. For example, in Glasgow, Scotland, the death rate rose from twenty-five deaths per thousand persons in 1820 to forty in 1840, an increase of 60 percent. See Werner Troesken, *The Great Lead Pipe Disaster* (Cambridge, MA: MIT Press, 2006), 156–59; Simon Szreter, "Economic Growth, Disruption, Deprivation, Disease, and Death: On the Importance of the Politics of Public Health for Development," *Population and Development Review* 23 (1997): 693–728. On the question of worsening disease environments during the early stages of industrialization in both the United States and Europe, see, generally, John Komlos,

"Shrinking in a Growing Economy? The Mystery of Physical Stature during the Industrial Revolution," *Journal of Economic History* 58.3 (1998): 779–802.

46. To the extent that immigration into cities was associated with reducing the average age of the population, crude mortality rates might understate the severity of the situation.

47. Contrary to historical accounts that portray the railroad as transforming the American landscape wholesale, the available evidence suggests that the rise of the railroads did little to stifle the agglomeration of populations in and around major waterways, and it is entirely possible that the emergence and extension of railroads made water transportation and port cities more attractive, not less. This is because of what economists call network externalities, whereby railroads and water transportation were complements in the production process rather than substitutes. Put more simply, for a given water port to be useful to inland locations, there has to be some easy way to transport goods between the port city and the interior. Absent economical linkages, farmers and manufactures at those interior locations will simply use another port. Historically, port cities, such as Mobile, Alabama, Galveston, Texas, and Pensacola, Florida, are said to have benefited significantly because of the construction of railroad lines linking those cities to other population centers. By the same token, Charleston, South Carolina, which during the colonial period was the fourth largest city in the United States, is often said to have stagnated over the course of the nineteenth century in part because of the difficulty of linking its port to inland population centers. See Patricia Beeson, David DeJong, and Werner Troesken, "Population Growth in U.S. Counties, 1840–1990," *Regional Science and Urban Economics* 31.6 (2001): 669–99; Jordan Rappaport and Jeffrey D. Sachs, "The United States as a Coastal Nation," *Journal of Economic Growth* 8.1 (2003): 5–46; Carl Bridenbaugh, *Cities in the Wilderness: The First Century of Urban Life in America, 1625–1742* (New York: Alfred Knopf, 1955); Carl Bridenbaugh, *Cities in Revolt: Urban Life in America, 1743–1776* (New York: Alfred Knopf, 1955); Robert Greenhalgh Albion, *The Rise of New York Port* (New York: Charles Scribner & Sons, 1939); and Harriet E. Amos, *Cotton City: Urban Development in Antebellum Mobile* (Tuscaloosa: University of Alabama Press, 1985).

48. Consider, for example, the experience of Pittsburgh, Pennsylvania, where the confluence of three rivers (the Ohio, Allegheny, and Monongahela) facilitated the rise of the steel industry by lowering the costs of transporting coal and iron ore into the city, and then making it easy to ship the finished steel out of the city on barges. On the significance of water and water transport in American economic development, see Robert W. Fogel, *Railroads and American Economic Growth: Essays in Econometric History* (Baltimore, MD: Johns Hopkins University Press, 1964); and Rappaport and Sachs, "The United States as a Coastal Nation," (2003), 5–46.

49. See Margaret Humphreys, *Yellow Fever and the South* (Newark, NJ: Rutgers University Press, 1992), 81,102; John M. Keating, *A History of the Yellow Fever: The Yellow Fever Epidemic of 1878, in Memphis, Tennessee* (Memphis: Printed for the Howard Association, 1879). See also *Report of the Portsmouth Relief Association to the Contributors of the Fund for the Relief of Portsmouth, Virginia during the Prevalence of the Yellow Fever in That Town in 1855* (Richmond, VA: H. K. Ellyson's Steam Power Presses, 1856).

50. See Jonathan B. Pritchett and Insan Tunali, "Strangers Disease: Determinants of Yellow Fever Mortality during the Yellow Fever Epidemic of 1853," *Explorations in Economic History* 32 (October 1995): 517–39.

51. The experience of the Chinese in San Francisco is described in chapter 3.

52. Walter Wyman, "Sanitation and Progress," *Journal of the American Medical Association* 36.10 (1901): 609–15, esp. 613.

53. See, for example, George C. Whipple, *Typhoid Fever: Its Causation, Transmission, and Prevention* (New York: John Wiley & Sons, 1908), 273–94.

54. See Edward Meeker, "The Social Rate of Return on Investment in Public Health, 1880–1910," *Journal of Economic History* 30.3 (1974): 392–421.

55. John M. Toner, "Boards of Health in the United States," *Public Health Reports and Papers Presented at the Meetings of the American Public Health Association in the Year 1873* (New York: Hurd and Houghton, 1875), 499–521; and John Duffy, *The Sanitarians: A History of American Public Health* (Champaign: University of Illinois Press, 1992), esp. 138–56.

56. Kenneth Kiple, ed., *Cambridge World History of Disease* (Cambridge: Cambridge University Press, 1999), 1059–68.

57. Frederick I. Knight, "Shall Anything Be Done to Prevent the Spread of Tuberculosis?" *Transactions of the American Climatological Association* 10 (1893): 285–97.

58. City of Somerville v. Commonwealth, 225 Mass. 589 (1917).

59. M. J. Rosenau, *The Milk Question* (Boston: Houghton Mifflin, 1912), 221. See also Alan L. Olmstead and Paul W. Rhode, "An Impossible Undertaking: The Eradication of Bovine Tuberculosis in the United States," *Journal of Economic History* 64.3 (2004): 1–37.

60. Rosenau, *The Milk Question*, 113–29, and 221.

61. See Michael R. Haines, "The Urban Mortality Transition in the United States, 1800–1940," Historical Paper 134 (Cambridge, MA: National Bureau of Economic Research, 2001); and Joseph P. Ferrie and Werner Troesken, "Death and the City: Chicago's Mortality Transition, 1850–1925," Working Paper 11427 (Cambridge, MA: National Bureau of Economic Research, 2005); American Public Health Association, *A Half Century of Public Health* (New York: American Public Health Association, 1921), 151.

62. On the summer peak in infant mortality and its strong correlation with bacteria counts in milk, see, generally, Rosenau, *The Milk Question*, 214–20.

63. In New York, for example, the ratio of summer mortality to nonsummer mortality for children under the age of five fell from around 1.4 in 1890 to 1 by 1914, a reduction of nearly 40 percent. See Lina Gutherz Straus, *Disease in Milk: The Remedy Pasteurization: The Life Work of Nathan Straus*, 2nd ed. (New York: E. P. Dutton, 1917), 90–91.

64. Edwin O. Jordan, "The Case for Pasteurization," *Transactions of the Fifteenth International Congress on Hygiene and Demography* 4 (September 1912), 627–39; Edwin O. Jordan, "The Protection of Milk Supplies by Pasteurization," *Creamery and Milk Plant Monthly* 1.2 (1922): 19–23. Jordan gives data for Boston and Chicago, consistent with the hypothesis that expansions in the practice of pasteurization led to reductions in typhoid rates. Jordan goes on to describe how in Washington, D.C., the lowest typhoid rates in the city were found along the route of the city's only milk dealer to pasteurize his milk.

65. See the unsigned article, "The Antitoxin Treatment of Diphtheria: The Discussion on Diphtheria Antitoxin at the German Medical Congress," *British Medical Journal*, 27 April 1895, 935–36; Robert Dawson, "The Use of Antitoxin in the Treatment and Prevention of Diphtheria," *British Medical Journal*, 9 May 1903, 1078–79; unsigned article, "Diphtheria Antitoxin," *Medical News*, 14 April 1900, 590–92; R. W. Marsden, "Diphtheria and Its Treatment by Antitoxin," *British Medical Journal*, 8 September

1900, 658–62; and J. W. Washbourne, E. W. Goodall, and A. H. Card, "A Series of 80 Cases Treated with Diphtheria Antitoxin," *British Medical Journal*, 22 December 1894, 1417–19.

66. See, again, Dawson, "Use of Antitoxin," and Marsden, "Diphtheria."

67. Again, this was a paradigmatic case, where the antitoxin worked very well to reverse the course of the fever; as such, it is only meant to show what the antitoxin could do when it worked as it was supposed to. There were certainly cases where the antitoxin failed to achieve this end, and the patient died. As explained above, the antitoxin did not reduce the case fatality rate from the disease to zero. On the contrary, case fatality rates remained as high as 15 to 20 percent.

68. American Public Health Association, *A Half Century of Public Health*, 153.

69. As the American Public Health Association explained in its jubilee celebration, *A Half Century of Public Health*, "Probably the chief cause of the phenomenal decline in the death rate from diphtheria has not been due to control of the spread of the disease, but to the use of antitoxin. That this valuable remedy has been so easily accessible has been due to the action of city and state officials" (153).

70. For patterns in other places, see Kiple, ed., *Cambridge World History of Disease*, 683; A. Jefferis Turner, "The Diphtheria Mortality of the Three Principal Australian Colonies for the Past Fifteen Years," *British Medical Journal*, 18 November 1899, 1409–12.

71. For a historical overview of these discoveries, see Martin V. Melosi, *The Sanitary City: Urban Infrastructure in America from Colonial Times to the Present* (Baltimore, MD: Johns Hopkins University Press, 2000), esp. 58–117. For shorter treatments, see Werner Troesken, *Water, Race, and Disease* (Cambridge: MIT Press, 2004), 17–25; George C. Whipple, *Typhoid Fever*, ix–xii (introductory essay by William Sedgwick); *Cambridge World History of Disease*, 642–49, 1071–77.

72. H. B. Anderson, *State Medicine: A Menace to Democracy* (New York: Citizens Medical Reference Bureau, 1920). See, for example, William M. Golden, "The Present Status of the Practical Therapeutic Value of Diphtheria Antitoxin," *Practical Medicine* 7.1 (1896): 241–44. For more details on the life and work of Harry Bernhart (H. B.) Anderson, see James Colgrave, *State of Immunity: The Politics of Vaccination in Twentieth Century America* (Berkeley and Los Angeles: University of California Press, 2006), 54–58.

73. Anderson, *State Medicine*.

74. See, for example, Charles M. Higgins, *Horrors of Vaccination Exposed and Illustrated* (New York: self-published, 1920), 41–55.

75. See John Duffy, *The Sanitarians: A History of American Public Health* (Champaign: University of Illinois Press, 1992), 196–97. Along the same lines, as one Canadian official explained in relation to measures requiring that physicians notify local authorities of all cases of tuberculosis they diagnosed and treated, "People will strenuously object as much to being pointed at as a consumptive, by the authorities, as to being called a leper, and the opposition to such legislation will be found to be vigorous. Up to the present the health authorities all over the world have dealt only with acute infections, except in the case of leprosy. Tuberculosis would naturally be classed as practically the same thing, and the people would oppose it to the full extent of their power" (142); quoted in John M. O'Donnell, "Tuberculosis: Its Restriction and Prevention," *Public Health Papers & Reports* 20.2 (1894), 137–43.

76. More recent evidence, however, suggests they were highly effective in curtailing the spread of tuberculosis. See Alex Hollingsworth, "The Impact of Sanitaria on Pulmo-

nary Tuberculosis Mortality: Evidence from North Carolina, 1932–1940," unpublished paper (University of Arizona, 16 March 2013).

77. Anderson, *State Medicine*, 101–6.

78. See, generally, Nancy Tomes, *The Gospel of Germs: Men, Women, and the Microbe in American Life* (Cambridge, MA: Harvard University Press, 1999); and Alan Kraut, *Silent Travelers: Germs, Genes, and the Immigrant Menace* (New York: Basic Books, 1994).

CHAPTER THREE

1. For a review of these epidemics, as well as a summary of the relevant data sources, see Patricia E. Beeson and Werner Troesken, "When Bioterrorism Was No Big Deal," Working Paper 12636 (Cambridge, MA: National Bureau of Economic Research, , 2006).

2. See Alexander Hamilton, John Jay, and James Madison, *The Federalist Papers: The Gideon Edition*, ed. George Carey and James McClellan [Indianapolis, IN: Liberty Fund, 2012], 11 and 48–51; hereafter cited as *FP* (with page references to the Liberty Fund edition).

3. In Tocqueville's words, "The authority of a king is purely physical, and it controls the actions of the subject without subduing his private will; but the majority possesses a power which is physical and moral at the same time; it acts upon the will as well as upon the actions of men, and it represses not only all contest, but all controversy" (*DIA*, 267).

4. See David Bernstein, *Only One Place of Redress: African Americans, Labor Regulations, and the Courts from Reconstruction to the New Deal* (Durham, NC: Duke University Press, 2001).

5. This logic is not especially new and can be found in *Federalist Papers*, esp. 78 and 79. See also Ivan C. Rand, "The Role of the Independent Judiciary in Preserving Freedom," *University of Toronto Law Journal* 9.1 (1951): 1–14.

6. Hamilton, Jay, and Madison, *FP*, 405.

7. Hamilton, Jay, and Madison, *FP*, 406. That the Founders valued judicial independence and believed it essential to the functioning of any free society is also evident in the Declaration of Independence. In one early passage, the Revolutionaries complain that King George "has made judges dependent on his Will alone, for the tenure of their offices, and the amount and payment of their salaries." This passage refers to a series of events in Massachusetts that helped inspire the War of Independence. See Barbara Aronstein Black, "Massachusetts and the Judges: Judicial Independence in Perspective," *Law and History Review* 3.1 (1985): 101–62.

8. See Werner Troesken, *Why Regulate Utilities? The New Institutional Economics and the Chicago Gas Industry, 1850–1924* (Ann Arbor: University of Michigan Press, 1996); and Werner Troesken, "The Sources of Public Ownership: Historical Evidence from the Gas Industry," *Journal of Law, Economics, and Organization* 13.1 (1997): 1–27.

9. See Stefan Voigt and Jerg Gutmann, "Turning Cheap Talk Into Economic Growth: On the Relationship between Property Rights and Judicial Independence," *Journal of Comparative Economics* 41.1 (2013): 66–73; Lars P. Feld and Stefan Voigt, "Economic Growth and Judicial Independence: Cross-Country Evidence Using a New Set of Indicators," *European Journal of Political Economy* 19.3 (2003): 497–527; and Paul G. Mahoney and Daniel Klerman, "The Value of Judicial Independence: Evidence from Eighteenth-Century England," *American Law and Economics Review* 7.1 (2005): 1–27.

10. Douglass C. North and Barry Weingast, "Constitutions and Commitment: The Evolution of Institutions Governing Public Choice in Seventeenth Century England," *Journal of Economic History* 49.4 (1989): 803–32.

11. United States Bureau of the Census, *Census Reports*, vol. 1, *Population, Part I* (Washington, DC: United States Census Office, 1901), cxix–cxxii.

12. See Thomas W. Joo, "Yick Wo Revisited: Nonblack Nonwhites and Fourteenth Amendment History," *University of Illinois Law Review* 2008 (2008): 1427–475; and David Bernstein, "Revisiting *Yick Wo v. Hopkins*," *University of Illinois Law Review* 2008 (2008): 1393–1426.

13. Wong Wai v. Williamson et al., 103 F. 1 (1900).

14. See chapter 2 for a discussion of the origins and implications of the Fourteenth Amendment and the Equal Protection Clause. See also *Wong Wai*, 103 F. 1.

15. *Wong Wai*, 103 F. 1 at 9.

16. Ibid.

17. The quotations and information in this paragraph are taken from a letter the San Francisco Board of Health wrote to the United States Treasury Department requesting a federal quarantine station at the city's port. The letter was dated July 25, 1882, and was signed by James Simpson, Henry Gibbons, and W. Andrew Douglas, all members of the San Francisco Board of Health. The letter was reprinted in the *Annual Report of the National Board of Health*, S. Exec. Doc. No. 5, 47th Cong., 2nd Sess., at 577–78 (1882) (Washington: Government Printing Office, 1883). More generally, see Alan Kraut, *Silent Travelers: Germs, Genes, and the Immigrant Menace* (New York: Basic Books, 1994).

18. Ho Ah Kow v. Nunan, 12 F. Cas. 252 (1879).

19. Yick Wo v. Hopkins, 118 U.S. 356 (1886). See, more generally, David Bernstein, "Revisiting *Yick Wo v. Hopkins*," *University of Illinois Law Review* 8 (2005): 1393–1404.

20. Kirk v. Board of Health, 83 S.C. 372 (1909).

21. See Judith Walzer Leavitt, "'Typhoid Mary' Strikes Back: Bacteriological Theory and Practice in Early Twentieth-Century Public Health," *Isis* 83.4 (1992): 608–29; and Judith Walzer Leavitt, *Typhoid Mary: Captive to the Public's Health* (Boston: Beacon Press, 1996).

22. See Michael Willrich, *Pox: An American History* (New York: Penguin Books, 2011), 50–53, 58, 90–91, and 103–09.

23. Barry R. Weingast, "The Economic Role of Political Institutions: Market-Preserving Federalism and Economic Development," *Journal of Law, Economics, and Organization* 11.1 (1995): 1–31; and (addressing critiques of Weingast) Daniel L. Rubinfeld, "On Federalism and Economic Development," *Virginia Law Review* 83.7 (1997): 1581–92.

24. Subsequent chapters document the first of these effects; this chapter is occupied mainly with documenting the second.

25. Federal Constitution, Art. 1, Sec. 8, Clause 3.

26. The definition of *commerce* has evolved over time and left many strict constructionists critical of modern-day jurisprudence, which interprets commerce far more broadly than the strict constructionists believe the Founders intended. By interpreting the word *commerce* more broadly than it had been historically, the claim is that the federal government has usurped the power of the states. See Randy Barnett, *Restoring the Lost Constitution: The Presumption of Liberty* (Princeton, NJ: Princeton University Press, 2004); and Randy Barnett, "The Original Meaning of the Commerce Clause," *University of Chicago Law Review* 68.1 (2001): 101–47. While the definition of commerce has evolved over time, this book focuses mainly on the nineteenth century, when the courts tended to adopt a more stable definition that emphasized a federalist approach to governance. The largest expansion in what constituted commerce and facilitated large expansions in federal power came during the New Deal, well after

the time of most of the material considered here. See Cass Sunstein, "Constitutionalism after the New Deal," *Harvard Law Review* 101.2 (1987): 421–501.

27. All quotations in this paragraph are taken from Stockton v. Baltimore & New York Railroad Co., 32 F. 9 (1887), 17.

28. See, generally, Richard C. Schragger, "Cities, Economic Development, and the Free Trade Constitution," *Virginia Law Review* 94.5 (2008): 1091–1164.

29. Borders can have significant effects on trade flows, independent of variations in tariffs, but many of these effects appear to stem from ethnicity. See Jenny C. Aker, Michael W. Klein, Stephen A. O'Connell, and Muzhe Yang, "Borders, Ethnicity, and Trade," Working Paper 15960 (Cambridge, MA: National Bureau of Economic Research, 2010).

30. Hamilton, Jay, and Madison, *FP*, 218–19.

31. Hamilton, Jay, and Madison, *FP*, 218–19. "We may be assured by past experience," Madison wrote, "that such a practice would be introduced by future contrivances: and both by that and a common knowledge of human affairs, that it would nourish unceasing animosities, and not improbably terminate in serious interruptions of the public tranquility" (218–19).

32. Ibid., 219. As he does throughout *The Federalist*, Madison does not limit himself to American history to highlight the wisdom of the new republic's Constitution and its commitment to free trade among the states; he also cites the experiences of continental Europe: "The necessity of a superintending authority over the reciprocal trade of confederated states, has been illustrated by other examples as our own." For example, of Switzerland, he writes, "Each canton is obliged to allow to merchandises, a passage through its jurisdiction into other cantons without an augmentation of the tolls." Similarly, among the states of the German empire, it was the law "that the princes and states shall not lay tolls or customs on bridges, rivers, or passages, without consent of the emperor and diets." That the various states did not always respect the law only served to highlight Madison's larger point. Madison also cites the "restraints imposed by the union of the Netherlands," where member states could not "establish imposts disadvantageous to their neighbors, without the general permission." (All quotations here are from *FP*, 219).

33. Charles M. Tiebout, "A Pure Theory of Local Expenditures," *Journal of Political Economy* 64.5 (1956): 416–24.

34. Jan K. Brueckner, "Fiscal Federalism and Economic Growth," *Journal of Public Economics* 90.10–11 (2006): 2107–20.

35. Weingast, "The Economic Role of Political Institutions," 1–31.

36. For a review and critique of the argument that corruption slowed municipal growth, see Rebecca Menes, "Graft and Growth in American Cities, 1880–1930," in *Corruption and Reform: Lessons from America's Economic History*, ed. Edward L. Glaeser and Claudia Goldin (Chicago: University of Chicago Press, 2006), 63–94. Menes argues that corruption might have helped foster growth by promoting large public works projects that were rife with patronage employment. For contrary evidence, see James E. Rauch, "Bureaucracy, Infrastructure, and Economic Growth: Evidence from U.S. Cities During the Progressive Era," *American Economic Review* 85.4 (1996): 968–80. Rauch presents statistical evidence that municipal reforms and institutional innovations designed to combat corruption were associated with increased investments in public infrastructure.

37. See Louis Cain and Elyce Rotella, "Epidemics, Demonstration Effects, and Investments in Sanitation Capital by U.S. Cities in the Early Twentieth Century," in *Quantitative Economic History*, ed. Joshua Rosenbloom (New York: Routledge, 2008), 34–58.

38. Gibbons v. Ogden, 22 U.S. 1 (1824).
39. See Thomas Gibbons v. Aaron Ogden, 17 Johns. 488 (1820).
40. *Gibbons*, 22 U.S. 1 at 4.
41. Ibid. at 88–89. Marshall wrote, "The inconveniences resulting from these powers of the States, gave rise to the new constitution. These inconveniences consisted principally in the impositions and taxes levied on property imported and exported by one State through another. There was no inconvenience as to the right of passing from State to State, as that was secured by the articles of confederation. The constitution applied the remedy to these evils in two ways: (1) By express prohibitions on the States, in those particulars in which the evils had been most sensibly felt, preventing them from levying any impost or duty of tonnage, without the consent of Congress. (2) By vesting Congress with a general power to regulate commerce with foreign nations and among the States."
42. Wabash, St. Louis, and Pacific Railway Company v. Illinois, 118 U.S. 447 (1886).
43. See, for example, In re Watson, 15 F. 511 (1882); McLaughlin v. City of South Bend, 126 Ind. 471 (1891); Welton v. State of Missouri, 91 U.S. 275 (1876); and McCall v. California, 136 U.S. 104 (1890).
44. See, for example, Swift v. Sutphin, 39 F. 630 (1889); and Ex parte Kieffer, 40 F. 399 (1889).
45. Scott v. Donald, 165 U.S. 58 (1897).
46. See Smith v. Turner, 48 U.S. 283 (1849); *McCall*; Norfolk and Western Railroad Company v. Pennsylvania, 136 U.S. 114 (1890); Guy v. Baltimore, 100 U.S. 434 (1880); and Brennan v. Titusville, 153 U.S. 289 (1894).
47. See Gary D. Libecap, "The Rise of the Chicago Packers and the Origins of Meat Inspection and Antitrust," *Economic Inquiry* 30.2 (1992): 242–62.
48. City of St. Louis v. McCoy, 18 Mo. 238 (1853).
49. Ibid.
50. On the significance of the distinction between incidental and purposive effects, see a nearly identical case decided by the United States Supreme Court, Compagnie Francaise de Navigation a Vapeur v. Louisiana State Board of Health, 186 U.S. 380 (1902).
51. Morgan's Steamship Company v. Louisiana Board of Health, 118 U.S. 455 (1886), 459.
52. Ibid. The Court wrote, "Although situated over a hundred miles from the Gulf of Mexico, it is the largest city which partakes of its commerce, and more vessels of every character come to and depart from it than any connected with that commerce. Partaking, as it does, of the liability to diseases of warm climates, and in the same danger as all other seaports of cholera and other contagious and infectious disorders, these are sources of anxiety to its inhabitants, and to all the interior population of the country who may be affected by their spread among them."
53. Ibid. at 459–60: "Whatever may be the truth with regard to the contagious character of yellow fever and cholera, there can be no doubt of the general belief, and very little of the fact, that all the invasions of these epidemics in the great valley of the Mississippi River and its tributaries in times past have been supposed to have spread from New Orleans, and to have been carried by steamboats and other vessels engaged in commerce with that city. And the origin of these diseases is almost invariably attributed to vessels ascending the Mississippi River from the West Indies and South America, where yellow fever is epidemic almost every year, and from European countries whence our invasions of cholera uniformly come."
54. Ibid.

55. Ibid., at 461–62: "The State now says you must submit to this examination. If you appear free of [objectionable disease], you are relieved . . . of all responsibility on that subject. If you are in a condition dangerous to the public health, you are quarantined and relieved in this manner. For this examination and fumigation you must pay. The danger comes from you, and though it may turn out that in your case there is no danger, . . . you belong to a class from which all this kind of injury comes, [and] you must pay for the examination which distinguishes you from others of that class. It seems to us that this is . . . clearly a fair charge against the vessel."

   That the requisite fees rose with the tonnage of the ship only reflected the fact that the costs (and benefits) of examining and fumigating the vessel rose with its size: "In the present case we are of [the] opinion that the fee complained of is not a tonnage tax . . . within the true meaning of that word . . . but is [instead] compensation for a service rendered." This idea—that the fee was not a tax but compensation for a service provided—was critical, because in a series of earlier cases, the Supreme Court had struck down tonnage taxes. A federal law passed in 1799 (as well as Article 1, Section 10, Clause 3, of the Federal Constitution) expressly forbade states from enacting tonnage taxes without the consent of Congress. See Peete v. Morgan, 86 U.S. 581 (1873); State Tonnage Tax Cases, 79 U.S. 204 (1871); and Blewett Harrison Lee, "Limitations Imposed by the Federal Constitution on the Right of the States to Enact Quarantine Laws," *Harvard Law Review* 2.7 (1889): 293–315.

56. "That the vessel itself has the primary and deepest interest in this examination it is easy to see. It is obviously to her interest, in the pursuit of her business, that she enter the city and depart from it free from the suspicion which, at certain times, attaches to all vessels coming from the Gulf. This she obtains by the examination and can obtain in no other way" *Morgan's Steamship Company*, 118 U.S. 455 at 461.

57. Ibid.: "If the law did not make this provision for ascertaining her freedom from infection, it would be compelled to enact more stringent and more expensive penalties against the vessel herself, when it was found that she had come to the city from an infected port or had brought contagious persons or contagious matter with her; and throwing the responsibility for this on the vessel, the heaviest punishment would be necessary by fine and imprisonment for any neglect of the duty thus imposed."

58. Ibid. at 465.

59. Ibid.: "[The law] arrests a vessel on a voyage which may have been a long one. It may affect commerce among the States when the vessel is coming from some other State of the Union than Louisiana, and it may affect commerce with foreign nations, when the vessel [quarantined] comes from a foreign port. This interruption of the voyage may be for days or for weeks. It extends to the vessel, the cargo, the officers and seamen, and the passengers. In so far as it provides a rule by which this power is exercised, it cannot be denied that it regulates commerce."

60. Ibid. at 464.

61. Ibid. at 465.

62. Ibid. According to the Court, two federal laws were particularly relevant. The first of these laws was enacted in 1799. This measure authorized the Treasury Department to deal with national public health matters, subject to the express conditions that the officers of the Treasury would recognize and respect the quarantine laws of the various states and that the Treasury Department would make its policies conform with state-level policies. The second law, passed in 1878, empowered the Surgeon-General of the Marine Service to assist in "preventing the importation of disease" into the United

States. Much like the 1799 legislation, this expansion in federal power was subject to the proviso that "there shall be no interference in any manner with any quarantine laws or regulations as they now exist or may hereafter be adopted under State laws."

63. Ibid., at 465.

64. Ibid., at 466: "For the period of nearly a century since the government was organized Congress has passed no quarantine law, nor any other law to protect the inhabitants of the United States against the invasion of contagious and infectious diseases from abroad, and yet during the early part of the present century, for many years the cities of the Atlantic coast, from Boston and New York to Charleston, were devastated by the yellow fever. In later times, the cholera has made similar invasions, and the yellow fever has been unchecked in its fearful course in the Southern cities, New Orleans especially, for several generations. During all this time the Congress of the United States never attempted to exercise this or any other power to protect the people from the ravages of these dreadful diseases."

65. Ibid.: "No doubt [Congress] believed that the power belonged to the States. Or if it ever occurred to any of its members that Congress might do something in that way, they probably believed that what ought to be done could be better and more wisely done by the authorities of the States who were familiar with the matter."

66. Ibid., at 465. "The matter is one in which the rules that should govern it may in many respects be different in different localities, and for that be better understood and more wisely established by the local authorities. The practice which should control a quarantine state on the Mississippi River . . . may be widely and wisely different from that which best for the harbor of New York."

67. See Missouri v. Illinois and the Sanitary District of Chicago, 1906 U.S. Lexis 1494 (Feb. 1904). There is evidence to suggest that St. Louis was mistaken in its claim that Chicago sewage was polluting its water supply. According Louis Cain, one study found that water from the Chicago River and polluted with Chicago sewage was clean by the time it reached Pekin and Peoria, Illinois, only to become polluted by those cities. Another expert witness found that water from the Illinois River (which the Chicago River eventually flowed into) was purer than water from the Mississippi River. See Louis P. Cain, *Sanitation Strategy for a Lakefront Metropolis: The Case of Chicago* (DeKalb: Northern Illinois University Press, 1978), 81.

68. "The instability, injustice, and confusion, introduced into the public councils, have, in truth, been the mortal diseases under which popular governments every where perished; as they continue to be the favorite and fruitful topics from which the adversaries to liberty derive their most specious declamations" (Hamilton, Jay, and Madison, *FP*, 42–43).

69. As suggested by the earlier discussion of the tyranny of the majority, Madison did not believe that democracy was itself a solution to the problem of faction. On the contrary, he believed that majoritarian factions and unfettered populism posed a great threat to individual liberty and the long-term viability of any state. "A pure democracy," Madison wrote, "can admit of no cure for the mischiefs of faction. A common passion or interest will, in almost every case, be felt by majority of the whole; a communication and concert, results from the form of government itself; and there is nothing to check the inducements to sacrifice the weaker party, or an obnoxious individual" (ibid.).

70. Ibid., 43–44.

71. The literature explaining and documenting the costs of rent-seeking and political corruption to human societies is large; some important contributions include Kevin M.

Murphy, Andrei Shleifer, and Robert W. Vishny, "Why Is Rent-Seeking So Costly to Growth?" *American Economic Review* 83.2 (1993): 409–14; Douglass C. North, *Structure and Change in Economic History* (New York: W. W. Norton, 1985); Gordon Tullock, "The Welfare Costs of Tariffs, Monopolies, and Theft," *Western Economic Journal* 5 (June 1967): 224–32; Anne Krueger, "The Political Economy of the Rent-Seeking Society," *American Economic Review* 74.3 (1974): 291–303; and Robert Eklund and Robert Tollison, *Mercantilism as a Rent-Seeking Society: Economic Regulation in Historical Perspective* (College Station: Texas A&M University Press, 1982).

72. That said, the discussion that follows suggests that other institutional and ideological factors could sometimes come into conflict with Commerce Clause jurisprudence and allow factions to form, especially around policies related to public health.

73. Minnesota v. Barber, 136 U.S. 313 (1890). See also Alan Olmstead and Paul Rhode, "An Impossible Undertaking: The Eradication of Bovine Tuberculosis in the United States," *Journal of Economic History* 64.3 (2004): 1–37.

74. *Minnesota*, 136 U.S. 313.

75. Ibid. at 326.

76. Whether the Court was correct in its assumption that meat slaughtered out-of-state was no less safe than meat slaughtered in-state is the subject of much scholarly debate. See, generally, Olmstead and Rhode, "An Impossible Undertaking"; and Libecap, "The Rise of the Chicago Packers."

77. As the Court wrote there,

> Undoubtedly, a State may establish regulations for the protection of its people against the sale of unwholesome meats, . . . [but] it may not, under the guise of exerting its policy powers, or of enacting inspection laws, make discriminations against the products and industries of some of the States in favor of the products and industries of its own or of other States. The owner of the meats here in question, although they were from animals slaughtered in Illinois [home to the Chicago stockyards and the Meat-packing Trust], had the right, under the Constitution, to compete in the markets of Virginia upon terms of equality with the owners of like meats, from animals slaughtered in Virginia or elsewhere. (Brimmer v. Rebman, 138 U.S. 78 (1891), 80).

78. Louisiana v. Texas, 176 U.S. 1 (1900), 2.

79. Ibid.

80. Ibid. at 20: "In as much as the vindication of the freedom of interstate commerce is not committed to the State of Louisiana, and that State is not engaged in such commerce, the cause of action must be regarded not as involving any infringement of the powers of the State of Louisiana, or any special injury to her property, but as asserting that the State is entitled to seek relief in this way because the matters complained of affect her citizens at large. Nevertheless, if the case stated is not on presenting a controversy between these States, the exercise of original jurisdiction by the court as against the State of Texas cannot be maintained."

81. Ibid., at 14–15. Specifically, the relevant section of the Constitution reads,

> The judicial power shall extend to all cases, in law and equity, arising under this Constitution, the laws of the United States, and treaties made, or which shall be made, under their authority; to all cases affecting ambassadors, other public ministers and consuls; to all cases of admiralty and maritime jurisdiction; to controversies to which the United States shall be a party; to controversies between two or more States; between a State and citizens of another State; between citizens of different States, between citizens of the same State

claiming lands under grants of different States, and between a State, or the citizens thereof, and foreign States, citizens or subjects. In all cases affecting ambassadors, other public ministers and consuls, and those in which a State shall be party, the Supreme Court shall have original jurisdiction. In all the other cases before mentioned, the Supreme Court shall have appellate jurisdiction, both as to law and fact, with such exceptions, and under such regulations as the Congress make.

Of this portion of the Constitution, Fuller went on to write,

The reference we have made to the derivation of the words "controversies between two or more States" manifestly indicates that the framers of the Constitution intended that they should include something more than controversies over "territory or jurisdiction"; for in the original draft as reported the latter controversies were to be disposed of by the Senate, and controversies other than those by the judiciary, to which by amendment all were finally committed. But it is apparent that the jurisdiction is of so delicate and grave a character that it was not contemplated that it would be exercised save when the necessity was absolute and the matter in itself properly justiciable.

82. Ibid., at 27–28: "An embargo, though not an act of war, is frequently resorted to as preliminary to a declaration of war, and may be treated under certain circumstances as a sufficient casus belli."

83. Ibid.

84. Ibid., at 22–23. Harlan wrote,

Taking the allegations of the bill to be true—as upon demurrer must be done—this suit cannot be regarded as one relating only to local regulations that incidentally affect interstate commerce and which the State may adopt and maintain in the absence of national regulations on the subject. On the contrary, if the allegations of the bill be true, the Texas authorities have gone beyond the necessities of the situation and established a quarantine system that is absolutely subversive of all commerce between Texas and Louisiana, particularly commerce between Texas and New Orleans. This court has often declared that the States have the power to protect the health of their people by police regulations directed to that end, and that regulations of that character are not to be disregarded because they may indirectly or incidentally affect interstate commerce. But when that principle has been announced it has always been said that the police power of a State cannot be so exerted as to obstruct foreign or interstate commerce beyond the necessity for its exercise, and that the courts must guard vigilantly against needless intrusion upon the field committed to Congress.

85. Herbert Hovenkamp, "The Political Economy of Substantive Due Process," *Stanford Law Review* 40.2 (1988): 379–447. Most legal dictionaries define substantive due process by contrasting it with procedural due process. Under substantive due process, the state is prohibited from infringing on fundamental constitutional liberties, under the assumption that those liberties are well defined. In contrast, procedural due process is about procedural limitations on the way in which a law is administered, applied, or enforced. In this way, procedural due process prohibits the government from arbitrarily depriving individuals of legally protected interests without first giving them notice and the opportunity to be heard. For an extended discussion, see the "Due Process" entry in *The Oxford Companion to American Law*, ed. Kermit Hall (New York: Oxford University Press, 2002).

86. See, for example, Hovenkamp, "Political Economy of Substantive Due Process"; Ronald M. Labbe and Jonathan Lurie, *The Slaughterhouse Cases: Regulation, Reconstruction, and the Fourteenth Amendment*, abridged ed. (Lawrence: University Press of Kansas, 2005), 172–75; and David Bernstein, *Rehabilitating Lochner: Defending Individual Rights from Progressive Reform* (Chicago: University of Chicago Press, 2011).

87. See, for example, Fertilizing Company v. Hyde Park, 97 U.S. 659 (1878). More generally, see Wendy E. Parmet, "From Slaughterhouse to Lochner: The Rise and Fall of the Constitutionalization of Public Health," *American Journal of Legal History* 40.4 (1996): 476–505; and William J. Novak, *The People's Welfare: Law and Regulation in Nineteenth-Century America* (Chapel Hill: University of North Carolina Press, 1996), 50, 61–62, 65–66, 222–33, and 340.

88. See Hovenkamp, "Political Economy of Substantive Due Process"; and Troesken, *Why Regulate Utilities?*

89. See, generally, Jonathan R. T. Hughes, *The Governmental Habit Redux: Economic Controls from Colonial Times to the Present* (Princeton, NJ: Princeton University Press, 1991).

90. Classic early treatments of this topic include Gabriel Kolko's two books, *Railroads and Regulation, 1877–1916* (Princeton, NJ: Princeton University Press, 1965), and *The Triumph of Conservatism: A Reinterpretation of American History, 1900–1916* (New York: Free Press, 1963).

91. See Kolko *Railroads and Regulation*; Albro Martin, *Enterprise Denied: Origins of the Decline of American Railroads, 1897–1917* (New York: Columbia University Press, 1971); and Christopher Grandy, "Can Government Be Trusted to Keep Its Part of a Social Contract? New Jersey and the Railroads, 1825–1888," *Journal of Law, Economics, and Organization* 5.2 (1989): 249–69. In their analysis of railroad regulation in Illinois, Mark Kanazawa and Roger Noll find evidence that, as administered in Illinois, railroad regulation was not captured by shippers, though it enjoyed their overwhelming support. Moreover, once implemented, state regulation, at least in Illinois, did not deter the development of the industry. See Mark T. Kanazawa and Roger G. Noll, "The Origins of State Railroad Regulation: The Illinois Constitution of 1870," in *The Regulated Economy: A Historical Approach to Political Economy*, ed. Claudia Goldin and Gary Libecap (Chicago: University of Chicago Press, 1995), 13–80. Having said this, cases such as *Smyth v. Ames* suggest that on at least some occasions, shippers did capture the regulatory process. See Smyth v. Ames 171 U.S. 361 (1898).

92. Mancur Olson, *The Logic of Collective Action: Public Goods and the Theory of Groups* (Cambridge, MA: Harvard University Press, 1971).

93. Troesken, *Why Regulate Utilities?* 55–78.

94. See Troesken, "Sources of Public Ownership"; Charles David Jacobson, *Ties That Bind: Economic and Political Dilemmas of Urban Utility Networks, 1800–1990* (Pittsburgh: University of Pittsburgh Press, 2000).

95. See Troesken, "Sources of Public Ownership" and Jacobson, *Ties That Bind*. Although the dramatic effects that water purification had on health and longevity are discussed in detail in chapter 5, another starting point is David Cutler and Grant Miller, "The Role of Public Health Improvements in Health Advances: The Twentieth Century United States," *Demography* 42.1 (2005): 1–22.

96. *Columbian Herald; or, The Patriotic Courier of North-America*, 26 April 1787, 2–3.

97. See the discussion that follows for evidence; also Barton H. Thompson, "The History of the Judicial Impairment Doctrine and Its Lessons for the Contract Clause," *Stanford Law Review* 44.6 (1992): 1373–1466; and Terry L. Anderson and P. J. Hill,

"Economic Growth in a Transfer Society: The United States Experience," *Journal of Economic History* 41.1 (1981): 113–19.

98. All quotations are from George C. Rogers Jr., "Aedanus Burke, Nathanael Greene, Anthony Wayne, and the British Merchants of Charleston," *South Carolina Historical Magazine* 67.2 (1966): 75–83, esp. 80.

99. Ibid.

100. As described in the text above, a stay law is a law that suspends a debtor's obligations to repay interest and/or principal on a debt obligation or otherwise forestalls collection by the creditor. Along the same lines, *Merriam-Webster* (online) defines a stay law as "a moratory law" or "a law suspending or providing a means of suspending execution of judgments or sale on foreclosure or otherwise suspending legal remedies for a limited time."

101. *The Scot's Magazine*, 17 November 1786, 566.

102. Ibid.; and *Pennsylvania Evening Herald and American Monitor*, 17 December 1785, 168.

103. *Independent Journal*, 15 February 1786, 2.

104. Ibid.: "After having our wants supplied, and our almost boundless appetites glutted, we object to pay our creditors; and why? Because our pride and lavish desires exceeded our abilities. What a shameful subterfuge! Who could be a better judge of our several necessities and our abilities? Was it for the British merchants to point out and dictate . . . what goods [we] ought to purchase, or to what amount? Surely not, the consumers are always the best judges of their wants or wishes, which, if they act prudently, they should limit to their circumstances."

105. Ibid.

106. Ibid.: "Is it by pouring all her wealth into the bosom of America, and for which she will never be paid, that Great Britain is to conquer us? Is it by beggaring her merchants, the fountain of her wealth and the support of her empire, that she forges the chains to enslave America? Common sense revolts at the idea, and contradicts the assertion! In short, is it possible that any man can pervert his understanding so much as to believe that half the merchants in Britain could be induced to involve themselves and their families in utter ruin, to serve the turn of a Minister, or to play a state trick?"

107. Ibid.

108. All quotations in this paragraph are from Daniel Webster, *The Works of Daniel Webster*, vol. 6 (Boston: Little, Brown, 1890), 34–35.

109. Ibid.

110. Hamilton, Jay, and Madison, *FP*, 31.

111. See *The Papers of Alexander Hamilton*, vol. 4, *1787–May 1788*, ed. Harold C. Syrett and Jacob E. Cooke (New York: Columbia University Press, 1962), 325, n. 16.

112. Robert L. Hale, "The Supreme Court and the Contract Clause," *Harvard Law Review* 57.4 (1944): 512–57; James L. Kainen, "Nineteenth-Century Interpretations of the Federal Contract Clause: The Transformation from Vested to Substantive Rights against the State," *Buffalo Law Review* 31.381 (1982).

113. On the economic benefits of the Contract Clause as well as a discussion of its historical evolution, see Richard A. Epstein, "Toward a Revitalization of the Contract Clause," *University of Chicago Law Review* 51.3 (1984): 703–51; Barton H. Thompson Jr., "The History of the Judicial Impairment 'Doctrine' and Its Lessons for the Contract Clause," *Stanford Law Review* 44.6 (1992): 1373–1466; Lee J. Alston, "Farm Foreclosure Moratorium Legislation: A Lesson from the Past," *American Economic Review* 74.3 (1984): 445–57.

114. See Alston, "Farm Foreclosure Moratorium Legislation," 445–57.

115. See Troesken, *Why Regulate Utilities?* 3–16.

116. For the history and evolution of franchise contracts, see Delos F. Wilcox, *Municipal Franchises: A Description of the Terms and Conditions Upon Which Private Corporations Enjoy Special Privileges in the Streets of American Cities*, vols. 1 and 2 (Rochester, NY: Gervaise Press, 1910); Herbert Hovenkamp, *Enterprise and American Law, 1836–1937* (Cambridge, MA: Harvard University Press, 1991), 109–20; Troesken, *Why Regulate Utilities?* 14, 15, and 91; and George L. Priest, "The Origins of Public Utility Regulation and the 'Theories of Regulation Debate,'" *Journal of Law and Economics* 36.2 (1993): 289–324. By the early 1900s, the courts were interpreting franchises much less strictly than they had during the early nineteenth century. Over time, the franchise grew to be more a set of loose suggestions than a formal contract.

117. See Dartmouth v. Woodward, 17 U.S. 518 (1819). Along similar lines, the Supreme Court even upheld private contracts when those contracts rested on legislation secured by bribery. See Fletcher v. Peck, 10 U.S. 87 (1810). For a fuller discussion of these cases and their significance for contracts, see Jonathan Hughes, *The Governmental Habit Redux* (Princeton, NJ: Princeton University Press, 1991), 77–79; and Hovenkamp, *Enterprise and American Law*, 20 and 32–34.

118. Troesken, *Why Regulate Utilities?* 3–16 and 91; Werner Troesken, "Typhoid Rates and the Public Acquisition of Private Waterworks, 1880–1920," *Journal of Economic History* 59.4 (1999): 927–48; Priest, "Origins of Public Utility Regulation," 289–324; and Jacobson, *Ties That Bind*, 26, 30–31, 33, 49–53, 55–56, 62–69, and 179–80.

CHAPTER FOUR

1. The quotations and data in this paragraph are taken from the following sources: Eugene Foster, "The Statistic Evidences of the Value of Vaccination to the Human Race, Past, Present, and Future," *Journal of the American Medical Association* 2.13 (1896): 672–77; Donald R. Hopkins, *The Greatest Killer: Smallpox in History* (Chicago: University of Chicago Press, 2002), 16–25; Yu Li, Darin S. Carroll, Shea N. Gardner, Matthew C. Walsh, Elizabeth A. Vitalis, and Inger K. Damon, "On the Origin of Smallpox: Correlating Variola Phylogenics with Historical Smallpox Records," *Proceedings of the National Academy of Sciences* 104.40 (2007): 15787–92; and M. Bray and M. Buller, "Looking Back at Smallpox," *Clinical and Infectious Diseases* 38.6 (2004): 882–89.

2. For a compact international comparison of smallpox rates around 1900, see Samuel W. Abbott, "Progress in Public Hygiene," *Boston Medical and Surgical Journal* 146.18 (1902): 465–67.

3. A. W. Hedrich, "Changes in the Incidence and Fatality of Smallpox in Recent Decades," *Public Health Reports* 51.14 (1936): 363–84.

4. See the discussion of Cuba and Puerto Rico later in this chapter.

5. See the rest of the chapter for evidence and documentation of the claims made in this paragraph, particularly the Jacobson case and the Leake and Force study. See also James Colgrove, *State of Immunity: The Politics of Vaccination* (Berkeley and Los Angeles: University of California Press, 2006), 24–80.

6. For explicit linkages between vaccination for smallpox and other infectious diseases, see James G. Hodge and Lawrence O. Gostin, "School Vaccination Requirements: Historical, Social, and Legal Perspectives," *Kentucky Law Journal* 90.1 (2002): 831–926.

7. Hopkins, *Greatest Killer*, 16–25; Yu Li et al., "On the Origin of Smallpox"; and Michael Willrich, *Pox: An American History* (New York: Penguin, 2011), 25–36.

8. Charles V. Chapin, "Municipal Sanitation," *American Journal of Public Hygiene* 15.3 (1905): 427–30; Alfred W. Crosby, "Smallpox," in *The Cambridge World History of Dis-*

ease, ed. Kenneth F. Kiple (Cambridge: Cambridge University Press, 1999), 1008–13; Bray and Buller, "Looking Back at Smallpox," 882–89. The case fatality rate refers to the proportion of all individuals infected with the disease who would ultimately perish from the disease.

9. On the connection between sanitation and smallpox among anti-vaccinationists, see Nadja Durbach, *Bodily Matters: The Anti-Vaccination Movement in England, 1853–1907* (Durham, NC: Duke University Press, 2005), 152–65.

10. See J. T. Biggs, *Leicester: Sanitation versus Vaccination* (London: Anti-Vaccination League, 1912), 357–410. Using city-level data from the nineteenth century in the United States and Great Britain, smallpox rates are regressed against death rates from tuberculosis, typhoid fever, and variety of proxies for sanitation. These regressions contradict the claim that sanitation and the broader disease environment influenced smallpox rates. (Results available upon request.)

11. See Hopkins, *Greatest Killer*, 29, 52, 87, 106–15, and 208–11; and Richard F. Tomasson, "A Millennium of Misery: The Demography of the Icelanders," *Population Studies* 31.3 (1977): 405–27.

12. A disease is said to be endemic when maintaining the disease in a given population does not require an external input or source of exposure. A disease is said to be epidemic when its incidence is higher than one would normally expect. A childhood disease refers to a disease that strikes mainly children. To the extent that children are the most likely members of a population to have no prior exposure to disease, and therefore no heightened immunity status, one expects that they would be the most vulnerable to both endemic and epidemic diseases.

13. Put more precisely, if there were one hundred cases of smallpox, ninety of these would have been in children five years old or younger, while the remaining ten would have been in individuals older than five years. On the age distribution of smallpox cases, see Charles Creighton, *A History of Epidemics in Britain* (London: The University Press, 1891), 524–37; and General Board of Health, *Papers Relating to the History and Practice of Vaccination, Presented to Both Houses of Parliament by Command of Her Majesty* (London: Her Majesty's Stationary Office, 1857), xxv–xxxiv.

14. Creighton, *History of Epidemics in Britain*, 524–37 General Board of Health, *History and Practice of Vaccination*, xxv–xxxiv.

15. Hopkins, *Greatest Killer*, 32–33, 295–96.

16. Crosby, "Smallpox," 1008–13; Hopkins, *Greatest Killer*, 45–51, 109–110, 114–21.

17. E. Huth, "Quantitative Evidence for Judgements on the Efficacy of Inoculation for the Prevention of Smallpox: England and New England in the 1700s," *Journal of the Royal Society of Medicine* 99.5 (2006): 262–66; and Hopkins, *Greatest Killer*, 109–12.

18. Crosby, "Smallpox," 1008–13; Hopkins, *Greatest Killer*, 84–85 and 274–75.

19. Crosby, "Smallpox,"1008–13; Marcus P. Hatfield, "Varicella, Variola, and Vaccination," in *The Medical Standard and the North American Practitioner* (Chicago: G. P. Engelhard, 1914), 23:522–28; *Second Report of the Royal Commission Appointed to Inquire into the Subject of Vaccination; with Minutes and Appendices* (London: Her Majesty's Stationary Office, 1890); and Robert D. Johnston, *The Radical Middle Class: Populist Democracy and the Question of Capitalism in Progressive Era Portland, Oregon* (Princeton, NJ: Princeton University Press, 2003), 184–88.

20. The quotation on Ceylon is from the *British Medical Journal*, 23 May 1896, 1267; other information is from Edward Belongia and Allison L. Naleway, "Smallpox Vaccine: The Good, the Bad, and the Ugly," *Clinical Medicine and Research* 1.2 (2003): 87–92; and *Second Report of the Royal Commission*.

21. Johnston, *Radical Middle Class*, 184. Johnston describes opposition to vaccination in India, Ghana, Kenya, Malaya, Algeria, and the Belgian Congo.
22. See Durbach, *Bodily Matters*, esp. 124–33; and Johnston, *Radical Middle Class*, 187.
23. See Henry S. Mathewson, "Prophylactic Value of Vaccination," *Pharmaceutical Era*, 13 February 1908, 205–7; and *Second Report of the Royal Commission*.
24. Colgrove, *State of Immunity*, 47. Even in this setting, vaccination could still be rational if one believed the risk of a future outbreak was high, or if the costs associated with contracting even a low-probability disease were very high.
25. As Nadja Durbach explains in *Bodily Matters* (26–34), if there were free trade in corn, why not medicine? Along the same lines, but with a broader European focus that also describes anti-vaccination movements in Continental Europe, see Peter Baldwin, *Contagion and the State in Europe, 1830–1930* (Cambridge: Cambridge University Press, 2005), 280–312. For other observations in this paragraph and the following, see *A Report on Vaccination and Its Results, Based on the Evidence Taken by the Royal Commission During the Years 1889–1897*, vol. 1, *The Text of the Commission Report* (London: New Sydenham Society, 1898); the *Second Report of the Royal Commission Appointed*; Crosby, "Smallpox," 1008–13; and Hopkins, *Greatest Killer*, 83–84, 93–95, 147, 289, and 292–93.
26. *The Vaccination Inquirer*, March 1885, 234.
27. See Baldwin, *Contagion and the State*, 278–79, 308–10. Baldwin also explains that anti-vaccination sentiments were strongest among non-established Protestant sects (292). Although Baldwin does not discuss this, the data on smallpox suggest that while the typical Catholic clergyman might have actively supported vaccination, rank-and-file Catholics continued to oppose the procedure. As shown by the data presented below, Catholic countries tended to have much higher smallpox rates than non-Catholic countries.
28. *The Vaccination Inquirer*, March 1885, 234.
29. See Durbach, *Bodily Matters*, 124–33, esp. 131.
30. William White, *The Story of a Great Delusion in a Series of Matter-of-Fact Chapters* (London: E. W. Allen, 1885), 595–96.
31. Ibid. To give White his due, it is possible that vaccination undermined incentives to maintain a sanitary living environment. If so, it might also have unintentionally generated more deaths from diseases highly correlated with poor sanitation, such as tuberculosis and typhoid fever. But, as previously noted, in an econometric analysis of death rates in nineteenth- and early twentieth-century Britain and the United States, I find no evidence to support such a conjecture.
32. On Lora Little, see Johnston, *Radical Middle Class*, 199–202. On anti-vaccinationist concern for colonial populations (as well as poor and working-class populations in England), see Durbach, *Bodily Matters*, 80–82.
33. Johnston, *Radical Middle Class*, 199–202.
34. Ibid., 201–7.
35. This evidence is reviewed and documented below.
36. For a detailed and reliable discussion of the risks of smallpox vaccination, see Johnston, *Radical Middle Class*, 185–88.
37. This suggests 1.5 deaths for every hundred thousand vaccinations. Other samples suggest similar fatality rates. See Mathewson, "Prophylactic Value of Vaccination," 205–7. For other assessments of the safety of the smallpox vaccine (that arrive at broadly similar conclusions), see *Second Report of the Royal Commission*. Ironically, efforts to preserve the vaccine with glycerin around the turn of the twentieth century,

at least in the short run, might have actually undermined the safety of the vaccine. See Willrich, *Pox: An American History*, 194–96. This episode suggests one probably should not think of safety in a static way. The safety of the vaccine varied over time and across place because of experiments with new techniques and production processes.

38. For the pre-1839 period, data on deaths are based on church burials. For the post-1839 period, the data are from the Registrar General of England's official death registry. One concern with these data is that before the introduction of official death registration in 1839, deaths from smallpox might have been under-reported. To the extent that the reporting of deaths became more reliable over time, however, figure 4.1 actually understates the beneficial effects of vaccination on London smallpox rates.

39. Ironically, Charles Creighton, a highly accomplished physician and medical historian, used the London data to support his claim that vaccination was ineffective and counterproductive. Looking at the data today, it is difficult to understand how Creighton arrived at that conclusion, but it is to his credit that he published the data for others to analyze and interpret.

40. See Edward J. Edwardes, *A Concise History of Smallpox Vaccination in Europe* (London: H. K. Lewis, 1902).

41. See Durbach, *Bodily Matters*, 152–59 and 162–65; Biggs, *Leicester: Sanitation versus Vaccination*, 208–14 and 357–410.

42. This can be seen in figures 4.1 and 4.2. After vaccination laws in England and Sweden were strengthened during the 1870s and early 1880s, smallpox rates in both London and Sweden fell to almost nothing, but when England reverted to a policy of voluntary vaccinations around the turn of the twentieth century, smallpox rates began to rise soon thereafter. Elsewhere in the world, laws mandating universal vaccination were also followed by precipitous drops in smallpox rates. See, for example, the discussion of Prussia and various US states presented later in this chapter.

43. The French rate was 22.6 deaths per thousand; the Prussian, 0.58.

44. Among the Prussians, the death rates for dysentery and typhoid were, respectively, 32.3 and 118.8 per thousand. Among the French, the same rates were 19.3 and 80.6.

45. This paragraph is based on data and the graph on p. 240 (appendix no. 2) of the *Second Report of the Royal Commission*.

46. See Ridolfo Livi, "On Vaccination and Small-Pox in the Italian Army," *British Medical Journal*, 29 April 1899, 1017–22.

47. A small fraction of this population achieved elevated immunity status not through vaccination but by contracting smallpox and surviving the disease.

48. Before joining the army, recruits (or their families) chose whether or not to get vaccinated and whether or not to live in environments with a high risk of smallpox.

49. *Yale Law Journal* 10.4 (1901): 158–59.

50. The relevant statute read, "The board of health of a city or town if, in its opinion, it is necessary for the public health or safety, shall require and enforce the vaccination and revaccination of all of the inhabitants thereof and shall provide them with the means of free vaccination. Whoever, being over twenty-one years of age and not under guardianship, refuses or neglects to comply with such requirement shall forfeit five dollars" (Commonwealth v. Pear, 183 Mass. 242 (1903), 243). For an overview of this case and a brief discussion of Jacobson's background, see Colgrove, *State of Immunity*, 38–43.

51. *Commonwealth*, 183 Mass. 242. On the contours of Henning's broader life and how he came to be an anti-vaccinationist, see Colgrove, *State of Immunity*, 38–43 and 48–49.

52. *Commonwealth*, 183 Mass. 242 at 245.

53. Ibid. at 246.
54. This, of course, presumes that not getting vaccinated imposes a cost on others. Most medical scientists believe not getting vaccinated for contagious diseases does, indeed, impose a significant risk on the rest of society, and few would argue that smallpox is not highly contagious. For a recent statement, see David Fisman, "The Sounds of Silence: Public Goods, Externalities, and the Value of Infectious Disease Control Programs," *Canadian Journal of Infectious Diseases and Medical Microbiology* 20.2 (2009): 39–46. For a historical statement along the same lines involving smallpox vaccination, see the unsigned article "The Smallpox and Vaccination," *London Journal*, 5 January 1839, 14–15, which concludes with the following comment: "Parents who are careless about vaccination are very culpable—neglectful of their own interests, *and that of society* [emphasis added]." More generally, the economics literature on vaccination treats vaccination as a public good and suggests that subsidies and taxes can help achieve economically optimal levels of vaccination. See the following article and the literature it cites: Bryan L. Boulier, Tejwant S. Datta, and Robert S. Goldfarb, "Vaccination Externalities," *The B. E. Journal of Economic Analysis and Policy* 7.3 (2007): 1–25. That said, some papers suggest that universal mandatory vaccination is neither efficient nor necessary to achieve complete eradication of disease, even in the face of externalities; see Dagobert L. Brito, Eytan Sheshinski, and Michael D. Intrilligator, "Externalities and Compulsory Vaccinations," *Journal of Public Economics* 45.1 (1991): 69–90. When one looks at the history of smallpox eradication during the twentieth century and its effective use of the so-called ring strategy, this seems plausible; see Frank Fenner, *Smallpox and Its Eradication* (New York: World Health Organization, 1989); and Johnston, *Radical Middle Class*, 187. One might argue, however, that this history highlights the effectiveness of a carefully focused and intensive strategy that is very close to compulsion.
55. See Goodwin Lu, "The First Justice Harlan," *California Law Review* 96.5 (2008): 1383–93; Edward Douglass White, "A Tribute to Mr. Justice Harlan," *North American Review* 195.676 (1912): 289–92; and Loren P. Beth, "Justice Harlan and the Uses of Dissent," *American Political Science Review* 49.4 (1955): 1085–1104.
56. Jacobson v. Massachusetts, 197 U.S. 11 (1905), 40–42.
57. Ibid. at 46. Harlan wrote, "If the mode adopted by the Commonwealth of Massachusetts for the protection of its local communities against smallpox proved to be distressing, inconvenient or objectionable to some, . . . the answer is that it was the duty of the constituted authorities primarily to keep in view the welfare, comfort and safety of the many, and not permit the interests of the many to be subordinated to the wishes or convenience of the few."
58. Ibid.
59. Willrich, *Pox: An American History*, 328–29; and Colgrove, *State of Immunity*, 42.
60. See Charles M. Higgins, *Horrors of Vaccination Exposed and Illustrated* (New York: self-published, 1920), vii–viii.
61. See, for example, "Schools and School Districts: Vaccination as Condition to Admission to Schools," *Virginia Law Register* 9.9 (1924): 702–9, esp. 707.
62. *Jacobson*, 197 U.S. 11 at 40–42.
63. James P. Leake, "The Essentials of Smallpox Vaccination," *Public Health Reports* 36.33 (1921): 1975–89.
64. Willrich, *Pox: An American History*, 73–74.
65. James G. Hodge and Lawrence O. Gostin, "School Vaccination Requirements: Historical, Social, and Legal Perspectives," *Kentucky Law Journal* 90.1 (2002): 831–86.

This article describes examples from New York in the 1920s involving parents who were jailed for refusing to have their children vaccinated. Robert J. Cynkar suggests that the Supreme Court's decision in *Buck v. Bell* (upholding a eugenics-inspired sterilization law in Virginia) helped pave the way for more draconian vaccination laws, policies, and enforcement. See Robert J. Cynkar, "*Buck v. Bell*: 'Felt Necessities' v. Fundamental Values," *Columbia Law Review* 81.7 (1981): 1418–61, esp. 1448–59. In the New York cases above, however, the city appears to have been in the midst of an outbreak of smallpox, and the parents were often given the option of paying a fine or going to jail. To make a point, they chose jail over paying a small financial penalty. See the *New York Times*, 16 December 1936, 49, and 15 April 1927, 2.

66. Leake, "Essentials of Smallpox Vaccination,"1975–89.

67. *Jacobson*, 197 U.S. 11 at 8–9; "Vaccination Made Compulsory in Province of Madrid," *Journal of the American Medical Association* 72.15 (1919): 1091; and "Vaccination," *Encyclopedia Britannica*, vol. 24, ed. Day Otis Kellogg (New York and Chicago: Werner Company, 1899), 23–29. This encyclopedia article, available on Google books, provides a short but comprehensive review of vaccination policies in Europe during the nineteenth and early twentieth centuries. See also Baldwin, *Contagion and the State*, 244–354. Baldwin provides a detailed account of the origins, evolution, and effects of vaccination policies in continental Europe.

68. Willrich, *Pox: An American History*, 38–39. The efficacy of the German approach is highlighted in figure 4.3 and the associated text.

69. Harlan wrote,

> The authority of the State to enact this statute is to be referred to what is commonly called the police power—a power which the State did not surrender when becoming a member of the Union under the Constitution. Although this court has refrained from any attempt to define the limits of that power, yet it has distinctly recognized the authority of a State to enact quarantine laws and 'health laws of every description'; indeed, all laws that relate to matters completely within its territory and which do not by their necessary operation affect the people of other States. According to settled principles the police power of a State must be held to embrace, at least, such reasonable regulations established directly by legislative enactment as will protect the public health and the public safety." (*Jacobson*, 197 U.S. 11 at 25–26)

70. The phrase "from a disease-prevention standpoint" is critical because it is possible that the populations in states without mandatory vaccination valued the absence of such coercive laws more than they did the absence of smallpox. Put another way, they might have strongly preferred a world with smallpox and no state coercion to a world without smallpox but greater coercion. A libertarian, for example, might argue that all infringements on personal liberty, even if well-intentioned and effective in some ways, impair long-term economic growth and political development.

71. Potts v. Breen, 167 Ill. 67 (1897), 15.

72. In Adams v. Burdge, 95 Wis. 390 (1897), 349, the Wisconsin Supreme Court ruled, "As the police power imposes restrictions and burdens upon the natural and private rights of individuals, it necessarily depends on the law for its support; and although of comprehensive and far-reaching character, it is subject to constitutional restrictions, and, in general, it is the province of the lawmaking power to determine in what cases or upon what conditions this power may be exercised."

73. See Alvah H. Doty, "On Vaccination," *Medical Record* 44.24 (1893): 743–45; and Baldwin, *Contagion and the State*, 316–19.

74. Willrich, *Pox: An American History*, 50–64; and Baldwin, *Contagion and the State*, 316–19. Some English sources suggest that Sweden also had a policy of compulsory revaccination, but Baldwin's review of the primary sources in Sweden suggests otherwise.
75. As noted above, the Supreme Court in *Jacobson* was not explicit on this question, and the Massachusetts Supreme Court expressly said that authorities could not compel vaccination through physical force. Uncertainty and ambiguity like this are a primary source of conflict and litigation. See George L. Priest and Benjamin Klein, "The Selection of Disputes for Litigation," *Journal of Legal Studies* 13.1 (1984): 1–55.
76. Leake, "Essentials of Smallpox Vaccination," 1975–89.
77. The difference is statistically significant at a .0001 confidence level.
78. Leake, "Essentials of Smallpox Vaccination," 1975–89.
79. See also the data for England and Sweden discussed above and described in figures 4.1 and 4.2, both of which show the same pattern as the US states: remove mandatory vaccination laws, and smallpox spikes upward.
80. Baldwin, *Contagion and the State*, 263–309; and D. G. Williamson, *Bismarck and Germany, 1862–1890* (London: Longman, 1998).
81. See, for example, Pierre-Yves Geoffard and Tomas Philipson, "Rational Epidemics and Their Public Control," *International Economic Review* 37.3 (1996): 603–24.
82. The phrase "from a disease-prevention standpoint" is, again, critical. As above, there is no way to compare the utility or well-being of anti-vaccinationists with that of vaccinationists. It is possible that the pain suffered by someone strongly opposed to vaccination exceeded the gain in utility enjoyed by those who internalized a reduction in disease risk because of that vaccination. There is no way to make such interpersonal comparisons of utility, and so it is difficult to speak about economic efficiency in the absence of a more formal model. That said, so long as getting vaccinated for a highly contagious disease reduces the risk of an outbreak, we can say that mandatory vaccination helps to forestall increases in the disease.
83. For a formal and extensive treatment of the behavioral logic that underlies herd immunity, see Chris T. Bauch and David J. D. Earn, "Vaccination and the Theory of Games," *Proceedings of the National Academy of Sciences* 101.36 (2004): 13391–94.
84. See, for example, Colgrove, *State of Immunity*, 75–78.
85. See Judith Walzer Leavitt, "Public Resistance or Cooperation? A Tale of Smallpox in Two Cities," *Biosecurity and Bioterrorism* 1.3 (2003): 185–93; Johnston, *Radical Middle Class*, 193–94; and Colgrove, *State of Immunity*, 24–26.
86. See J. W. Kerr, "Vaccination: An Analysis of the Laws and Regulations Relating Thereto in Force in the United States," in *Public Health Bulletin* 52 (January), Treasury Department (Washington, DC: Government Printing Office, 1912).
87. On the costs and benefits of free trade, generally, see Douglas A. Irwin, *Free Trade Under Fire* (Princeton, NJ: Princeton University Press, 2002), 21–70.
88. Johnston, *Radical Middle Class*, 208–10.
89. See *British Medical Journal*, 28 January 1899, 216–17. Lay opposition to vaccination among Catholics is surprising because, as noted earlier, the Catholic clergy tended to support government vaccination programs. See Baldwin, *Contagion and the State*, 292.
90. Two outliers in the figure are Austria and France, which appear to have unusually high smallpox rates (and presumably low vaccination rates). As the previous note explains, this could be the result of the two countries' adherence to Catholicism.
91. It is true that for a time smallpox vaccination was mandatory in England, but that was a highly contentious policy that legislators were ultimately forced to abandon in the face of opposition from anti-vaccinationists. See also, Baldwin, *Contagion and*

the State, 330–33. Baldwin provides an overview of how political cultures and social attitudes toward individual liberty shaped vaccination policies. He focuses mainly on France, Sweden, Germany, and Great Britain. He does note some oddities, however, and these oddities are reflected in the data presented in figure 4.6. Unlike England and Wales, which abandoned compulsory vaccination in the face of public protest, Scotland and Ireland did not. Similarly, in Germany, it was not conservative and authoritarian Prussia that was the first to implement compulsory vaccination, but Bavaria. In France, under the first Napoleon, smallpox vaccination policy was laissez-faire according to Baldwin, but grew more draconian during the liberal Third Republic.

92. Massachusetts was, for example, among the first states to develop a state board of public health and a system for the registration of vital statistics. It was also at the forefront of efforts to control water pollution and eradicate waterborne diseases, such as typhoid. During the early twentieth century, while most scientists and physicians were minimizing the potential dangers of lead poisoning, Massachusetts officials were working hard to mitigate lead exposure through water and other environmental sources. See John M. Toner, "Boards of Health in the United States," in *Public Health Reports and Papers Presented at the Meetings of the American Public Health Association in the Year 1873* (New York: Hurd and Houghton, 1875), 499–521; and Werner Troesken, *The Great Lead Water Pipe Disaster* (Cambridge, MA: MIT Press, 2006).

CHAPTER FIVE

1. This paragraph is based on George C. Whipple, *Typhoid Fever: Its Causes, Transmission, and Prevention* (New York: John Wiley & Sons, 1908), esp. 21–69.

2. Ibid.

3. Whipple, *Typhoid Fever*; H. Curschmann, *Typhoid Fever and Typhus Fever* (Philadelphia: W. B. Saunders, 1901), 37–42; William T. Sedgwick, *Principles of Sanitary Science and the Public Health, with Special Reference to the Causation and Prevention of Infectious Diseases* (New York: Macmillan, 1902), 166–68.

4. Whipple, *Typhoid Fever*; Curschmann *Typhoid Fever and Typhus Fever*, 37–42; and Sedgwick, *Principles of Sanitary Science*, 166–68. See also Werner Troesken, *Water, Race, and Disease* (Cambridge: MIT Press, 2004), 23–36.

5. See Louis I. Dublin, "Typhoid Fever and Its Sequelae," *American Journal of Public Health* 15.11 (1915): 1016–19.

6. See William Budd, "Typhoid Fever: Its Nature, Mode of Spreading, and Prevention," *American Journal of Public Health* 8.7 (1873 repr.): 610–12; Martin V. Melosi, *The Sanitary City: Urban Infrastructure in American from Colonial Times to the Present* (Baltimore, MD: Johns Hopkins University Press, 2000), 1–43, 60–61, and 110–13.

7. For a survey of the effectiveness of water filtration (and other modes of improving water quality) in reducing typhoid rates, see Whipple, *Typhoid Fever*, 228–66. On the Pittsburgh experience, see Troesken, *Water, Race, and Disease*, 27 and 56. For papers on the effectiveness of sewers and other measures promoting sanitary sewage disposal, see Lionel Kestenbaum and Jean-Laurent Rosenthal, "Income Versus Sanitation: Mortality Decline in Paris, 1880–1914," unpublished MS, California Institute of Technology (2014); Jeffrey K. Beemer, Douglas L. Anderton, and Susan Hautaniemi Leonard, "Sewers in the City: A Case Study of Individual-Level Mortality and Public Health Initiatives in Northampton, Massachusetts, at the Turn of the Century," *Journal of the History of Medicine and Allied Sciences* 60.1 (2005): 42–72; Joseph P. Ferrie and Werner Troesken, "Death and the City: Chicago's Mortality Transition, 1850–1925,"

Working Paper 11427 (Cambridge, MA: National Bureau of Economic Research, 2005); and C. E. Terry, "Extermination of the House Fly in Cities, Its Necessity and Possibility," *American Journal Public Health* 2.1 (1912): 14–22. Of all these articles, those by Beemer et al. and by Kestenbaum and Rosenthal describe the largest effects of sewers on overall mortality. The Terry article explains that in well-sewered cities it is not so important to eradicate the house fly, but in cities with poor sewer systems, such as those in the South, the house fly was an important disseminator of disease, especially typhoid fever. In Jacksonville, the passage of an ordinance mandating that all privies be screened had an enormous effect in reducing typhoid rates, particularly for poor socioeconomic groups. For the effects of this measure, see Troesken, *Water, Race, and Disease*, 80–87. Although not a sewer per se, a screened privy had a similar (and cheaper) effect: to assure more sanitary waste disposal.

8.   W. T. Sedgwick and J. Scott MacNutt, "On the Mills-Reincke Phenomenon and Hazen's Theorem Concerning the Decrease in Mortality from Diseases Other Than Typhoid Fever Following the Purification of Public Water Supplies," *Journal of Infectious Diseases* 7.4 (1910): 489–564.

9.   See Emanuel B. Fink, "American Mortality Statistics and the Mills-Reincke Phenomenon," *Journal of Infectious Diseases* 21.1 (1917): 62–94; and Joseph P. Ferrie and Werner Troesken, "Water and Chicago's Mortality Transition, 1850–1925," *Explorations in Economic History* 45.1 (2008): 553–75.

10. While the flow of the Chicago River was formally reversed in 1871 (it had been informally reversed before 1871), that reversal could be overwhelmed by heavy storms, in which case the river and the sewage the river inevitably carried would flow into Lake Michigan. The Sanitary and Ship Canal, which was completed in 1900, guaranteed that even in the worst weather the river flowed away from the lake. See Chicago Bureau of Public Efficiency, *The Water Works System of the City of Chicago* (n.p., 1917); and Louis P. Cain, *Sanitation Strategy for a Lakefront Metropolis* (DeKalb: Northern Illinois University Press, 1977). Quoting an earlier commentator, Cain summarizes the effects of this last change as follows:

> As early as 1865 the problem of sewage disposal led the city to obtain from the state permission to lower the summit level of the canal sufficiently to insure such flow of water from Lake Michigan as would carry the sewage from the Chicago River through the canal into the Des Plaines (River). This improvement, completed in 1871, at an expenditure of approximately $3,000,000, . . . met the sanitary requirements for nearly a decade. By 1881, however, the collection of debris in the prism of the canal, the lowering of the lake level, and the increasing amount of sewerage to be carried, combined to render the canal ineffective as an outlet." (63)

11. For these projects and dates, see Chicago Bureau of Public Efficiency, *Water Works System*; and the *Chicago Daily Inter-Ocean*, 1 January 1894, 13.

12. Louis P. Cain, in *Sanitation Strategy for a Lakefront Metropolis* (57), dates chlorination as starting in 1912. But it is important to be clear that in the years immediately following 1912, chlorination was experimental and limited to a few pumping stations. It was not until 1916 that the entire city enjoyed chlorinated water. As reported in *Municipal and County Engineering* 56.1 (1918), "Treatment of [Chicago] water by the hypochlorite of lime method was tried experimentally early in 1912 at the Edward F. Dunne intake crib, supplying the Roseland pumping station. In July, 1912, this treatment was extended to the 68th street crib. . . . In August 1913, a similar experimental plant was also placed in operation at the Lake View intake crib. Many difficulties

were encountered at these installations" (6). Once these difficulties were addressed and chlorine gas replaced the hypochlorite used at the early experimental stations, the city extended chlorination to the rest of the city. The article from *Municipal and County Engineering* cited above provides exact dates for when the city's various pumping stations were brought online and chlorinated. The same dates are provided in Chicago Bureau of Public Efficiency, *Water Works System*.

13. The link between improvements in the city's water supply and reductions in typhoid rates did not escape notice in the medical press. After the completion of the Four Mile Intake Crib, *Medical News* reported that "the four mile intake crib of the Chicago water-supply reduced the typhoid fever death rate from 104 in 1892 to 42 and 31 in 1893 and 1894, respectively per 100,000" (21 November 1896, 586). The same sentiments are expressed in an article in the *Chicago Daily Inter-Ocean*, a prominent Chicago newspaper (1 January 1894, 13). Similarly, the Chicago Department of Health, quoted in the *Bulletin of the Chicago School of Sanitary Instruction* 900.9 (1921), explained that "it has been discovered that chlorine makes polluted water safe to drink, . . . [and] this is why we chlorinate Chicago's drinking water. Before this process of treating the water was adopted, Chicago had a pretty high death rate from typhoid fever. Since chlorination has been adopted, Chicago's death rate from this filth disease has decreased each year, until now for three consecutive years, Chicago has had the lowest death rate from typhoid fever of any city of its class in the United States" (34).

14. The total death rate is defined as deaths from all causes per thousand persons, from 1853 through 1925.

15. Figure 5.3, it should be noted, understates the variability observed in the total death rate between 1853 and 1880, as three epidemic years—when death rates were as high as sixty deaths per thousand—are dropped from the time-series so that trends can be more easily established.

16. Other plausible mechanisms include laws mandating milk pasteurization, the introduction of the diphtheria antitoxin, and behavioral changes on the part of individuals. These other possible mechanisms are ruled out in a more extensive analysis published in Ferrie and Troesken, "Death and the City."

17. Note that if typhoid had had a higher case fatality rate (so that more people would have died before ever experiencing any sequelae), the impact on non-typhoid deaths would have been smaller.

18. See Ferrie and Troesken, "Water and Chicago's Mortality Transition.

19. See David M. Cutler and Grant Miller, "The Role of Public Health Improvements in Health Advances: The Twentieth Century United States," *Demography* 42.1 (2005): 1–22. Cutler and Miller find that for every one death from typhoid fever prevented by water purification, there were four deaths from other causes that were also prevented. That finding is lower than the finding for Chicago, but they focus on the period from 1900 to 1920, after the largest reductions in typhoid rates had already been achieved.

20. Between 1850 and 1950, life expectancy for whites increased by 29.5 years; and 60 percent of 29.5 is 17.7. Along the same lines, between 1850 and 1950, life expectancy for nonwhites rose by 38 years; and 60 percent of 38 is 22.8. (See chapter 1 for more details.)

21. See Moses N. Baker, *The Manual of American Water-Works* (New York: Engineering News Publishing Company, 1897), pp. b–k; and Melosi, *Sanitary City*, 74 and 120. See also Werner Troesken and Rick Geddes, "Municipalizing American Waterworks, 1897–1915," *Journal of Law, Economics, and Organization* 19.2 (2003): 546–67.

22. David Cutler and Grant Miller, "Water, Water Everywhere: Municipal Finance and Water Supply in American Cities," in *Corruption and Reform: Lessons from America's Economic History*, ed. Edward L. Glaeser and Claudia Goldin (Chicago: University of Chicago Press, 2006), 152–83.

23. The Chicago Sanitary District is discussed in greater detail below. See that discussion for citations to the relevant secondary literature.

24. The data in table 5.1 come from the following sources: Stanley L. Engerman and Kenneth L. Sokoloff, "Digging the Dirt at Public Expense," in *Corruption and Reform: Lessons from America's Economic History*, ed. Edward L. Glaeser and Claudia Goldin (Chicago: University of Chicago Press, 2006), 95–124; Melosi, *Sanitary City*, 128–29, 376–77; Cain, *Sanitation Strategy*; Noel Mauer and Carlos Yu, *The Big Ditch: How America Took, Built, Ran, and Ultimately Gave Away the Panama Canal* (Princeton, NJ: Princeton University Press, 2011).

25. See T. C. Simonton, *A Treatise on the Law of Municipal Bonds of the Municipal Corporations of the United States* (New York and Albany: Banks & Brothers, Law Publishers, 1896), 361–63; John Joseph Wallis, "Constitutions, Corporations, and Corruption: American States and Constitutional Change, 1842–1852," *Journal of Economic History* 65.1 (2005): 211–56; and Gelpcke et al. v. The City of Dubuque, 68 U.S. 175 (1863).

26. Howard F. Beebe, "Municipal Bonds as Popular Investments: Why Are Municipal Bonds Growing More Popular as Investments; and What Effect Is the War Having Upon Municipal Financing," *National Municipal Review* 4 (April 1915): 245–53; quotes on 246.

27. Lawrence Chamberlain, *The Principles of Bond Investment* (New York: Henry Holt, 1911).

28. On the creation and powers of municipal corporations, see William Novak, *The People's Welfare: Law and Regulation in Nineteenth-Century America* (Chapel Hill: University of North Carolina Press, 1996), 10–11, 21, 49, 66–70, 99–100, 128–30, 137–142, and 212–15; Hendrik Hartog, *Private Property and Public Power: The Corporation of the City of New York in American Law, 1730–1870* (Chapel Hill: University of North Carolina Press, 1983); Werner Troesken, "The Sources of Public Ownership: Historical Evidence from the Gas Industry," *Journal of Law, Economics, and Organization* 13.1 (1997): 1–25; and Werner Troesken, *Why Regulate Utilities? The New Institutional Economics and the Chicago Gas Industry, 1849–1924* (Ann Arbor: University of Michigan Press, 1996), 12–13, 39, 49, 55, 58, and 73–75.

29. The following court cases illustrate the power of state constitutions and municipal charters to constrain county, school district, and municipal borrowing: David McNutt v. Lemhi County, 12 Idaho 63 (1906); Elizabeth A. Russell v. The High School Board of Education, 212 Ill. 327 (1904); City of South Bend et al. v. Reynolds, 155 Ind. 70 (1900); and N.W. Halsey and Company v. City of Belle Plain, 128 Iowa 467 (1905). See also the relevant discussions in John Forrest Dillion, *Commentaries on the Law of Municipal Corporations* (New York: James Cockcroft, 1873); and Chamberlain, *Principles of Bond Investment*.

30. On the importance of such commitment mechanisms in reducing the interest rates on sovereign debts, see Douglass C. North and Barry R. Weingast, "Constitutions and Commitment: The Evolution of Institutions Governing Public Choice in Seventeenth-Century England," *Journal of Economic History* 49.4 (1989): 803–32.

31. Under the Missouri constitution, municipalities could not underwrite the bonds of private enterprises or in any way subscribe to the capital stock of corporations. Nor could municipalities issue any debt unless approved by voters in a local referendum, and then only if total debt in the municipality did not exceed 5 percent of the value of all taxable property. Similarly, in Wisconsin, cities could not borrow in excess of

5 percent of assessed valuation, and the state's constitution made explicit a list of activities and projects that cities were authorized to borrow for; if a project from a particular class was not on this list (e.g., railroads), cities in the state could not borrow to build or underwrite building for that purpose. In Kentucky, under the state's 1891 constitution, debt limits were tied to city size: larger cities had larger debt limits. An article in the constitution of the State of New York stated that cities and towns could only borrow for municipal purposes and could not engage in more speculative ventures, such as underwriting railroads. A similar provision in the Connecticut constitution was more direct, explicitly stating that no municipality "shall ever subscribe to the capital stock of any railroad corporation, or become the purchaser of the bonds, or make donation to, or loan its credit in aid of, any such corporation. These examples all are taken from *Commercial and Financial Chronicle, State and City Supplement* 69 (October 1899): 39–40, 106, and 118; and Chamberlain, *Principles of Bond Investment*, 181.

32. For example, under the constitution of the State of Washington, municipal corporations were authorized to incur debt for water, sewer, and artificial light work over and above the normal debt limit of municipalities (5 percent of the value of all taxable property), so long as all borrowing in the municipality did not exceed 10 percent of the value of all taxable property in the municipality. In Alabama, all towns and cities with populations in excess of six thousand were subject to a debt limit of 7 percent of assessed property valuation, excluding debt for waterworks and sewers. Information and quotations about Washington and Alabama are from Dillion, *Law of Municipal Corporations* , vol. 1 (1878), 443–44. The constitution of South Carolina was more complex than either Washington's or Alabama's, but expressed the same basic principles. Towns and cities in the state could not incur any debt exceeding 8 percent of the assessed value of all taxable property, except for water-related debt in a handful of larger towns and cities, which was not constrained in any way. In Wyoming, the constitution stated that no "city, town, or village" could borrow in excess of 2 per cent of assessed property valuation, but may be authorized to create an additional indebtedness not exceeding 4 percent on the assessed value of taxable property . . . for the purpose of building sewerage." Moreover, debts "contracted for water" had no limitations whatsoever (435).

33. Wells v. City of Sioux Falls et al., 16 S.D. 547 (1903), 552.

34. Sinking funds could fail during moments of extreme financial distress, such as the Great Depression; see, Bankers Life Col. v. City of Littlefield, 93 F. 2d. 152 (1937). In addition, Chamberlain describes a number of problems with the way municipalities administered sinking funds during the early 1900s that undermined their effectiveness (*Principles of Bond Investment*, 97–236). The Texas Supreme Court provided an elaborate justification for sinking funds rooted in the state's history of municipal profligacy during the railroad boom. This justification comports nicely with the logic spelled out in the text. According to the court, at the time the Texas constitution "was framed, the history of the country and of the State afforded examples of municipal corporations which had become bankrupt through the reckless and extravagant management of their governing bodies." The "framers doubtless had under consideration the evils" that resulted, both to the "taxpayers" and to the "creditors" of such municipalities "from an unlimited power to create debts." Hence, in framing the state's new constitution, the legislature kept two goals "prominently in view": to protect "the inhabitants of municipalities against oppressive taxation"; and to protect "creditors" and "preserve the financial honor" of municipalities. The latter goal

would protect not just creditors and the honor of municipal governments, but also help assure that later Texas municipalities would have access to a large and reasonably priced market for debt (The City of Terrell v. L.C. Dessaint, 71 Tex. 770 (1888), 773–74).

35. United States, Department of Commerce and Labor, Bureau of the Census, *Statistics of Cities Having a Population of Over 30,000: 1906* (Washington, DC: Government Printing Office, 1908), 248–53.

36. These fifteen states were California; Georgia; Idaho; Illinois; Iowa; Kentucky; Michigan; Missouri; New Hampshire; North Dakota; Oklahoma; Pennsylvania; South Dakota; Texas; and Wisconsin.

37. Chamberlain, *Principles of Bond Investment*, 188 and 214–26.

38. The charter of the City of Vicksburg, Mississippi, mandated that the city levy new taxes to meet interest payments on its debt; see Chamberlain, *Principles of Bond Investment*, 189. Similarly, when the New Jersey legislature granted the City of Rahway the authority to construct and operate a waterworks, it also required the city to estimate receipts and expenses, including all interest due on the bonds issued to construct the works. Should receipts fall short of expenses, the legislature required the city to raise taxes to cover any shortfall and meet the interest payments on the bonds. The impact of both the Vicksburg and Rahway measures was, once again, to help assure bondholders that they would be repaid, which in turn would have reduced the cost of borrowing and promoted lending to the city. Subsequent litigation suggests that these measures were effective in this regard. In 1886, twenty years after the initial law was passed, the board of commissioners that operated the Rahway water system found that receipts had dipped below expenses and that, absent a tax increase, the water board would not be able to meet the interest due on the bonds. The City of Rahway declined to raise taxes and tried to let the bonds fall into default. Bondholders, however, sued, arguing that by law the city was required to meet any shortfalls with a tax increase. In the Supreme Court of New Jersey, the bondholders won, and the city was forced to meet its debt obligations. State law effectively blocked the City of Rahway from defaulting on its water bonds; see The State, ex rel, the Rahway Savings Institution v. The Mayor and Common Council of the City of Rahway, 1887 N.J. Sup. Ct., Lexis 78.

39. North and Weingast, "Constitutions and Commitment, 803–32.

40. See the discussion of the Howard Beebe article in the text above. See also Beebe, "Municipal Bonds as Popular Investments."

41. John Joseph Wallis, "Constitutions, Corporations, and Corruption: American States and Constitutional Change, 1842 to 1852," *Journal of Economic History* 65.1 (2005): 211–56.

42. For evidence on these arguments, see Werner Troesken, "Race, Disease, and the Provision of Water in American Cities, 1890–1921," *Journal of Economic History* 61.3 (2001): 750–77; and Werner Troesken, "Typhoid Rates and the Public Acquisition of Private Waterworks, 1880–1920," *Journal of Economic History* 59.4 (1999): 927–48.

43. See R. E. McDonnell, *Rates, Revenues, and Results of Municipal Ownership of Water Works in the U.S.* (Kansas City: Burns & McDonnell Engineering Co., 1932).

44. Both quotations from the North Carolina Board of Health are taken from Troesken, "Race, Disease, and the Provision of Water." The other quotation is from McDonnell, *Municipal Ownership of Water Works in the U.S.*

45. Based on data calculations from the following source: *Water, Gas, and Electric Light Plants Under Private and Public Ownership*, H.R. Doc. 56-107, No. 713 (1899, 1st.

Sess.) (Fourteenth Annual Report of the Commissioner of Labor) (Washington, DC: Government Printing Office, 1900).

46. Sam Peltzman, "Pricing in Public and Private Enterprises: Electric Utilities in the United States," *Journal of Law and Economics* 14.1 (1971): 109–47.

47. See Troesken, "Race, Disease, and the Provision of Water"; and Troesken and Geddes, "Municipalizing American Waterworks," 546–67.

48. See McDonnell, *Municipal Ownership of Water Works in the U.S.*

49. Troesken, "Race, Disease, and the Provision of Water."

50. On municipalization in Duluth, see Ronald K. Huch, "Typhoid Truelsen, Water, and Politics in Duluth, 1896–1900," *Minnesota History* 47.5 (1981): 189–99.

51. The federation wrote, "Over nine-tenths of the people of any community do not boil the water they drink, so that a low typhoid rate is the best test of the healthfulness of the water" (National Civic Federation, *Municipal and Private Operation of Public Utilities*, vol. 1, pt. 1 [New York: National Civic Federation, 1907], 191).

52. The logic here is the same as that used to explain the externalities associated with refusing to get vaccinated for smallpox. See chapter 4 and the associated citations to the relevant economics literature.

53. See Delos F. Wilcox, *Municipal Franchises: A Description of the Terms and Conditions Upon Which Private Corporations Enjoy Special Privileges in the Streets of American Cities*, 2 vols. (Rochester, NY: Gervaise Press, 1910); Herbert Hovenkamp, *Enterprise and American Law, 1836–1937* (Cambridge, MA: Harvard University Press, 1991), 109–20; Troesken, *Why Regulate Utilities?* 4, 15, and 91; George L. Priest, "The Origins of Public Utility Regulation and the 'Theories of Regulation' Debate," *Journal of Law and Economics* 36.2 (1993): 289–324; and Troesken, "Sources of Public Ownership."

54. See National Waterworks Company v. Kansas City, 62 Fed. 853 1894, 856; Weatherly v. Birmingham Waterworks Company, 185 Ala. 383 (1913); City of Topeka v. Topeka Water Co., 49 Pac. 79 (1897); and Troesken and Geddes, "Municipalizing American Waterworks," 546–67.

55. Troesken and Geddes, "Municipalizing American Waterworks," 546–67. See also Troesken, "Typhoid Rates"; and Hamilton v. Madison Water Company, 116 Me. 157 (1917); and Keeler v. City of Mankato, 113 Minn. 55 (1911).

56. The source for this survey is *Water, Gas, and Electric Light Plants*, H.R. Doc. 107 (see n. 46 above). The years this survey covers, around 1898 and 1899, are an ideal time for assessing variation in water filtration across public and private ownership. The rise of municipal ownership in the water industry took place between 1880 and 1920. Moreover, at this time, there was still much variation in the filtration practices across cities. By 1920, almost all large cities were filtering their water or otherwise taking steps to assure water quality. Alternatively, before 1890, filtration was uncommon among both public and private plants. See Troesken, "Typhoid Rates"; and Melosi, *Sanitary City*, 117–48.

57. See Troesken, "Typhoid Rates"; and Melosi, *Sanitary City*, 117–48.

58. The results of this analysis also indicate that the decision to filter water depended on the nature of the company's water supply. For example, companies that drew their water from springs (underground wells) were 16 (17) percentage points less likely to have installed filters than were companies that drew their water from rivers. These patterns are consistent with prior work showing that cities located on rivers required the largest and most expensive filtration systems because of upstream polluters, while cities that used underground wells or springs required less elaborate systems because of the purity of their water sources. See Troesken, "Typhoid Rates."

59. See the examples of Billings, Montana, and Akron, Ohio, discussed below. For more systematic quantitative evidence, particularly as it relates to extensions in water mains, see Troesken and Geddes, "Municipalizing American Waterworks, 1897–1913," 546–67.

60. See Troesken, "Typhoid Rates"; and Troesken and Geddes, "Municipalizing American Waterworks," 546–67.

61. This can be seen in the following data. As of 1915, there were 201 cities in the United States with a population greater than 30,000 persons. Of these cities, 41 municipalized their water systems sometime between 1890 and 1915; and of the 41, litigation erupted in at least 16. For the number of companies municipalized during this period, see United States, Bureau of the Census, General Statistics of Cities (1915), 144–45. Cities involved in litigation over their water systems were identified via a LexisNexis search.

62. See Troesken and Geddes, "Municipalizing American Waterworks," 546–67; Oliver Williamson, The Economic Institutions of Capitalism (New York: Free Press, 1985), 327–64; Charles David Jacobson, Ties That Bind: Economic and Political Dilemmas of Urban Utility Networks, 1800–1900 (Pittsburgh: University of Pittsburgh Press, 2000), 22–73; Victor Goldberg, "Regulation and Administered Contracts," Bell Journal of Economics 7.3 (1976): 426–52; and Troesken, Why Regulate Utilities?

63. See, for example, Long Island Water Supply Company v. Brooklyn, 166 U.S. 722 1897; and City of Leavenworth et al. v. Leavenworth City and Fort Leavenworth Water Company, 76 Pac. 451 (Kansas, 1904).

64. In the words of the Tennessee Supreme Court, "The argument is made that the city authorities, by oppressive legislation and ordinances, may make the plant unproductive and less valuable, in order to secure it at less than it is worth." See Mayor v. Knoxville Water Company, 64 S.W. 1075 (Tennessee, 1901), 1086.

65. See National Waterworks Company v. Kansas City, 62 Fed. 853 (1894).

66. Ibid. at 856.

67. According to a federal court, section 4 of the franchise required the city to purchase the plant at the end of twenty years if it did not renew the company's franchise. Given this, the court dissented "from the claim of the city that at the lapse of the 20 years the title to this property, with the right of possession, passed absolutely to it, without any payment or tender of payment, leaving only to the company the right to secure compensation by agreement or litigation, as best it could." See National Waterworks, 62 Fed. 853 at 863.

68. In Birmingham, Alabama, the local water company had for years drawn water from a creek that served as drainage for homes, outhouses, farms and diaries, and railroad shops. Even though the creek was frequently polluted, in the court's words, by "disease germs, bacteria, excrement, and other unwholesome matter," the water company had for years refused to do anything to clean up the source or begin filtering its water. The state's attorney general eventually filed suit. See State v. New Orleans Water Supply Company 111 La. 1049 (1904); State ex rel. Weatherly et al. v. Birmingham Waterworks Company 185 Ala. 383 (1913); and City of Topeka v. Topeka Water Company 49 Pac. 79 (Kansas, 1897).

69. Topeka v. Topeka Water Company, 58 Kan. 349 (1897).

70. Waterworks Co. v. City of Burlington, 43 Kan. 725 (1890); and City of Winfield v. Water Co., 51 Kan. 125 (1893).

71. Walla Walla Waterworks v. City of Walla Walla, 172 U.S. 1 (1898), 17–18.

72. See Skaneateles Waterworks Co. v. Village of Skaneateles, et al., 55 N.E. 562 (1899, New York), esp. 567–68.

73. In the words of the United States Supreme Court, "Grants of franchises and special privileges are always to be construed most strongly against the donee, and in favor of the public." The impact of this interpretive principle is illustrated by a case in which a city included in the franchise of a private water company a provision promising that the city would, under no circumstances, "grant to any other person or corporation" the privilege of furnishing water to the city. Twenty years later, when the city in question built its own waterworks to compete with that same private water company, the private company sued for injunctive relief. Ruling against the company, the United States Supreme Court held that the franchise merely implied that the city did not have the right to build a competing works; apparently the phrase "any other person or corporation" might, or might not, have included the city itself. See Knoxville Water Company v. Knoxville, 200 U.S. 22 (1906), esp. 28.

74. White et al. v. City of Meadville, 35 A. 695 (1896), 698.

75. Gloucester Water Supply Company v. City of Gloucester, 60 N.E. 977 (1901), 980. During the late nineteenth century, Massachusetts passed similar laws for many other cities in the state. Although *Gloucester* did not challenge the constitutionality of required-purchase laws, the Massachusetts Supreme Court used the case to explain why the legislature passed such legislation. "It is plain," the court said, "that a private water company . . . cannot hope to compete with a city, which can rely upon taxes to supply a deficit in operating expenses. For that reason, it is also plain that, if the legislature had not required the city to buy the water company's property, the company's property would have been practically, though not legally, confiscated" (981).

76. Despite the economic logic that appears to have undergirded required-purchase laws, they did not enjoy universal support among state courts. In both Montana and North Carolina, for example, state supreme courts struck down required-purchase laws because they violated provisions in the state constitution. See Helena v. Steele, 195 U.S. 383 (1904); and Asbury v. Town of Albemarle, 162 N.C. 247 (1911).

77. See *Engineering News*, 2 March 1911, 277; and *Twenty-Seventh Annual Report of the State Board of Health of the State of Ohio, for the Year Ending, December 31, 1912* (Columbus, OH: F. J. Heer Printing, 1913), 254–60.

78. See *Engineering News*, 18 February 1915, 365.

79. See Attorney General v. City of Salem, 103 MA 138 (1869).

80. James Sinclair & others v. Mayor of Fall River & others. Same v. Charles P. Brightman & another, 198 Mass. 248 (1908).

81. Sebastian Galiani, Paul Gertler, and Ernesto Schargrodsky, "Water for Life: The Impact of Privatization of Water Services on Child Mortality," *Journal of Political Economy* 113.1 (2005): 83–120.

82. See Joseph P. Ferrie, "Internal Migration" in *Historical Statistics of the United States, Earliest Times to the Present: Millennial Edition*, ed. Susan B. Carter, Scott Sigmund Gartner, Michael R. Haines, Alan L. Olmstead, Richard Sutch, and Gavin Wright, chap. Ac (New York: Cambridge University Press, 2006). Available online at http://dx.doi.org/10.1017/ISBN-9780511132971.Ac.ESS.01.

CHAPTER SIX

1. Recent laboratory experiments indicate that yellow fever has many strains and that the pathogenic properties of these strains differ markedly, so that case fatality rates can differ markedly across epidemics. For an overview of what is known about the disease today, see Elizabeth Barnett, "Yellow Fever: Epidemiology and Prevention," *Clinical Infectious Diseases* 44.6 (2007): 850–56.

2. Khaled J. Bloom, *The Mississippi Valley's Great Yellow Fever Epidemic of 1878* (Baton Rouge: Louisiana State University Press, 1993), 1.

3. Data for yellow fever deaths are from J. M. Toner, "On the Natural History and Distribution of Yellow Fever in the United States, from A.D. 1668 to A.D. 1774" (American Public Health Association, 1873). Reprinted from the *Annual Report of the Marine Hospital Service* (Washington, DC: Government Printing Office, 1873); and Patricia Beeson and Werner Troesken, "When Bioterrorism Was No Big Deal," Working Paper 12636 (Cambridge, MA: National Bureau of Economic Research, 2006).

4. In 1880, Carlos Finlay hypothesized that mosquitoes might play a role in the transmission of yellow fever, and in 1881 he identified the specific type of mosquito that carried the disease. However, it would take another twenty to thirty years before Finlay's theorizing would be established and accepted as fact through a series of experiments conducted by Walter Reed. See John R. Pierce and James V. Writer, *Yellow Jack: How Yellow Fever Ravaged America and Walter Reed Discovered Its Deadly Secrets* (Hoboken, NJ: John Wiley and Sons, 2005); P. L. Bres, "A Century of Progress in Combating Yellow Fever," *Bulletin of the World Health Organization* 64.6 (1986): 775–86; and Walter Reed, "Recent Researches Concerning the Etiology, Propagation, and Prevention of Yellow Fever, by the United States Army Commission," *Journal of Hygiene* 2.2 (1902): 101–19.

5. Southerners, it should be noted, were willing to accept federal intrusion into state matters when it suited their own ends, as was the case with the Fugitive Slave Law and the Dred Scott decision. See Timothy S. Huebner, "Roger B. Taney and the Slavery Issue: Looking Beyond—and Before—Dred Scott," *Journal of American History* 97.1 (2010): 17–38; and Scott J. Basinger, "Regulating Slavery: Deck-Stacking and Credible Commitment in the Fugitive Slave Act of 1850," *Journal of Law, Economics, and Organization* 19.2 (2003): 307–42.

6. Samuel Hogg, "An Account of the Epidemic Fevers of Natchez, Mississippi, in the Years 1837–38–39," *Western Journal of Medicine and Surgery* (June 1842): 401–24; Margaret Humphreys, *Yellow Fever and the South* (Baltimore, MD: Johns Hopkins University Press, 1992), 23–42; Bloom, *Mississippi Valley's Great Yellow Fever Epidemic*, 2–45; John M. Keating, *A History of the Yellow Fever: The Yellow Fever Epidemic of 1878, in Memphis, Tenn.* (Memphis: Howard Association, 1879), 77–98; John H. Griscom, *A History, Chronological and Circumstantial, of the Visitations of Yellow Fever at New York* (New York: Hall Clayton & Co., 1858); Bres, "A Century of Progress"; and Carl Spinzig, *Yellow Fever; Nature and Epidemic Character* (St. Louis, MO: Geo. O. Rumbold, 1880), 155–74.

7. Deanne Love Stephens, "The 1878 Yellow Fever Epidemic in Mississippi," PhD diss., University of Southern Mississippi, 1996; Margaret Humphreys, *Yellow Fever and the South* (Baltimore, MD: Johns Hopkins University Press, 1999), 23–42; Bloom, *Mississippi Valley's Great Yellow Fever Epidemic*; Kenneth F. Kiple and Virginia H. Kiple, "Black Yellow Fever Immunities, Innate, and Acquired, as Revealed in the American South," *Social Science History* 1.3 (1977): 419–36.

8. See Pierce and Writer, *Yellow Jack*; Bres, "A Century of Progress"; and Reed, "Recent Researches."

9. Bloom, *Mississippi Valley's Great Yellow Fever Epidemic*, 20–28.

10. Having said this, Toner acknowledged that he undoubtedly missed a few epidemics, but at the same time he was "confident that such localities will be found within the region of this general distribution, as here indicated." See Toner, "On the Natural History and Distribution of Yellow Fever," 3.

11. *Medical Times and Gazette*, 15 February 1873, 169. By the same token, yellow fever was unknown in Europe until Columbus's expedition to the Americas, when he and his crew described a new and unknown disease in the West Indies that appears to have been yellow fever. Soon after that, the disease "found a home in Spain and Portugal, along the south shore of the Mediterranean Sea, and along the West Coast of Africa" (Toner, "On the Natural History and Distribution of Yellow Fever," 3).

12. For example, in Texas, the coastal towns of Sabine and Matagorda had only engaged in coastwise and domestic commerce before the Civil War and had always been "exempt" from yellow fever. This only changed when the Union Army established a blockade around the Port of Galveston and took possession of New Orleans. After this, Sabine and Matagorda became "convenient" ports for "blockade runners," and once they became convenient international ports, they also started to suffer from occasional yellow fever epidemics. See *Medical Times and Gazette*, 15 February 1873, 169.

13. The number of deaths in 1855, 1867, 1873, were 220, 550, and 2,000, respectively. By contrast, the number of deaths from the 1878 epidemic was 5,150. See Bloom, *Mississippi Valley's Great Yellow Fever Epidemic*, 30, 55–56, 59, 70, and 77–80.

14. Toner, "On the Natural History and Distribution of Yellow Fever"; Keating, *History of the Yellow Fever.*

15. Spinzig, *Yellow Fever*, 111–12.

16. S. B. Grubbs, *Vessels as Carriers of Mosquitoes*, Yellow Fever Institute, Bulletin No. 11 (March) (Washington, DC: Government Printing Office, 1912), 25–28 (quotation on 27). Along the same lines, see H. R. Carter, *Are Vessels Infected with Yellow Fever? Some Personal Observations*, Yellow Fever Institute, Bulletin No. 9 (July) (Washington: Government Printing Office, 1902), 7–15. There is also direct quantitative evidence linking the level of trade with the incidence of yellow fever in particular ports. A formal quantitative study of trade and yellow fever epidemics at ports throughout the United States shows that yellow fever epidemics typically occurred in years of unusually high trading activity, or immediately following a year of unusually high activity. See Beeson and Troesken, "When Bioterrorism Was No Big Deal."

17. Monette wrote,

> The same was true of all our ports during the war of revolution, from 1776 to 1785. But so soon as peace was confirmed, and a brisk trade was carried on with the West Indies, the yellow fever began to prevail in all our most important ports, from 1790; and it prevailed extensively in some of the principal ports, nearly every other year, until the embargo in 1808 and the war of 1812 so interrupted the commercial intercourse with the West Indies, that epidemic yellow fever was not known in the United States until the year 1817, when a constant commercial intercourse with the West Indies had become again established. Since that time the intercourse with tropical America has been uninterrupted, and yellow fever as an epidemic has not failed to visit our most important ports, almost every other summer." (John W. Monette, *Observations on the Epidemic Yellow Fever of Natchez and of the Southwest* [Louisville, KY: Prentice and Weissinger, 1842], 139–40)

18. D. W. Hand, "Yellow Fever: Its History in the United States; An Account of the Recent Epidemic in the South and the Conclusions of the Yellow Fever Conference at Richmond, Va., in 1878." Reprinted in *Seventh Annual Report of the State Board of Health of Minnesota* (Minneapolis, MN: Johnson, Smith, and Harrison, 1879).

19. See Douglas A. Irwin, "Revenue or Reciprocity? Founding Feuds over Early US Trade Policy," in *Founding Choices: American Economic Policy in the 1790s*, ed. Douglas Irwin and Richard Sylla (Chicago: University of Chicago Press, 2011), 89–120, esp. 96.

20. See also Douglas A. Irwin, "New Estimates of the Average Tariff Rate of the United States, 1790–1820," *Journal of Economic History* 63.2 (2003): 506–13. Irwin's estimates are similar to those reported here.

21. Hamilton, Jay, and Madison, *FP*, 59.

22. Ibid., 58–59.

23. Ibid., 103.

24. The Laffer Curve construct is typically applied to an income tax. It suggests that tax revenues from the income tax will be minimized at rates of 0 percent and 100 percent. At the former the government will collect no revenue despite the fact taxpayers are earning income. At the latter, taxpayers decline to work because all their income will be taxed away and therefore tax revenues will be zero (assuming that all revenues are collected from work-related earnings). This suggests that tax revenues are maximized at some intermediate rate between 0 and 100 percent. Hamilton's logic for the tariff is similar (but not identical) to this.

25. Hamilton, Jay, and Madison, *FP*, 103. The tension between Hamilton's logic and modern libertarianism should be noted. In the latter, tariffs are anathema; more than any other form of taxation, they distort personal choices and undermine market forces. See Douglas A. Irwin, *Against the Tide: An Intellectual History of Free Trade* (Princeton, NJ: Princeton University Press, 1996). But in Hamilton's logic they are an institution that, on net, preserves and promotes individual freedom: while it is true that tariffs might alter relative prices and induce consumers to make decisions that they otherwise would not make, tariffs might also supplant other forms of taxation more vulnerable to political excess. The fatal flaw in Hamilton's reasoning, however, is that tariffs are not just about revenue. Politically connected and well-organized groups can use tariffs to protect bloated and inefficient businesses from foreign competition, raising consumer prices and slowing technological innovation. See J. J. Pincus, "Pressure Groups and the Pattern of Tariffs," *Journal of Political Economy* 83.4 (1975): 757–78.

26. See Irwin, "Revenue or Reciprocity," esp. 98.

27. See Linda K. Salvucci, "Atlantic Intersections: Early American Commerce and the Rise of the Spanish West Indies (Cuba)," *Business History Review* 79.4 (2005): 781–809.

28. Other countries with different and perhaps less commercially friendly institutions also experienced growth in trade during this period, so clearly institutions are, at most, only part of the explanation. For a history of international trade and economic performance during the nineteenth century, see Kevin H. O'Rourke and Jeffrey G. Williamson, *Globalization and History: The Evolution of the Nineteenth Century Atlantic Economy* (Cambridge, MA: MIT Press, 1999), esp. 225–46.

29. See T. W. Van Metre, G. G. Huebner, and D. S. Hanchett, *History of Domestic and Foreign Commerce of the United States* (Washington, DC: Carnegie Institution of Washington, 1922), 1:16.

30. Ibid.

31. Ibid., 19–20.

32. See H. H. Powers, "Expansion and Protection," *Quarterly Journal of Economics* 13.4 (1899): 361–78; and Charles Lyon Chandler, "United States Commerce with Latin America at the Promulgation of the Monroe Doctrine," *Quarterly Journal of Economics* 38.3 (1924): 466–86.

33. Humphreys, *Yellow Fever*, 148, 151.

34. William C. Gorgas, "Sanitary Conditions as Encountered in Cuba and Panama, and What Is Being Done to Render the Canal Zone Healthy," *Medical Record* 67.5 (1905): 161–63.

35. Sheldon J. Watts, *Epidemics and History: Disease, Power, and Imperialism* (New Haven, CT: Yale University Press, 1999), 255.

36. See Samuel Choppin, "History of the Importation of Yellow Fever Into the United States, from 1693 to 1878," *Public Health Papers and Reports* 4.2 (1878): 190–206.

37. Rubert William Boyce, *Yellow Fever Prophylaxis in New Orleans* (London: Williams & Norgate, 1906), 3.

38. See Francisco Castillo Najera, "The Campaign Against Yellow Fever in Mexico," *American Journal of Public Health* 12.3 (1922): 181–87; George Miller Sternberg, United States Public Health Service, Marine Hospital Service, *Report on the Etiology and Prevention of Yellow Fever* (Washington, DC: Government Printing Office, 1890), 40–43; United States, *Bulletin of the Yellow Fever Institute* (1902): 1–17, quotation at 12; and Edward Stuart, "Sanitation in Brazil," *American Journal of Public Health* 4 (1914): 1159–72.

39. According to T. C. Lyster, "By enforcing [Liceaga's] plans for the destruction of breeding places both within and without the city, Vera Cruz become practically free from mosquitoes and thus insured against the spread of yellow fever. While the elimination of yellow fever from Vera Cruz was but one of Liceaga's many sanitary achievements, it was a most worthy one and all America should to claim him as one of the brilliant products of the Western Hemisphere." See T. C. Lyster, "Liceaga and Yellow Fever," *Proceedings of the Second Pan American Scientific Congress* 8.1 (1916); *Public Health and Medicine* (Washington, DC: Government Printing Office, 1917), 9:106.

40. Liceaga's untitled address appears in *Transactions of the Third International Sanitary Conference of the American Republics*, held at the National Palace, City of Mexico, 2–7 December 1907 (Washington, DC: International Bureau of the American Republics, 1909), 19–22.

41. Kris Mitchener and Marc Weidenmier, "Empire, Public Goods, and the Roosevelt Corollary," *Journal of Economic History* 65.3 (2005): 658–92.

42. *Annual Report of the Surgeon General*, US Army, to the Secretary of War (Washington, DC: Government Printing Office, 1915), 128–31.

43. For the history of the National Board of Health given below, I draw primarily from Humphreys, *Yellow Fever*.

44. See J. M. Eager, "The Early History of Quarantine—Origin of Sanitary Measures Directed Against Yellow Fever," Yellow Fever Institute, Treasury Department, Public Health and Marine-Hospital Service, Bulletin No. 2, February, 1903; Harrison, *Contagion: How Commerce Has Spread Disease* (New Haven, CT: Yale University Press, 2013), 1–23; and Keating, *History of the Yellow Fever*, 284–369.

45. See Eager, "Early History of Quarantine"; Harrison, *Contagion*, 1–23; Keating, *History of the Yellow Fever*, 284–369.

46. See, generally, *Proceedings and Debates of the Third National Quarantine and Sanitary Convention*, held in New York, 27–30 April 1859, Document No. 9 (New York: Edmunde Jones, 1859); Bloom, *Mississippi Valley's Great Yellow Fever Epidemic*, 150–55, 215–19, and 273–74; and S. Oakley Van Der Poel, "General Principles Affecting the Organization and Practice of the Quarantine," *Public Health Reports and Papers Presented at the Meetings of the American Public Health Association in the Year 1873* (New York: Hurd and Houghton, 1875), 402–26.

47. Griscom, *A History*, 22.

48. Toner, "On the Natural History and Distribution of Yellow Fever."

49. Griscom, *A History*.

50. A concern one might have with this discussion is the rise of New Orleans as a port. To the extent that the expansion of New Orleans caused New York's trade with the

West Indies to decline in absolute terms over time, it is possible that this trade diversion is what caused the reduction in yellow fever in New York. In this regard, it is notable that yellow fever disappeared from Philadelphia around the same period of time. For a qualitative overview of trade patterns in New York, particularly trade with the West Indies, during the late eighteenth and early nineteenth centuries, see Robert Greenhalgh Albion, *The Rise of New York Port* (New York: Charles Scribner & Sons), 165–93. It is, however, easy to overstate the relative significance of New Orleans as a rival port of New York. As late as 1868, imports into New York exceeded imports into New Orleans by a factor of 25 ($277.5 million versus $11.1 million in nominal dollars); see Bureau of Labor Statistics, Department of the Treasury, *Statistical Abstract of the United States, 1893* (Washington, DC: Government Printing Office, 1894), 78. Furthermore, as explained in the text, New York continued to successfully interdict vessels with sick passengers, suggesting that, had those passengers or the mosquitoes that followed them landed on shore, there was the risk of yellow fever erupting.

51. See *Macon Weekly Telegraph*, 23 July 1878, 2.

52. New York was, in many respects, a mercantile city more than an industrial city, and preserving trade flows would have been important to both policymakers and merchants.

53. There are clearly exceptions to this line of thought, however. As explained later in the chapter, business groups also sometimes hijacked the quarantine process and used quarantines as a sort of strategic trade measure (much like a tariff) to promote their interests at the expense of broader societal interests. See also the discussion in Harrison, *Contagion*, 24–79.

54. See Herbert Hovenkamp, *Enterprise and American Law, 1836–1937* (Cambridge, MA: Harvard University Press, 1992), 139–40.

55. As an example of a powerful public health official who advocated very strict quarantine measures, consider Samuel Choppin, the president of the Louisiana State Board of Health and the second president of the American Public Health Association. According to Choppin, "The only certain and sure preventive of yellow fever, in my humble opinion, is absolute non-intercourse with ports where yellow fever is indigenous, from the first April to the first of November of each year." In Choppin's view, absolute autarky was required because no "conditional quarantine" could ever be made to work. Choppin believed that any quarantine law that was not "absolute in its restrictions" would fail, no matter how incorruptible and zealous were the agents who administered it. The difficulty in his view was the "cupidity of commercial men," who, because they had "large interests at stake," would "always move heaven and earth to evade successfully all quarantine laws and regulations." As evidence of the efficacy of absolute autarky with infected ports and places, Choppin pointed to cities like Natchez, Mississippi, which, as already explained, imposed a shotgun quarantine during the epidemic of 1878: "The experience of [1878] with regard to the efficacy of a strict quarantine goes to sustain the theory of importation and portability of yellow fever. Witness . . . Shreveport, Monroe, La. [and] Natchez, Miss., with their shotgun quarantines turning away the pestilence." See Choppin, "History of the Importation of Yellow Fever."

56. The race-to-the-bottom argument has been applied in many contexts, including environmental regulation, taxes, minimum wage laws, labor market regulations, and welfare. The empirical and theoretical support for the argument is, however, mixed: some studies find evidence of a race-to-the-bottom among competing polities, but others find no supportive evidence. See the following: Ronald B. Davies, "A Race to

the Bottom in Labor Standards? An Empirical Investigation," *Journal of Development Economics* 103.2 (2013): 1–14 (finds evidence of race-to-the-bottom in labor standards, especially among developing countries); Enrique G. Mendoza and Linda L. Tesar, "Why Hasn't Tax Competition Triggered a Race to the Bottom? Some Quantitative Lessons from the EU," *Journal of Monetary Economics* 52.1 (2005): 163–204 (develops a model showing that there are few gains from coordinating tax policies for labor and suggests the behavior of tax rates in the European Union is consistent with this model); Neal D. Woods, "Interstate Competition and Environmental Regulation: A Test of the Race-to-the-Bottom Thesis," *Social Science Quarterly* 87.1 (2006): 174–89 (finds evidence of a race-to-the-bottom in state-level environmental policies); Jan K. Brueckner, "Welfare Reform and the Race to the Bottom: Theory and Evidence," *Southern Economic Journal* 66.3 (2000): 505–25 (builds a model and reports evidence consistent with the hypothesis that there is a race-to-the-bottom among American states with regard to welfare policies); and Richard L. Revesz, "Federalism and Environmental Regulation: A Public Choice Analysis," *Harvard Law Review* 115.2 (2001): 553–641 (presents evidence against the idea that there is a race-to-the-bottom among American states with regard to environmental policy).

57. *Proceedings and Debates of the Third National Quarantine and Sanitary Convention*, 331.

58. Ibid., 322.

59. Ibid., 323.

60. Ibid., 348–55.

61. See *Tenth Report of the State Board of Health of Minnesota* (St. Paul, MN: Pioneer Press), 35; Treasury Department, US Marine Hospital Service, *Answer of the Supervising Surgeon General of the National Board of Health*, 12 March 1884 (Washington, DC: Government Printing Office, 1884), 3–27.

62. See, for example, Peete v. Morgan, 86. U.S. 581 (1874).

63. On the widespread adoption of quarantines during the 1878 epidemic, see Bloom, *Mississippi Valley's Great Yellow Fever Epidemic*, 150–55 and 211–19; and Humphreys, *Yellow Fever in the South*, 104–6. For accounts of quarantines in the popular press during the 1878 and 1879 yellow fever epidemics, see the articles in the following issues of the *New York Times*: 6 September 1878, 2; 22 July 22 1879, 1; 11 August 1878, 9; 10 August 1878, 1; 1 August 1879, 5; 16 August 1878, 7; and 12 July 1879, 1. Articles from other papers document quarantines in additional cities during the 1878 epidemic. See the following: *Columbus Daily Enquirer*, 27 July 1878, 1; *Philadelphia Inquirer*, 28 July 1878, 8; *New Orleans Times Picayune*, 28 July 1878, 2; *Baltimore Sun*, 29 July 1878, 1; *Chicago Daily Inter-Ocean*, 30 July 1878, 2, and 13 July 1878, 1; *New Orleans Times Picayune*, 1 August 1878, 1; *New Hampshire Sentinel*, 1 August 1878, 2 (reporting that "quarantine regulations are being adopted quite generally throughout the Southwest"); and *New Orleans Times Picayune*, 6 August 1878, 8.

64. See Harrison, *Contagion*, 1–76.

65. See Humphreys, *Yellow Fever and the South*, 83 and 88–89. In addition to the evidence cited by Humphreys and the other evidence presented later in this chapter, see the discussion of the *Louisiana v. Texas* case in chapter 3.

66. Humphreys, *Yellow Fever and the South*, 59–61, 96–97.

67. National Board of Health, *Annual Report* (1881), 287.

68. Ibid. For example, on September 23, 1880, the Louisiana State Board of Health issued the following resolution: "Resolved, That this board has solemnly pledged itself to promptly communicate to the country the existence within our city and State of any epidemic or contagious diseases, [and] it requests the press of the United

States not to attach any credence to any report in relation to the public health of our city or State that does not bear the official sanction of this board."

69. Ibid., 287–88.

70. Ibid., 288–89. According to the National Board of Health, "the present generation of the Mississippi Valley" would "not likely forget" this incident.

71. Ibid.

72. Humphreys, *Yellow Fever and the South,* 72–73.

73. On the sanitary conditions of nineteenth-century cities, see Joel Tarr, *The Search for the Ultimate Sink* (Akron, OH: University of Akron Press, 1996); and Melosi, *Sanitary City.*

74. As Margaret Humphreys explains, "In a like manner, business men taking part in southern politics were motivated to a certain extent by the desire to elevate their cities' commercial advantage by improving its health, and at the same time sought to direct public health efforts along avenues not inimical to business interests" (*Yellow Fever and the South,* 81). See also Stanley K. Schultz and Clay McShane, "To Engineer the Metropolis: Sewers, Sanitation, and City Planning in Late-Nineteenth-Century America," *Journal of American History* 65.2 (1978): 389–411. Similar statements can be found in the popular press; see, for example, "Shutting Out Disease: It Is Policy to Take Time by the Forelock," *Knoxville Journal,* 4 April 1888, 4; "Its Commercial Aspect: A Talk on the Actual Money Value of Proper Sanitary Measures," *Omaha World Herald,* 30 March 1890, 7; "The Waterworks Problem: Plenty of Good Potable Water Is Essential to the Comfort and Growth of the City," *Dallas Morning News ,* 6 May 1900, 24; and "A Conference on City Health Board," *New Orleans Daily Picayune,* 5 June 1900, 14. Along these lines, Southerners were often heard to argue that their cities lagged behind those in the Northeast because of the backward state of public health in the South. Yet census data indicate that, with two notable exceptions (Baltimore and New Orleans), cities in the American South did not lag behind their Northern counterparts in terms of the extensiveness of their local water and sewer systems, and in some respects, they might have been ahead of cities in the North. See Werner Troesken, *Water, Race, and Disease* (Cambridge: MIT Press, 2004), 32–56.

75. This paragraph is based on the following sources: John H. Ellis, "Memphis' Sanitary Revolution, 1880–1890," *Tennessee Historical Quarterly* 23.2 (1964): 59–72; John H. Ellis, "Disease and the Destiny of a City: The 1878 Yellow Fever Epidemic in Memphis," *West Tennessee Historical Society Papers* 38.2 (1974): 75–89; and Keating, *History of the Yellow Fever.*

76. "Report of Sanitary Survey of Memphis, Tenn.," in *Annual Report of the National Board of Health, 1880* (Washington: DC: Government Printing Office, 1881), 416–41 (appendix L).

77. It should be noted, however, that business groups in Memphis strongly opposed the city's strict quarantine measures during the epidemic, and their pressures eventually forced the city to pull back. See "Memphis' Sanitary Revolution, 1880–1890"; Ellis, "Disease and the Destiny of a City," 75–89; Keating, *History of the Yellow Fever;* Joan Hassell, *Memphis, 1800–1900,* vol. 3, *Years of Courage, 1870–1900* (New York: Nancy Powers, 1982).

78. On the population of Memphis, see *Historical Statistics of the United States, Earliest Times to the Present: Millennial Edition,* ed. Susan B. Carter, Scott Sigmund Gartner, Michael R. Haines, Alan L. Olmstead, Richard Sutch, and Gavin Wright, Series Aa854 (New York: Cambridge University Press, 2006), 1–110.

79. Prior to the 1878 epidemic, Memphis like all other Southern cities, did not hire black policemen. A desirable and well-paying job by the standards of the day, it was

reserved for whites. But in the midst of the yellow fever epidemic, the city officials ran short of healthy white men and were forced to turn to African Americans. Memphis remained one of the few Southern cities to use black police officers throughout the late nineteenth century. See Dennis C. Rousey, "Yellow Fever and Black Policemen in Memphis: A Post-Reconstruction Anomaly," *Journal of Southern History* 51.3 (1985): 357–74.

80. Humphreys, *Yellow Fever and the South* 100–107.

81. John H. Ellis, *Yellow Fever and Public Health in the New South* (Lexington: University of Kentucky Press, 1992), 113–15; Lynette Bonney Wrenn, "The Memphis Sewer Experiment," *Tennessee Historical Quarterly* 44.3 (1985): 340–49; and Troesken, *Water, Race, and Disease*, 62–74. Historically, it was not uncommon for health departments and the federal government to identify diarrhea as a cause of death. Hence, the three waterborne diseases considered in Memphis were cholera, typhoid, and diarrhea. See United States, Department of Labor, "Condition of the Negro in Various Cities," *Bulletin of the Department of Labor* 10 (Washington, DC: Government Printing Office, 1897).

82. See Hovenkamp, *Enterprise and American Law*, 118–21.

83. Ibid., 119–20.

84. Wendy E. Parmet, "From Slaughter-House to Lochner: The Rise and Fall of the Constitutionalization of Public Health," *American Journal of Legal History* 40.4 (1996): 484.

85. Keating, *History of the Yellow Fever*, 317n (referring to State Medical Society of Tennessee).

86. John Bell, "Report on the Importance of and Economy of Sanitary Measures to Cities," in *Proceedings and Debates of the Third National Quarantine and Sanitary Convention*, 614.

87. "The Plague in the Southwest: The Great Yellow Fever Epidemic in 1853," *De Bow's Review and Industrial Resources, Statistics, etc.*, 15 (1853): 595–606 (quotation on 600).

88. See, for example, this excerpt from an editorial in the *New Orleans Times-Picayune*, the city's major newspaper and a strident opponent of the Slaughterhouse Monopoly Act (20 February 1869), 1: "About the [law's] requirement which seems to aim at improving the health of the city by removing the slaughterhouses and the stock landings below the city Waterworks, we have little complaint to make."

89. Ibid. *The New Orleans Times-Picayune* queried, "How too are we to have milk brought us in the morning fresh from the cow, if this bill is to become law?" It was too far, the paper believed, to have fresh milk brought in from outside the city.

90. See Herbert Hovenkamp's discussion of the Dunning School in *Enterprise and American Law*, 116–118. See also, Parmet, "From Slaughter-House to Lochner," 473–99.

91. Slaughter-House Cases, 83 U.S. 36 (1873), p. 39.

92. Ibid. at 62.

93. Ibid.

94. Ibid.

95. Ibid. at 61–63.

96. See Michael B. Ross, "Justice Miller's Reconstruction: The Slaughter-House Cases, Health Codes, and Civil Rights in New Orleans, 1861–1873," *Journal of Southern History* 64.4 (November 1998): 649–76. Most critiques of the Slaughterhouse decision focus not on the end result of the decision (upholding the Slaughterhouse Monopoly Act) but on the flawed constitutional reasoning the court used to get there. For less critical and more practical views aligned with the argument developed here, see John Harrison, "Reconstructing the Privileges or Immunities Clause," *Yale Law Journal* 101.7 (1992): 1385–1474; William Novak, *The People's Welfare: Law and Regulation in Nineteenth-Century America* (Chapel Hill: University of North Carolina Press,

1996), 230–33; Ronald M. Labbe and Jonathan Lurie, *The Slaughterhouse Cases: Regulation, Reconstruction, and the Fourteenth Amendment* (Lawrence: University of Kansas Press, 2003); and Hovenkamp, *Enterprise and American Law*, 116–24. Although it focuses on later decisions, the following article helps put the Slaughterhouse decision in broader context: Pamela Brandwein, "A Judicial Abandonment of Blacks? Rethinking the 'State Action' Cases of the Waite Court," *Law and Society Review* 41.2 (2007): 343–86.

97. See *Sanitary Record*, 2 November 1905, 390; Ian MacLachlan, "'The Greatest and Most Offensive Nuisance That Ever Disgraced the Capital of a Kingdom': The Slaughterhouses and Shambles of Modern Edinburgh," unpublished MS; and Ian MacLachlan, "A Bloody Offal Nuisance: The Persistence of Private Slaughterhouses in Nineteenth Century London," *Urban History* 34.2 (2007): 227–54; Christine Meisner Rosen, "Knowing Industrial Pollution: Nuisance Law and the Power of Tradition in a Time of Rapid Economic Change, 1840–1864," *Environmental History* 8.4 (2003): 565–97; "A Discussion On the Regulation of the Slaughterhouse of Animals for Human Food," *British Medical Journal*, 11 August 1895, 513–15; and "Dublin Slaughterhouses," *British Medical Journal*, 7 September 1893, 590–91. Although the article on Dublin covers regulatory efforts in the city during the early 1890s, it makes the point that this particular European city employed the same basic regulatory apparatus (a public slaughterhouse) as did New Orleans.

98. See Elizabeth C. Tandy, "The Regulation of Nuisances in the American Colonies," *American Journal of Public Health* 13.10 (1923): 810–813; Novak, *People's Welfare*, 222–33; Parmet, "From Slaughter-House to Lochner," 473–499. See also Tanner v. Trustees of the Village of Albion, 5 Hill 121 (1843) (explaining that a municipality was authorized to regulate "slaughter-houses and nuisances generally"); Brick Presbyterian Church v. City of New York, 5 Cow. 528 (1826) (suggesting that it was common knowledge that cities possessed the authority to regulate the location business activities considered to be nuisances); John Glenn v. Mayor and City Council of Baltimore, 1833 Md, Lexis 17; Duck v. The Chief Burgess, 7 Watts 181 (1838); Dimmett and Others v. Eskridge, 20 Va. 308 (1819).

CHAPTER SEVEN

1. See Richard Pipes, *Property and Freedom* (New York: Vintage, 2000); and Milton Friedman and Rose Friedman, *Free to Choose: A Personal Statement* (New York: Mariner Books, 1990).

2. Arthur Wollaston Hutton, *The Vaccination Question* (London: Methuen, 1895), 143–51; Henry Hylyn Hayter, *Victorian Yearbook for 1890–1891* (Melbourne: Sands & McDougall, 1891), 363.

INDEX

The letter f following a page number denotes a figure, and the letter t denotes a table.

Aedes aegypti, 139–40; arrival of in ships, 143, 155; requirement of clear water to breed and, 140, 167, 169. *See also* mosquito eradication

African Americans: discriminatory enforcement of smallpox measures for, 45, 75; disenfranchisement of, 26, 187n42; elevated immunity to yellow fever in, 139, 164, 165; increase in life expectancy of, 10, 183n23; in Louisiana legislature during Reconstruction, 171; as Memphis policemen, 166, 223n79; oppressed by democratic majority, 41, 45; Reconstruction Amendments and, 25–26; water systems benefiting, 10, 11

Ames, Smyth v., 199n91

Anderson, H. B., 3–4, 36–37, 182n12

anti-tuberculosis campaigns, 32–33, 37–38, 190nn75–76

anti-vaccinationists, 73–76; appeal to legal precedent and the Constitution and, 3–4, 37; in Asia, 72–73; beliefs of about causes of smallpox, 2, 3, 70, 74–75, 79, 203n31; beliefs of about dangers of vaccination, 2, 73–75, 203n31; difficulty in making utility analysis of, 207n82; disproportionate legislative influence of, 96; in England, 4, 73–74, 75, 207n91; free trade arguments of, 73, 203n25; *Jacobson* decision and, 86, 87; jurisdictional sorting of, ix, 89, 177; libertarian ideology of, 3–4; Lora Little as, 75–76, 97, 178; modern movement of, 12, 69, 73; Robinson's 1919 *Rhea* decision and,

2. *See also* nontraditional medicine; smallpox vaccination, mandatory

Articles of Confederation: decline of credit markets under, ix, 60–65; failure of trade policies under, 45, 46–47, 50, 148, 194n41; lack of national taxing power under, 145–46

autocratic societies, public health in, vii, viii

Baldwin, Peter, 203n27, 207n91

Baltimore Jennerian Society, 20

bankruptcy, of city and state governments, 116, 117; of Memphis, Tennessee, 165

bankruptcy law, and stable credit markets, 63, 65

Barber, Henry E., 54–55

Barber v. Minnesota, 54–55, 197n76

Beebe, Howard, 116

Behring, Emil, 34

Blaisdell decision, 65

Blane, Gilbert, 68

Blunt, William, 55

boards of health. *See* Louisiana State Board of Health; municipal boards of health; National Board of Health

bonus bonds, 116

Brazil: eradication of smallpox in, viii; yellow fever problem in Rio de Janeiro, 151, 152

Brown, Henry Billings, 56–57

Budd, William, 35–36, 105–6

Burke, Aedanus, 61, 62–63

Butchers Benevolent Association (BBA), 171–73